FOOD&**WINE**

Wine Guide
2009

WINE GUIDE 2009

editor in chief **Dana Cowin**
art director **Patricia Sanchez**
executive editor **Lettie Teague**
volume editor **Kristen Wolfe Bieler**
design/production **James Maikowski**
deputy editor **Ray Isle**
senior editor **Christine Quinlan**
editor **Colleen McKinney**
copy editor **Anne O'Connor**
chief researcher **Janice Huang**
researchers **Mollie Battenhouse, Jenny Choi,
Kathryn O'Shea-Evans, Paola Singer**
tastings coordinator **Robbin Gheesling**
indexer **Andrea Chesman**

produced for FOOD & WINE magazine by gonzalez defino, ny
www.gonzalezdefino.com
principals **Joseph Gonzalez, Perri DeFino**

map illustrations **Ethan Cornell**

cover photography **Tina Rupp**
food stylist **Alison Attenborough**
prop stylist **Alistair Turnbull**
cover credits: "Sommeliers Chardonnay" glasses by Riedel from
Williams-Sonoma, 877-812-6235 or williamssonoma.com

AMERICAN EXPRESS PUBLISHING CORPORATION
president/ceo **Ed Kelly**
senior vice president/chief marketing officer **Mark V. Stanich**
cfo/senior vice president/corporate development & operations **Paul Francis**
vice president/general manager **Keith Strohmeier, Frank Bland**

vice president, books & products/publisher **Marshall Corey**
director, book programs **Bruce Spanier**
director, customer retention & loyalty **Greg D'Anca**
senior marketing manager, branded books **Eric Lucie**
assistant marketing manager **Lizabeth Clark**
director of fulfillment & premium value **Phil Black**
manager of customer experience & product development **Charles Graver**
director of finance **Thomas Noonan**
associate business manager **Desiree Bernardez**
corporate production manager **Stuart Handelman**

FOOD&WINE

Wine Guide
2009

by Anthony Giglio

FOOD&WINE
BOOKS

American Express Publishing Corporation
New York

contents

old world

new world

old & new worlds

foreword

There are plenty of annual wine guides around—some offer inside news from key wine-producing countries, some focus on bottles favored by collectors and others feature lists of great bargain wines. Our 2009 FOOD & WINE Wine Guide has all of this—and a great deal more besides. Indeed, there's a tremendous amount of information packed into this year's edition, written by New York–based author Anthony Giglio. In addition to a lively writing style, Giglio has contributed expanded lists of star producers throughout the book, as well as longer and more detailed tasting notes of the nearly 1,000 selected wines—most of which you can actually find in stores! The handy pairing chart has been updated and organized according to popular dishes, e.g., grilled salmon (Pinot Gris), hamburgers (Zinfandel), roast chicken (Pinot Noir) and steak (Cabernet Sauvignon, of course). There are also tips on how to buy wine in restaurants (always ask to speak to the sommelier), online (check out wine-searcher.com) and in shops (ask for the 10 percent case discount). Finally, you'll find updates on what's going on around the world from our trusted correspondents, each an authority in his or her field. Burgundy correspondent Daniel Johnnes, wine director for the Daniel Boulud restaurant group, reports that prices for the vaunted 2005 wines will only continue to rise and advises looking at the 2004 and 2006 Burgundy vintages for better value. Meanwhile, Fiona Morrison reports from Bordeaux that the mood is a bit bleaker there, given the poor to middling quality of the 2007 vintage. And that's just a (very) brief look at what's inside. There's a lot to read in this latest guide—and we hope that you will do so with a glass of wine in hand.

Dana Cowin
Editor in Chief
FOOD & WINE

Lettie Teague
Executive Wine Editor
FOOD & WINE

acknowledgments

The author would like to thank the following people *not* named in the masthead, without whose help this seemingly small book would have been a far bigger task:

Wine authorities David Lynch, Jeffery Lindenmuth and Tara Q. Thomas, for their brilliant resourcefulness and generous spirit: Without you I'd still be buried.

Researchers extraordinaire Daniel J. Murphy, Stephanie McKinnon McDade and Roxanne Downer, whose tireless background work is now in the foreground of each page. Thanks, also, to fact-finder Letitia White-Washington.

Jennifer Spiering, Rosemarie Giglio (yes, my mom) and Lisa Giglio Kawalek (my sister), for tracking down winery contacts in a big hurry.

For sorting thousands of bottles into neat little (and not-so-little) tasting flights, Amy E. Hawley, Scott Rosenbaum, Michelle Lachman and Holland Cowger.

A toast to Maximilian Riedel, CEO of Riedel Crystal of America, for his generous donation of dozens of his company's lovely Vinum glasses to the Wine Guide's tasting room.

The staffs at Turnstile Entertainment and Shade Global, for putting up with one heck of a mess during the height of red wine tasting in their pristine office suite.

My predecessor, Jamal A. Rayyis, who graciously offered advice and counsel.

And finally, my wife, Antonia LoPresti Giglio, and our two greatest vintages, Sofia and Marco, for their patience during my long absences while writing this book.

how to use this book

All of the wines in this Guide are for sale this year. For ease of reference, the wines are listed alphabetically by producer name, followed by the vintage year. The quality and price symbols used to rate each wine are described below; price ranges have been updated this year to reflect a general uptick in prices.

You may note that certain wines have significantly older vintage dates than others. This is because some wines are released within months after harvest, while others are aged for years before release. Though most wines are thoroughly drinkable when they are put on the market, some will taste better if they've had a few more years to age in the bottle. These are usually wines that are heavy in tannin, such as Cabernet Sauvignon or Barolo. There are no guarantees, however, that aging a wine in your cellar will improve it.

Certain producers have proven themselves capable of making excellent wines every year without fail. Wineries that are second to none in their categories are highlighted in the "Star Producers" sections throughout the Guide.

For even more expert advice from FOOD & WINE magazine on bottles to buy and perfect food pairings, go to foodandwine.com/wine.

Key to Symbols

QUALITY

★★★★ **OUTSTANDING** Worth a search

★★★ **EXCELLENT** Top-notch of its type

★★ **VERY GOOD** Distinctive

★ **GOOD** Delicious everyday wine

PRICE

$$$$ **OVER $60**

$$$ **$31 TO $60**

$$ **$15 TO $30**

$ **UNDER $15**

the year in wine

Champagne News

France's *Institut National de l'Origine et de la Qualité* (INAO) voted unanimously in March 2008 to extend the Champagne region's heretofore sacrosanct boundaries by as much as 2,500 acres. Unchanged since 1954, the existing growing areas could soon be augmented by as many as 40 new communes, bringing the total number to 357. Approval is still pending, however, and the notoriously appellation-protective INAO plans years of terroir-testing to make sure the new areas measure up in terms of quality.

South America Sizzles

The numbers from South America's other winemaking countries are suddenly grabbing headlines: The most recent figures available show that in the last five years Brazilian wine exports increased fourfold, while Uruguay's total wine export revenues more than doubled. Meanwhile, stalwarts Chile and Argentina continue to battle for continental supremacy: Chile's wine exports to the U.S. grew by 8 percent from 2006 to 2007, while Argentine exports increased 25 percent in the same period. The boom is fueled in part by the emergence of new wine regions in both countries, such as Bío Bío and Limarí in Chile and Salta in Argentina.

Merlot Revisited

Sales of California Merlot have risen for most of the past decade and rose another 5 percent in 2007. The easy-to-drink, round-textured, fruity wine reigned supreme among casual U.S. red wine drinkers throughout the 1990s. Then, thanks to a substantial number of subpar bottles and a fervent anti-Merlot sentiment popularized by the 2004 movie *Sideways*, drinking Merlot became passé. Yet the wine never really went away: Even when its reputation was under attack, Merlot's supermarket sales were more than double those of Pinot Noir, and when all was said and crushed in 2007, the 300,000-plus tons of Merlot grapes put into production were more than triple the amount of Pinot Noir.

Dollar Decline

Fans of imported wines have been nervously watching for anticipated price increases as the dollar falls and shipping costs skyrocket. While some import prices have been holding steady—thanks in part to exporters, importers, distributors, retailers and producers absorbing some of the costs—many have risen significantly, particularly for European wines. A bottle of Moët et Chandon's 1999 Dom Pérignon Champagne, for example, which cost about $120 in 2007, was selling in some markets for nearly $160 by mid-2008; non-vintage versions were edging over $50 from about $35 to $40 in 2007. As far as we can tell, import prices are up by as much as 30 percent and are likely to continue climbing.

Robert Mondavi Remembered

Robert Mondavi, the man who made Napa Valley one of the world's great wine destinations, died in May 2008 at age 94. Mondavi founded his winery in 1966 in Oakville, where he blended New World techniques with Old World reverence, and later forged partnerships with Bordeaux's Baron Philippe de Rothschild (Opus One) and Tuscany's Frescobaldi family (Luce). He'll perhaps be best remembered as California's outspoken wine ambassador to the world.

2005: A Very Good Year Across the Globe

Bordeaux and Burgundy wines from the 2005 vintage (first sampled in 2007) sparked a frenzy among collectors who either bought them on the futures market or waited with bated breath for shipments to arrive. And it's not just France that benefited from a relatively long, dry growing season: 2005 was a stellar year for wines around the world, including California and Washington State, across Italy, Germany and Spain, and down in Chile, Argentina and Australia. Blame global warming, but 2005 is one of those nearly "universal" vintages (like 1990 and 2000) that make ordering wine at a restaurant so much easier.

food & wine's american wine awards 2008

In the world of American wine, few honors are as important as FOOD & WINE magazine's annual American Wine Awards. F&W editors polled a select group of wine professionals including writers, retailers, restaurateurs, sommeliers and past award winners, and the results are in. Here are our picks for the year's top winemaker, best importer, most promising new winery and most outstanding American wines.

winemaker of the year

Celia Masyczek (pronounced ma-CHESS-key) is widely considered one of Napa Valley's most talented consulting winemakers. The Oregon-born daughter of a wine enthusiast and amateur vintner, Masyczek graduated from the oenology program at the University of California, Davis, in 1982 and has been making wines ever since. She has worked at Silverado Vineyards, Robert Pepi and Staglin Family Vineyard, and today, in addition to making her own wine (Corra), Masyczek crafts wines for an array of top-notch vineyards, including the hottest new label in Napa, Scarecrow.

wine importer of the year

Rosenthal Wine Merchant, Ltd. For Neal Rosenthal and his wife, Kerry Madigan, *terroir* is the very foundation upon which they've built their company and reputation. Throughout the 30 years they've been in business, their objective has always been to work as closely as possible with vintners dedicated to producing limited quantities of quality wines made with a passion for what Rosenthal calls "that ephemeral sense of place." The company now represents 75 producers in Italy, France and California.

most promising new winery

Breggo Cellars In 2000, Douglas Stewart and his wife, Ana Lucia Benítez-Stewart, bought 203 acres in the heart of Anderson Valley to plant a vineyard. The land was once home to sheep (hence the name Breggo, which means "sheep" in Boontling, a 19th-century dialect of the nearby town of Boonville), and though only 30 percent of the land was fit for vines, that part proved perfect for Pinot Noir and Pinot Gris. Breggo's first estate fruit will be ready for harvest in 2010. In the meantime, the couple is using purchased local grapes to make some of Anderson Valley's most extraordinary wines.

best wines

Brander | 2007 | SAUVIGNON BLANC $20 AND UNDER

Cliff Lede Napa Valley | 2007 | SAUVIGNON BLANC OVER $20

Foxglove | 2007 | CHARDONNAY $20 AND UNDER

Ramey Ritchie Vineyard | 2005 | CHARDONNAY OVER $20

A to Z Oregon | 2006 | PINOT NOIR $20 AND UNDER

Talley Vineyards Rosemary's Vineyard | 2005 | PINOT NOIR OVER $20

R Collection by Raymond California | 2005 | MERLOT $20 AND UNDER

Shafer Napa Valley | 2005 | MERLOT OVER $20

Columbia Crest H3 Horse Heaven Hills | 2005 | CABERNET SAUVIGNON $20 AND UNDER

Harlan Estate | 2004 | CABERNET SAUVIGNON OVER $20

Edmeades Mendocino County | 2006 | ZINFANDEL $20 AND UNDER

Bella Lily Hill Estate | 2005 | ZINFANDEL OVER $20

Qupé Central Coast | 2006 | SYRAH $20 AND UNDER

Tensley Colson Canyon Vineyard | 2006 | SYRAH OVER $20

Schramsberg Blanc de Blancs | 2004 | SPARKLING WINE

Dominus | 2005 | BORDEAUX-STYLE BLEND

wine tasting guide

Tasting wine is like any other acquired skill: The more you practice, the better you become. Most of us possess the necessary tools to taste wine. Our tastebuds can detect sweet, salty, bitter and sour sensations, plus "umami," the savory flavor found in mushrooms and meat. And our noses can differentiate between hundreds of aromas. The most important thing to learn is how to pay attention to the wine in your glass. Here are a few tips to help get your palate into tasting shape.

set the mood For each wine you want to taste, find a clear, stemmed glass that is comfortable to hold. Choose a well-lit place that's relatively odor-neutral. It is best not to wear perfume or scented lotion.

set the scene Pour just enough wine in the glass so it barely reaches the widest part of the bowl. This way you'll have room to swirl the wine without spilling it.

check the color A light color generally indicates a light-bodied wine; a darker color, a fuller-bodied wine. Also, white wines deepen in color with age; reds get lighter and take on an orangish or even brown hue. If you've poured more than one wine, compare the colors and guess which wine will taste more concentrated. Young wines that appear brown may be the result of poor winemaking or storage.

swirl & sniff Hold the glass by its stem and swirl it gently to release the wine's aromas. Sniff. What do you smell? Sniff again. Do you smell fruit? What sort? The wine might evoke herbs, flowers, spices, vanilla or wood. Some wines smell like bell pepper, leather, roasted meat or even manure. Don't worry about cataloguing every aroma. Just articulate what you smell. Doing so will help you tell the difference between one wine and another. Sharing your impressions will help you learn and remember. Noxious smells like sulfur or must might dissipate with air. If the wine smells bad, give it a few minutes and swirl the glass to bring more contact with oxygen. If the wine still has an unappealing odor, move on to another one. If a wine smells like wet, moldy cork or cardboard, it may be "corked," meaning it has been infected by an unpleasant-smelling compound called TCA that can be found in corks. TCA is harmless, but it makes wine taste bad.

sip & swish Sip the wine and swish it around in your mouth. Try to suck air into your mouth while wine is still in it (this takes practice). This allows the wine to release more aromas. How does it feel? Does it coat your mouth? Is it light, prickly and refreshing? Does it taste bitter or sweet? Does it recall specific fruits or spices? Smell again. Does it smell like it tastes? Do you like it? There are no wrong answers; it's all about what you perceive.

to spit or swallow? If you're tasting more than a couple of wines at one sitting and want to be able to detect as much as possible from every glass (and remember your impressions tomorrow), it's important to spit.

taste in context In a horizontal tasting, you sample a range of wines that are alike in all but one way. This could be a group of wines from the same region and vintage, but made by different producers, or a group of wines from the same producer, same grape and same vintage, but from different vineyards. Comparing the differences among such similar wines will expand your knowledge. In a vertical tasting, you sample the same wine from the same producer made in different years. It's a great demonstration of how vintage can make a difference, as well as how age can change a wine's look and taste.

wine terms

You won't find much fussy wine jargon in this guide, but some of the terms commonly used to describe the taste of wine might be unfamiliar or used in an unfamiliar way. Many tasting notes mention specific flavors or describe a wine's texture. These references to flavors and textures other than "grape" are meant to serve as analogies: All the wines in this guide are made from grapes, but grapes have the ability to suggest the flavors of other fruits, herbs or minerals. A wine said to taste like "raspberries," for example, isn't infused with raspberries. Rather, it evokes flavors similar to those of raspberries. Here's a mini-glossary to help you become comfortable with the language of wine.

acidity The tart, tangy or zesty sensations in wine. Ideally, acidity brightens a wine's flavors like a squeeze of lemon brightens fish. Wines lacking acidity taste "flabby."

balance The harmony between acidity, tannin, alcohol and sweetness in a wine.

body How heavy or thick a wine feels in the mouth. Full-bodied or heavy wines are often described as "big."

corked Wines that taste like wet cork or newspaper are said to be "corked." The cause is trichloroanisole (TCA), a contaminant sometimes transmitted by cork.

crisp A term used to describe well-balanced, light-bodied wines that are high in acidity.

dry A wine without perceptible sweetness. A dry wine, however, can have powerful fruit flavors.

earthy An earthy wine evokes flavors like mushrooms, leather, damp straw or even manure.

finish The length of time a wine's flavors and sensations linger on the palate. A long finish is the hallmark of a more complex wine.

fruity Wine with an abundance of fruit flavors. Sometimes fruity wines can give the impression of sweetness, though they are not actually sweet.

herbaceous Calling a wine "herbaceous" or "herbal" can be positive or negative. Wines that evoke flavors of wild herbs and fresh-cut grass can be delicious. However, wines that show flavors of green beans or green pepper are less than ideal; such wines are also referred to as "vegetal."

mineral Flavors that reflect the minerals found in the soil in which a wine's grapes were grown. The terms "steely," "flinty" and "chalky" are also used to describe these mineral flavors.

nose How a wine smells; its bouquet, or aroma.

oaky Wines that transmit the flavors of the oak barrels in which they were aged. An often used synonym is "toasty."

oxidized Wines that have a tarnished quality due to exposure to air are said to be oxidized. When intended, as in the case of Sherry (see p. 265), oxidation can add fascinating dimensions to a wine. When unintentional, oxidation can make a wine taste tired and unappealing.

powerful Wine that is full of flavor, tannin and/or alcohol.

rustic Wine that is a bit rough and unsophisticated, though it can be charming.

tannin A component of grape skins, seeds and stems as well as of oak barrels, tannin is most commonly found in red wines. It imparts a puckery sensation similar to oversteeped black tea. Tannin also gives a wine its structure and enables some wines to age well.

terroir A French term that refers to the particular attributes a wine acquires from the specific environment of a vineyard, i.e., the climate, soil type, elevation and aspect.

wine buying guide

Buying wine should be fun and easy, yet for many people, it often isn't. Thankfully, there are several ways to gain confidence and make wine buying enjoyable no matter where you do your shopping.

in shops

scope out the shops Visit the wine shops in your area and determine which has the most helpful and knowledgeable sales people, the best selection and, of course, the best prices. Find out what sort of discounts they offer on 12-bottle cases, and if they permit you to mix and match your own assorted case. At a minimum, you should expect a 10 percent discount; some stores will offer 20 percent. Finally, pay attention to store temperature: The warmer the store, the more likely the wines could have problems.

ask questions Most wine-savvy salespeople are eager to share their knowledge and to steer you toward some of their favorite wines. Let them know your preferences, your budget and anything else that might help them select a wine you'll love.

become a regular The better the store's salespeople know you, the better they can suggest wines that will please you. They may also alert you about sales in advance.

online

know your options The two most common ways to buy wine online are via online retailers or directly from wineries. Retailers may offer bulk discounts if you buy a case and shipping discounts if you spend a certain amount. Wineries don't often discount, but their wines can be impossible to find elsewhere. A great advantage of online shopping is price comparison: Websites like wine-searcher.com allow you to compare prices at retailers around the world.

know the rules The difference between browsing for wine online and actually purchasing it has everything to do with where you live and how "liberal" your state is about interstate wine shipments. The laws governing direct-to-consumer interstate shipments differ from state to state. If you're considering buying wine from an out-of-state vendor, find out first whether it can ship to your state.

in restaurants

check out the list Most good lists feature wines in all price ranges. A poor list might be limited in selection, have too many wines from one producer or fail to list vintages. When faced with a bad wine list, order the least expensive bottle that you recognize as being reasonably good.

ask questions Treat the wine list as you would a food menu. You should ask how the Bordeaux tastes in comparison to the California Cabernet as readily as you'd ask the difference between two fish dishes. The first question should always be "May I speak to the wine director?" Then, tell that person the type of wine you're looking for—the price range, the flavor profile—as well as the dishes you will be having. With this information, the wine director should be able to recommend several options.

taste the wine When the bottle arrives, make sure it's exactly what you ordered—check the vintage, the producer, the blend or variety. If it's not, speak up. If the listed wine is out of stock, you might prefer to choose something else. You may be presented with the cork. Ignore it. Instead, sniff the wine in your glass. If it smells like sulfur, cabbage or skunk, tell your server that you think the wine might be flawed and request a second opinion from the wine director or the manager. If there's something truly wrong, they should offer you a new bottle or a new choice.

france

For most wine drinkers, France *is* wine. The very name of the country conjures up notions of quality and prestige. Indeed, France makes more fine wine than any other country, and for centuries French wines served as the paradigm against which all others were judged. Today, however, global competition has forced the country's vintners to raise their own standards higher, which means French wines have never been better.

Principal Wine Region

Paris ☆

· Reims

Champagne

Strasbourg ·

Alsace

Orléans ·

Loire Valley

· Dijon

~ Nantes

Burgundy

Atlantic Ocean

· Limoges

· Lyon

Bordeaux ·

Rhône Valley

Bordeaux

· Avignon

Nîmes ·

· Nice

Southwest

Provence

Marseille

Languedoc-Roussillon

Mediterranean Sea

France: An Overview

France is home to a vast amount of vineyard land, and wine-making takes place throughout the country, but there are five major wine regions that distinguish themselves as superior, based on the quality and track records of their wines over the centuries. Red wines reign in three of these regions: Bordeaux, Burgundy (which is also celebrated for its white wines) and the Rhône Valley. The remaining two principal regions, Alsace and the Loire Valley, both specialize in white wine. France has maintained its longstanding position as the center of the wine universe partly because almost all of the world's most recognized and esteemed grape varieties are French, including Chardonnay, Cabernet Sauvignon, Merlot, Pinot Noir, Syrah and Sauvignon Blanc. However, grape varieties, as important as they are—and as strictly regulated as to where and how they're allowed to be planted in France—mean far less to the French than the place from which a wine hails. The idea of *terroir,* a term that refers to all the distinguishing elements of a place such as climate, sun exposure, soil makeup and surrounding flora, is fundamental to French winemaking philosophy. It is the belief that nature and geography make the wine, not man. Perhaps that's why, surprisingly, there is no French word for winemaker; someone who makes wine is a *vigneron*—literally, a vine grower.

French Wine Labels

France's emphasis on terroir is so emphatic that most French labels list appellation (i.e., region or subregion), but not the grape variety used to make the wine. (Alsace labels are an exception; see p. 23.) A wine bearing its appellation name is required to satisfy certain regulations designed to guarantee quality and authenticity. The system governing these regulations is known as the *Appellation d'Origine Contrôlée* (AOC), or "controlled region of origin." The AOC hierarchy from top to bottom is:

- **AOC** This category encompasses the majority of French wines imported to the U.S. and insures that the wines meet regional requirements. While standards vary from region to region, they typically spell out permitted grapes, winemaking practices, minimum alcohol levels (higher alcohol levels mean riper grapes, which yield more flavorful wines) and harvest size (overly large grape harvests yield dilute wines). There are AOC regions *within* larger AOC regions as well, and generally, the more specific the subregion, the higher the standards. In Burgundy, for example, a wine bearing a district name like Côte de Nuits Villages must meet more stringent requirements than those labeled with the region-wide appellation Bourgogne Rouge. Wines from the Vosne-Romanée, a village within the Côte de Nuits, must conform to even stricter standards. Those from Vosne-Romanée Les Suchots, a *Premier Cru* appellation of Vosne-Romanée, must meet more demanding standards still.

- **VIN DÉLIMITÉ DE QUALITÉ SUPÉRIEURE (VDQS)** Wines designated VDQS adhere to standards that are often less rigid than those required of AOC wines and are considered minor players within the French wine hierarchy. But if a particular VDQS region produces enough wines of sufficiently high quality, the region might be promoted to AOC status.

- **VIN DE PAYS** Translated as "country wines," Vins de Pays are subject to lower standards than AOC or VDQS wines, but they are allowed to list the wine's region and grape. Most Vins de Pays are forgettable, but there are a growing number of innovative winemakers who wish to work beyond the restraints of AOC requirements, and many are producing exemplary wines with this designation.

- **VIN DE TABLE** The lowest rung on the quality ladder of wines that fail to meet AOC requirements, Vins de Table (literally, "table wines") are not permitted to mention vintages or grape varieties on their labels, or give a place of origin more specific than "France." Most are dull, but certain iconoclasts who've chosen to ignore some of the AOC demands (which they believe inhibit quality production) are currently making some remarkable Vins de Table.

alsace

Thanks to a history of being passed back and forth between Germany and France, Alsace is unique among all other French wine regions in its culture, cuisine and viticultural traditions. Alsace's historical ties and proximity to Germany, just across the Rhine River, influence everything from the grapes grown to the way wines are labeled—by variety, not region. And yet, they taste remarkably different from German wines, mainly because the majority are dry.

Alsace Grapes & Styles

Two of the area's most noble grapes are German: Riesling and Gewurztraminer. Unlike German versions, however, most Alsatian examples are completely dry. French Pinot Blanc, Pinot Gris, Muscat and Auxerrois make up the bulk of Alsace's other white varieties and are all widely planted. Pinot Noir is the region's only red variety. Alsace is also known for its wonderful dessert wines (see p. 271) and for Crémant d'Alsace, a Champagne-style sparkling wine.

Alsace Wine Labels

Unlike other French regions, Alsace labels its wines by grape variety. While European Union standards require that the listed grape compose at least 85 percent of the bottle's contents, Alsatian standards insist that it make up 100 percent. (Pinot Blanc is an exception; see p. 24.) Most Alsace wines fall into one of three categories: regular, reserve or late-harvest. Blended white wines are called "Edelzwicker" or "Gentil," or they may be named after the vineyard from which the grapes came. Wines labeled "Réserve," a term used fairly liberally in Alsace, may also list a place name. Alsace vineyards officially designated superior to all others can add "Grand Cru" to their labels. The integrity of this designation, however, is a matter of debate, and some wineries with Grand Cru sites prefer to use only the vineyard name, or proprietary names like Hugel & Fils "Cuvée Les Amours" Pinot Blanc. These names have no legal meaning but are mostly applied to premium wines.

ALSACE

pinot blanc & pinot gris

As their names imply, Pinot Blanc and Pinot Gris are indeed related, yet they can produce radically different wines. Pinot Blanc is softer, yielding subtle pear, citrus and nut flavors, while Pinot Gris is headier, with vibrant apricot and orange peel aromas. And although Pinot Gris is technically the same grape as the high-acid Pinot Grigio of Italy, they are very different in style, with Italian versions much lighter in body. Curiously, many wines labeled "Pinot Blanc" are blended with (and sometimes even made entirely of) the grape Auxerrois. Until recently Pinot Gris was labeled "Tokay d'Alsace," but to avoid confusion with the wines from Hungary's Tokaji region (made from Furmint), regulations now demand that it be called simply "Pinot Gris."

pinot blanc recommendations

Domaine Mittnacht Frères Terre d'Etoiles | 2006 |
★★ $ $ Winemaker Christophe Mittnacht employs organic and bio-dynamic practices in the crafting of all the wines from his up-and-coming estate. This clean and appley white has crisp acidity and only the slightest hint of residual sugar.

Josmeyer Mise du Printemps | 2005 |
★★ $ $ While this Pinot Blanc's peach and apple flavors are subtle, its mineral, flint and gunpowder qualities are immediately apparent. Biodynamically produced, the wine has a nice texture, good structure and a hint of tannins; it's slightly chalky on the lean, dry finish.

Lucien Albrecht Cuvée Balthazar | 2006 |
★★ $ $ The Albrecht family has been making wine since 1425. Their Cuvée Balthazar offers pretty yellow apple and citrus flavors and a very interesting nose: herbal, with an oregano and bay leaf quality. Medium-bodied, the wine has nice acidity, too.

Pierre Sparr Réserve | 2006 |
★ $ $ Sparr's "Réserve" line represents the estate's fuller-bodied wines, drawn from 20-to-35-year-old vines. This white's restrained pear aromas are combined with a distinct stony mineral quality, and the palate is nicely rounded with green apple fruit.

pinot gris recommendations

Domaine Ehrhart Grand Cru Brand | 2004 |
★★★ $ $ $ Reminiscent of a summer fruit salad with spearmint leaves, this gorgeous wine offers heaps of fresh apples and apricots and a greenness that's slightly spinachlike. The fruit flavors linger and show subtle highlights of honey.

Domaine Marcel Deiss | 2004 |
★★★ $ $ $ By using wild yeasts and gentle pressing techniques, Jean-Michel Deiss aims to let terroir truly shine in his wines. This terrifically minerally white is firm and well structured, a combination of green and yellow pear and a touch of melon and smoke. It's somewhat juicy on the palate, with generous acidity and a dry finish.

Domaines Schlumberger Grand Cru Spiegel | 2005 |
★★★ $ $ Aromas of apricot, peach and quince introduce Schlumberger's off-dry Spiegel. Then the fruit explodes on the palate with a seductively sweet quality. The wine is full, rounded and plump in texture, with mineral nuances taking a backseat to the pure, sweet fruit.

Josmeyer Le Fromenteau | 2005 |
★★ $ $ This mineral-driven white is somewhat restrained with its fruit but offers a honeyed, beeswax-candle aroma that's quite lovely. Flavors of smoky flint meet a touch of steely peach fruit.

Lucien Albrecht Grand Cru Pfingstberg | 2003 |
★★ $ $ $ The Pfingstberg vineyard's chalky and micaceous sandstone soils yield wines of great intensity. This fruit-packed white boasts green apple candy, mango and kiwi flavors; the initial fruit sweetness is balanced with great acidity.

ALSACE

riesling & gewurztraminer

Of Alsace's two preeminent grapes, Riesling is the more popular, thanks to its elegance and grace. Alsace Rieslings are generally medium-bodied and dry, possessing citrus and peach flavors and a flintiness unique to the terroir. While many wine drinkers appreciate Gewurztraminer's exotic, intensely flavored exuberance, it is not for everyone. Big and brash, Gewurztraminer yields wines bursting with lychee aromas and wonderful spiciness (*Gewürz* means "spice" in German).

riesling recommendations

Binner Vignoble de Katzenthal | 2004 |

★★ $ $ Distinctive and terroir-driven, this lean wine is extroverted and floral, with scents of both white flower and marigold, and a leafy-green quality. The wine's fruit flavors are also very green, and it has an acidity that practically crackles.

Domaines Schlumberger Les Princes Abbés | 2006 |

★★ $ $ Made with grapes from several Grand Cru vineyards (as well as some from a few less-recognized sites), this wine is approachable while young: It's steely and firm on the palate, with nice acidity that's crisp and clean; whiffs of petrol appear on the aroma.

Domaine Weinbach Cuvée Ste-Catherine | 2006 |

★★★ $ $ $ Imagine what the Capuchin monks who founded Weinbach in 1612 would think of their winery being run by women—Colette Faller and her daughters Catherine and Laurence. Any skepticism would end with a sip of this creamy, citrus-kissed powerhouse Riesling; it's dripping with peach and tropical fruit and has racy acidity.

Lucien Albrecht Cuvée Henri | 2005 |

★★ $ $ $ This is spot-on Riesling, humming with the grape's typical peach fruit aromas and subtle hints of petrol. Great acidity, tart green apple flavors and rocky mineral nuances are all in balance; the wine also has a slight almond, peach-pit quality.

Trimbach | 2005 |

★★ $ $ Here's a racy, steely Riesling that smells like kaffir lime and white flowers and grips the palate with laser-beam acidity. It's a great everyday white from a reference-point winery that's been a fixture in the Alsatian village of Ribeauvillé since the 17th century.

gewurztraminer recommendations

Binner Kaefferkopf | 2005 |

★★ $ $ Rose, lilac and violet dominate this incredibly aromatic, dry wine. Made from organically grown grapes, it's almost perfumelike, with lingering lychee and rose flavors and prickly, up-front acidity.

Domaine Weinbach Cuvée Théo | 2006 |

★★★ $ $ $ Weinbach's spicy, rose-scented Gewurztraminers are among the world's best, and this off-dry beauty is memorable. Its baked apple and smoky spice aromas meld with candied ginger and apricot on the wine's velvety palate, kissed by a spritz of grapefruit.

Hugel & Fils Hugel | **2006** |

★ ★ **$ $** Alsatian icon Hugel & Fils turns out consistently delicious whites, many of them crafted in the family's original 17th-century winery buildings. Though dry, this mineral-laden, glycerine-rich offering is a powerful, aromatic nectar with a huge apricot-scented finish.

Léon Beyer | **2005** |

★ ★ **$ $** At first sniff, this wine is like a basketful of rose petals. On the palate, however, it's a touch herbal, with nice peach fruit and green almond flavors, far more austere and bone-dry than its floral, flirtatious aroma implies.

Willm | **2007** |

★ ★ **$** Plush but not cloying, this well-priced white offers all of Gewurztraminer's exotic flavors—white peach, wildflowers, Asian spice—without any excess sweetness or weight. The oily viscosity of the grape is here, but the overall effect is bright and refreshing.

star producers
alsace

Domaine Ehrhart

The vineyards at Philippe and Corinne Ehrhart's relatively small estate have been farmed sustainably for two generations and are certified organic.

Domaine Marcel Deiss

At the helm of one of Alsace's best Riesling producers is Jean-Michel Deiss, a terroirist who created the region's first single-vineyard field blends with great success.

Domaines Schlumberger

Uncle and niece vintners Alain and Séverine Schlumberger work with grapes from Alsace's largest vineyard holdings to craft their organic wines.

Domaine Weinbach

Colette Faller and her daughters run this landmark winery, which was founded by 17th-century monks and produces some of the finest white wines in the world.

Hugel & Fils

This family-owned and operated winery has thrived for most of its 13 generations. Hugel's outstanding wines reflect their motto: "The wine is already in the grape."

Lucien Albrecht

Jean Albrecht carries on a long family tradition as winemaker and vineyard manager, crafting excellent, versatile whites.

other alsace whites

Alsace is France's only major region that champions its single-variety wines, yet many excellent blended wines are made here, sometimes called "Edelzwicker" or "Gentil." Blends usually contain Sylvaner, Auxerrois or Chasselas—good, if uncelebrated, varieties. Superior blends contain noble grapes, such as Riesling, Gewurztraminer or Pinot Gris. The two kinds of Muscat grown in Alsace are usually blended together, not with other grape varieties, and tend to deliver aromatic flavors of honeysuckle and citrus.

other alsace white recommendations

Albert Seltz Sono Contento Vieilles Vignes Sylvaner | 2003 |
★★ $ $ $ Sylvaner tends to create rounder and more viscous wines than its cousin, Riesling. This bottling is floral and honeyed, a petrol-scented giant that'll stand up to a funky cheese drizzled with honey.

Domaine Bott-Geyl Les Pinots d'Alsace Metiss | 2005 |
★★ $ $ This golden-hued, off-dry blend combines Pinots Blanc, Auxerrois, Gris and Noir to rich, honeyed effect. A small amount of botrytis-affected fruit lends depth and complexity to this unique wine.

Domaine Ehrhart Val St. Gregoire Pinot Auxerrois | 2005 |
★★ $ $ Made from a Pinot Noir clone originating in Alsace, this Pinot Auxerrois–based white is restrained in aroma, offering subtle tropical fruit and marshmallow with a touch of smoke. Enjoyable and refreshing, the wine is a touch peppery, with bright acidity.

bordeaux

Bordeaux is likely the world's most recognized wine region. Its legendary reputation is based on its formidable, long-lived reds, many made by world-famous châteaux. The Bordelais know how to maximize their terroir, and by good fortune the grapes that perform best here, like Cabernet and Merlot, are among the most celebrated on the planet. The superb 2005 vintage, which garnered record prices for the top wines, helped draw attention to the potential of the region's less-expensive offerings, of which there are many.

Bordeaux Grapes & Styles

When most people think of Bordeaux, they think of red wine, but many excellent whites are made here, too, with Sauvignon Blanc, Sémillon, Muscadelle or some combination thereof. Some of the best whites, made in the Graves and Médoc districts, are dry with stone fruit flavors. Those from the vast Entre-Deux-Mers area are light and citrusy. The greatest Bordeaux blancs are the sweet wines from Sauternes and its satellite regions (see p. 271). Bordeaux's iconic red wines are made from some combination of Cabernet Sauvignon, Merlot, Cabernet Franc, Malbec, Petit Verdot and/or Carmenère. Cabernet Sauvignon excels on the Left Bank of the Gironde, and Merlot is at its best on the Right Bank, though blending is vital in all Bordeaux regions.

Bordeaux Wine Labels

Bordeaux wines are labeled by region, and, generally, the more specific the regional designation, the better the wine. Wines labeled simply "Bordeaux" can be made anywhere in Bordeaux. The next level up is "Bordeaux Supérieur"; these wines are required to be higher in alcohol, which implies they were made from riper grapes—often a measure of better quality. Wines from Bordeaux's districts—such as Médoc, Graves and St-Émilion—are required to meet even higher standards. And within the districts are communes— Pauillac and Margaux, for example—which must meet more stringent requirements still. Bordeaux's system for ranking wines was established with the famous 1855 classification, which created a hierarchy of wineries (or châteaux) considered superior based on the prices their wines commanded over time. Known as the "Cru Classé" system, the ranking grouped 61 superior wineries by cru (growth), from first ("Premier Cru") on top to fifth. Châteaux that didn't make the cut, but were still considered good, received the rank "Cru Bourgeois." The 1855 system is limited to châteaux in the Médoc and Sauternes, and one in Graves. In 1955, a similar system was established to rank wines from St-Émilion, but it is subject to revision every decade or so. The famed wines of Pomerol are not ranked.

bordeaux whites

Bordeaux's reputation may be founded upon its reds, but white Bordeaux—especially the highly regarded examples from the Pessac-Léognan subregion of Graves—are worth seeking out for their flavors of citrus, peach, grass and stone. The vast majority of Bordeaux whites come from the region of Entre-Deux-Mers, and while they display similar flavors, most tend to be less impressive.

bordeaux white recommendations

Château Bonnet | 2006 | ENTRE-DEUX-MERS

★ $ Green melon and pear aromas introduce this fresh, unoaked, screw-cap white from Bordeaux impresario André Lurton. It would be terrific with *moules marinières* (or any shellfish).

Château Carbonnieux Grand Cru | 2005 | PESSAC-LÉOGNAN

★★★★ $ $ $ Pessac-Léognan's gravelly soils are known to produce Bordeaux's most structured whites, and the excellent 2005 vintage also helped make this benchmark bottling a standout: This is tightly wound yet expansive wine, loaded with beeswax aromas and peach flavors framed by well-etched minerality.

Château Les Tuileries | 2006 | ENTRE-DEUX-MERS

★★ $ The smell of this white blend is assertively mineral, as if you struck two rocks together trying to create a spark. On the palate, Sauvignon Blanc's lemon-skin tartness and herbaceous savor is fleshed out by smaller percentages of Sémillon and Muscadelle.

Château Olivier Grand Cru | 2005 | PESSAC-LÉOGNAN

★★★ $ $ $ The historic Château Olivier is the rare Bordeaux estate that's heralded for its white wines as well as its reds. This ripe 2005 white showcases the honeyed texture of its foundation grape, Sémillon. Floral and chalky at first, the wine spreads like a delicious oil slick across the palate.

Château Tour de Mirambeau Réserve | 2006 | BORDEAUX SUPÉRIEUR

★★ $ A team of consultants guided by prominent oenologist Michel Rolland has a hand in the making of this melony, substantial white from vineyards in Entre-Deux-Mers. It's labeled as generic Bordeaux but drinks like something from a higher classification, with good texture and hints of tropical fruit.

Château Villa Bel-Air | 2004 | GRAVES

★★ **$ $** Jean-Michel Cazes, owner of Château Lynch-Bages, purchased the Villa Bel-Air estate in 1988 and delivers consistent, value-priced wines from the property. This mineral-laced white is softened by aromas of honey and smoke and balanced with crisp acidity.

Domaines Barons de Rothschild Lafite Réserve Spéciale | 2006 | BORDEAUX

★ **$ $** Bright, lemony aromas dominate the nose of this quaffable white marketed by the Rothschild family of Château Lafite fame. Melon flavors show honey accents upheld by a refreshing crispness.

Vieux Château Gaubert | 2006 | GRAVES

★★ **$ $** Crafted from equal parts Sauvignon and Sémillon fermented in oak and aged for a short period *sur lie* (the yeasty sediment left after fermentation), this wine layers a little ripe melon and cream across the mid-palate before finishing up with a snappy acidic kick.

bordeaux reds

Over 80 percent of all Bordeaux wines are red, composed mostly of Cabernet Sauvignon and Merlot, plus Cabernet Franc, Petit Verdot and Malbec. Each subregion yields wines with distinctive characteristics: Those from Pauillac tend to be full-bodied and tannic; those from St-Julien are more taut. The wines of Margaux are typically more delicate, and those from St-Émilion are round and plush. Most Bordeaux reds share a common earthiness and finesse.

bordeaux red recommendations

Château Brane-Cantenac Grand Cru | 2005 | MARGAUX
★★★★ $ $ $ This superb second-growth blend offers both power and elegance. Brimming with juicy blackberries and black cherry confiture, it possesses perfectly integrated tannins that are balanced with plenty of acidity on a seemingly never-ending finish.

Château de Bel-Air | 2005 | LALANDE DE POMEROL
★★ $ $ Aged for a minimum of 16 months, this plump, hearty blend is primarily Merlot bolstered by Cabernets Sauvignon and Franc and Malbec, and shows dark chocolate flavors and a dense structure.

Château de Pez Cru Bourgeois | 2005 | ST-ESTÈPHE
★★★ $ $ $ From the gravelly soils of St-Estèphe, this is another excellent 2005, full of black and red currant flavors and aromas of freshly ground black pepper, leading into a bright, velvety finish.

Château d'Issan Grand Cru | 2005 | MARGAUX
★★★ $ $ $ $ Big, earthy and powerful, this stunning Margaux showcases a lovely mix of forest floor and mushroom aromas followed by a pleasant heat in the mouth.

Château Haut-Brion Grand Cru | 2005 | PESSAC-LÉOGNAN
★★★★ $ $ $ $ This opulent blend of Merlot, Cabernet Sauvignon and a little Cabernet Franc is over the top with succulent fruit and earthy nuances: black currants, dried plums, figs, tobacco, coffee and just enough tannins on the finish to guarantee a very long life.

Château La Fleur-Pétrus | 2005 | POMEROL
★★★★ $ $ $ $ This chunky, massive Pomerol is proof-positive of the greatness of the 2005 Bordeaux vintage. In this bottling, a violet and lavender bouquet kicks into high gear with sweet cocoa and dark chocolate flavors, rounded out by savory tannins.

Château Lagarosse | 2005 | PREMIÈRES CÔTES DE BORDEAUX
★ ★ **$** Made primarily of Merlot (plus 10 percent each of Cabernets Franc and Sauvignon), this wine has dark fruit and cedar aromas that lead to a cherry-filled palate. Oak and nice acidity round out the finish.

Château Lagrange Grand Cru | 2005 | ST-JULIEN
★ ★ ★ ★ **$ $ $ $** Taking advantage of its high-altitude, gravelly St-Julien terroir, this bright, concentrated wine combines violet aromas with vanilla flavors (imparted by new oak barrels) and notes of chalk.

Château Lascombes Grand Cru | 2005 | MARGAUX
★ ★ ★ ★ **$ $ $ $** This wonderful, muscular wine is a blend of Cabernet and Merlot plus a splash of Petit Verdot. Its dark, dense fruit flavors are marked by notes of iron, pencil lead and chalk. Delicious.

Château La Serre Grand Cru | 2005 | ST-ÉMILION
★ ★ **$ $ $** Grown in clay- and limestone-rich soil and then barrel-aged for 15 to 18 months, this lively wine is dark and ripe but not too earthy. It has fresh acidity, notes of pepper and medium tannins.

star producers
bordeaux reds

Château Haut-Brion
This first-growth château is one of Bordeaux's most consistent producers of world-class wines, even in off years.

Château La Fleur-Pétrus
This famous Right Bank winery, overseen by Christian Moueix (of legendary Pétrus), lives up to its fans' expectations beautifully, year after year.

Château Latour
Located in the famed Pauillac district, the iconic Latour is renowned for being dependably great. It dates back to medieval times, but today boasts a state-of-the-art, ultra-modern facility.

Château Lynch-Bages
This Pauillac producer's famous wines may be classified as fifth-growth, but their quality is comparable to that of many more expensive wines.

Château Margaux
Margaux's history has been tumultuous, but for the past quarter-century its glory has been restored by general director Paul Pontallier.

Château Mouton Rothschild
Mouton's high-quality wines are also celebrated for their artist-decorated labels, which have featured the work of Salvador Dalí and Keith Haring.

Château Latour Grand Cru | 2005 | PAUILLAC

★ ★ ★ ★ $ $ $ $ Latour cellar master Pierre-Henri Chabot doesn't mince words when describing this blend: "This wine has everything—it's perfect." And he's right. This wine is perfect, with an intense purity straddling jammy fruit and soft, elegant tannins.

Château le Puy | 2004 | CÔTES DE FRANCS

★ ★ $ $ $ Jean-Pierre Amoreau crafts this organic, biodynamic wine from his perch atop the "Plateau of Wonders," where his family has run Château le Puy since 1610. The wine's ripe, red fruit aromas lead into black currant flavors and a long, brightly acidic finish.

Château Lynch-Bages Grand Cru | 2005 | PAUILLAC

★ ★ ★ ★ $ $ $ $ The Cazes family has worked for more than 70 years to elevate the image of this fifth-growth wine with such success it's unofficially considered a second growth. The 2005 is a brilliant blend of sweet currant fruit layered with notes of cedar, thyme, licorice and olives. It balances earth and elegance with great finesse.

news from a wine insider

bordeaux by Fiona Morrison, Bordeaux-based Master of Wine and international journalist

Most Significant Trends

The prices of the famous châteaux continued to climb in 2007, and with new markets in Russia, India and China fueling demand, there seems to be no limit to what some collectors will pay for the best bottles. At the same time, it's becoming increasingly difficult to sell lower-end Bordeaux. Interestingly, the demand for the top wines seems to bear little relation to vintage quality. While 2006 was generally regarded as a difficult vintage in Bordeaux, buyers grumbled that the "en primeur" prices still did not fall by much as a result.

In the News

Much to the relief of growers, the 2006 classification of St-Émilion châteaux, which had been suspended in March 2007 following a court case brought by four demoted properties, was ratified, enabling producers to list either "Grand Cru Classé" or "Premier Grand Cru Classé" on their labels, as usual. A similar classification of the Médoc Cru Bourgeois was repealed. In its place, the Alliance des Cru Bourgeois hopes to adopt a "Label Cru Bourgeois" qualification system, not as a classification but as a mark of quality.

Château Lynch-Moussas Grand Cru | 2005 | PAUILLAC

★★★ $ $ $ Lynch-Moussas proprietor Philippe Castéja, who also owns Château Batailley, has worked hard to improve the image of this fifth-growth winery, and with the 2005 vintage, his effort shows: Rich and round, this medium-bodied wine neatly packages together aromas of dried black fruits, dates, figs and smoke, with juicy, ripe tannins and a lengthy finish.

Château Margaux Grand Cru | 2005 | MARGAUX

★★★★ $ $ $ $ Margaux's general director Paul Pontallier describes the 2005 vintage as "one of the most magical" in 50 years. His intense blend of Cabernet and a bit of Merlot is proof: It possesses layers of dark, ripe fruit, eucalyptus, tobacco and cedar.

Château Mouton Rothschild Grand Cru | 2005 | PAUILLAC

★★★★ $ $ $ $ This deep, dark, gorgeous wine, brimming with red and black fruit, is amazingly concentrated. A blend of 85 percent Cabernet Sauvignon, with the remainder made up of Merlot and a touch of Cabernet Franc, it weighs in at an unprecedented 13.2 percent alcohol, by far the highest level ever recorded for a Mouton.

Château Palmer Alter Ego | 2005 | MARGAUX

★★★★ $ $ $ $ The "other self" of the venerable 164-year-old Château Palmer, this wine is intended to showcase a younger, more fruit-forward style: It's rich, with soft fruits, smoke, fine cocoa powder and cassis and has all the complexity and sophistication of its big sister.

Château Pibran Cru Bourgeois | 2005 | PAUILLAC

★★★ $ $ $ Label readers take note: Though Pibran is technically a Cru Bourgeois (hence the $40 price tag), its neighbors include Châteaux Mouton Rothschild and Lynch-Bages. This bottling is packed with blackberry and raspberry fruit and bright acidity and is anchored by powerful tannins; earth notes impart elegance and balance.

Château Pichon-Longueville (Baron) Grand Cru | 2005 | PAUILLAC

★★★★ $ $ $ $ The second-growth Pichon-Longueville estate, today owned by the seemingly ubiquitous Cazes family, has produced a powerful wine that's akin to a bowlful of fresh berries tossed with cassis and purple flowers. In the mouth it's full-bodied and ripe, with wonderful depth and richness that goes on and on (and on).

Château Villa Bel-Air | 2003 | GRAVES

★★ $ $ Already mature and ready to drink now, this well-integrated wine evolves nicely in the mouth. A red brick color and a slightly cooked, molasses flavor make it just right for smoked meat or game.

burgundy

Burgundy is a relatively small region that manages to rival Bordeaux as one of the most recognized appellations in the wine world, celebrated for its ethereal, mineral-laden, smoky wines. Burgundy is one of the northernmost and coolest red grape–growing regions in France, and its climate plays an unusually large hand in the all-important terroir factor that is paramount to French wines. The result, unfortunately, is highly variable (and often disappointing) vintages and wines. In good years, and under the tutelage of a great *vigneron,* white Burgundies can be extraordinarily complex and rich, and reds can be downright sensual, embodying characteristics that bond them inextricably with their place of origin.

Burgundy Grapes & Styles

Burgundy's fame is tied to two grape varieties: Chardonnay and Pinot Noir. Basically, all white wines here are made from Chardonnay, except for small amounts of Sauvignon Blanc (grown in and around St-Bris) and Aligoté (mostly from the Côte Chalonnaise)—both of which are indicated on labels—and tiny amounts of Pinots Blanc and Gris. Pinot Noir is responsible for the lion's share of Burgundian reds, with the significant exception of Beaujolais, where wines are produced from the Gamay grape. Though considered part of the region of Burgundy, Beaujolais has a distinctly different climate, terroir and style of wine. Another unique, if less important, appellation is Irancy; its reds are made from a blend of Pinot Noir and the local grape César.

Burgundy Wine Labels

All wine labels in Burgundy list region, some also list subregion and a small number add the vineyard name. Generally, the more specific the place information on a label, the finer the wine, but the producer and vintage carry far greater weight when it comes to assessing quality in this region. Over the years, certain vineyards achieved distinction for their consistently outstanding wines. But it's smart to research well in Burgundy, as a poor producer can make a disappointing wine from even the best grapes, while less-prestigious grapes can yield a terrific wine in a good year or in the hands of a dedicated producer.

• **REGION** The most basic wines of Burgundy are labeled with the name of the region, "Bourgogne," and occasionally the grape type. Though unassuming, some of these wines nonetheless offer good quality at an excellent price.

• **DISTRICT** A district appellation (such as Chablis) is the next step up in terms of quality. The grapes must be grown exclusively in that district. Wines labeled with the word "Villages" after the district name are theoretically superior.

- **VILLAGE** A wine may take the name of a specific village if all its grapes have been grown within that village's boundaries. This is often a good sign, as wines from the same terroir typically have similar characteristics.
- **PREMIER CRU** Certain vineyards with a history of producing superior wines have earned the distinction "Premier Cru." Premier Cru wines account for only about 10 percent of Burgundy's wines, and they must be made with grapes from these designated vineyards, which are sometimes included in the name (Meursault-Genevrières Premier Cru, for example). This is the second highest distinction in Burgundy after Grand Cru. (Confusingly, in Bordeaux it's the reverse: Premier Cru is the more prestigious rank.)
- **GRAND CRU** Burgundy's Grand Cru vineyards are so elite (fewer than 2 percent hold the honor), and the wines so famous, that some, like Montrachet, don't even include the "Grand Cru" title on their labels. These are the region's finest wines, requiring years of age to reach their full potential.

So great is the prestige of these wines that some villages added the name of the local Grand Cru vineyard to their own name decades ago. Thus the wines from Chassagne, for example, became Chassagne-Montrachet; while many of them are superb, they're not true Montrachet.

BURGUNDY

chablis

For many connoisseurs, Chablis is one of the world's premier wines. Unfortunately, knockoff producers have tarnished its reputation by labeling inferior bottles with the Chablis name. Located in the north of Burgundy, the Chablis region has a cool climate and limestone-rich soil, perfect for yielding high-acid, mineral-laden wines. That, along with the grape's lively citrus flavors and its uncanny ability to age (especially the Premier Cru and Grand Cru varieties), makes Chablis one of France's most fascinating wines. Petit Chablis, made from grapes grown throughout the region, is technically not Chablis, but can be quite nice.

chablis recommendations

Albert Bichot Les Vaucopins Domaine Long-Depaquit
| 2005 | **CHABLIS PREMIER CRU**

★ ★ ★ **$ $ $** This delightfully round and fleshy bottling from the superb 2005 vintage was sourced from a subsection of the south-facing Vaucoupin Premier Cru vineyard. The wine's soft acidity and creamy, yeasty texture is a result of 11 months spent aging on the lees.

Domaine Christian Moreau Père & Fils Valmur | 2006 |
CHABLIS GRAND CRU

★ ★ ★ **$ $ $ $** From one of only seven Grand Cru Chablis vineyards comes this splendid Chardonnay. Fermented half in steel and half in barrel, it's a luxurious mix of pear and apple fruit and lemony acidity.

Domaine Laroche Les Clos | 2005 | **CHABLIS GRAND CRU**

★ ★ ★ **$ $ $ $** Some might question using a screw-cap for Grand Cru wine since there is speculation as to how wines with this closure evolve with time. However, this white is so voluptuous you may not want to wait to see how it ages: Flavors of apple and banana have a viscous, mouth-coating texture and are perfectly delicious now.

Domaine Oudin Les Serres | 2005 | **CHABLIS**

★ ★ **$ $** Lemon-lime aromas and chalky acidity define this tightly wound Chablis, which comes from vineyards adjacent to the Vaucoupin Premier Cru. Aged only in steel, and extremely sharp and focused as a result, it's a solid 2005 at a nice price.

Gilbert Picq & ses Fils | 2006 | **CHABLIS**

★ ★ **$ $** This is an expressive village-level wine from a small father-and-sons operation in the village of Chichée. Fermented only in stainless steel, this racy white displays the terrific mineral-and-acid ferocity of Chardonnay grown in the limestone-laden soils of Chablis.

Louis Michel & Fils Montmain | 2006 | **CHABLIS PREMIER CRU**

★ ★ ★ ★ **$ $ $** Jean-Loup Michel oversees this brilliant, wildflower-scented white, which derives its opulence not from oak but from impeccable grapes from a celebrated cru. Aged only in stainless steel, it glistens with purity, seamlessly integrating its stony, citrusy tartness with a velvety, clotted cream richness.

Simonnet-Febvre | 2006 | **CHABLIS**

★ ★ **$ $** Here's a straightforward Chablis from a *négociant* house owned by Beaune's Maison Louis Latour. Lime-rind aromas lead you to believe that the wine will be sharp and tight, when in fact it's plush and creamy, ready for immediate enjoyment.

William Fèvre Montmains | 2005 | **CHABLIS PREMIER CRU**
★★★ $ $ $ An ageworthy, beautiful white, this is crafted from one of the best of the 40 Premiers Crus of Chablis. Montmains faces southeast, taking in morning sun and producing powerful yet accessible wines. This one has a deep apple-pear richness balanced by classic Chablis minerality.

Vincent Mothe Fourchaume | 2005 | **CHABLIS PREMIER CRU**
★★ $ $ $ A fairly broad-shouldered Chablis, this wine has a lactic, creamy texture that almost masks its fine-grained minerality; overall, however, it's a pleasurable, drink-now quaffer.

BURGUNDY

côte d'or

The Côte d'Or is Burgundy's premier winemaking region. Literally translated as "slope of gold," the region is split into two halves: Côte de Nuits in the north and Côte de Beaune in the south. In the Côte de Nuits, such renowned villages as Nuits-St-Georges, Gevrey-Chambertin and Chambolle-Musigny produce some of the region's finest reds, bursting with cherry flavors underscored by a pronounced minerality. The Côte de Beaune is noted for its whites from villages such as Puligny-Montrachet and Meursault, though the villages of Pommard, Volnay and Aloxe-Corton are known for some excellent reds as well.

côte d'or recommendations

WHITES

Albert Bichot Domaine du Pavillon | 2005 | **MEURSAULT**
★★★ $ $ $ This elegant Chardonnay is from one of three estates that make up the core of this increasingly prominent domaine—now run by fifth-generation Albéric Bichot. Floral and delicate, with citrus and apple fruit, the wine grows spicier and nuttier toward the finish.

Bouchard Père & Fils Beaune du Château | 2005 |
BEAUNE PREMIER CRU
★★★ $ $ $ Bouchard's blend of grapes from 19 Premier Cru Beaune parcels amounts to one delicious (and very concentrated) wine, brimming with pear, apple and guava fruit, lush, mouthwatering acidity and bright citrus and fresh pineapple notes.

Chanson Père & Fils Clos des Mouches | 2005 |
BEAUNE PREMIER CRU

★★★★ **$ $ $ $** Here's a white Burgundy that more than delivers on the promise of the amazing 2005 vintage. Layers of apple, lemon zest and mineral aromas are followed by bright acidity, all balanced by lovely apple flavors and a terrific pear-fruit creaminess. Outstanding.

Domaine Arnoux Père et Fils Les Picotins | 2006 |
SAVIGNY-LÈS-BEAUNE

★★★ **$ $** Pascal Arnoux now runs the longtime Arnoux family label, and if this 2006 selection—creamy, butter-scented and bursting with notes of apple, pear and herbs—is typical of his style, he'll carry the family name on to even greater heights.

Domaine Bruno Clair | 2005 | **MARSANNAY**

★★★ **$ $** Bruno Clair's Chardonnay–Pinot Gris blend from the Côte de Nuits's northernmost appellation shows wonderfully complex aromas of flowers, apple pie and smoke. A substantial white with a lengthy finish, it's filled out with crisp apple and pear flavors.

star producers
côte d'or

Albert Bichot
Managing director Albéric Bichot has raised the quality standard at his family's winery, eschewing herbicides and chemical fertilizers in favor of natural farming methods.

Bouchard Père & Fils
Best known for its excellent domaine bottlings, this Burgundy institution also makes first-rate village wines.

Chanson Père & Fils
Chanson is one of the oldest established wine producers in Burgundy, and its vineyards comprise some of the region's most coveted property.

Domaine Henri Gouges
Domaine Henri Gouges's 36-plus acres in Nuits-St-Georges yield legendarily tight, dense wines that can take years to soften—but are worth the wait.

Jean-Marc Boillot
Overachiever Jean-Marc Boillot has a rare talent for crafting great whites *and* great reds. His Burgundies offer solid values with class and finesse.

Joseph Drouhin
The celebrated 2005 vintage was 37-year-old Drouhin oenologist Jérôme Faure-Brac's first with the producer—and bodes well for his future.

Domaine Désertaux-Ferrand | 2005 | BOURGOGNE

★★ $ $ The Désertaux-Ferrand family continues their generations-old practice of wine production in the Côte de Nuits with this fresh-scented white Burgundy. Abundant peach and apricot aromas are layered in the mouth with honey, hazelnuts and a hint of oak.

Domaine Guy Bocard Vieilles Vignes | 2005 | MEURSAULT

★★ $ $ $ An extended period of barrel aging gives this wine lovely balance. Flower and grass aromas are rounded out with peach and apricot flavors and underscored with acidity.

Domaine Henri Gouges Pinot Blanc | 2006 | BOURGOGNE

★★ $ $ $ Since 1930, the Henri Gouges estate has bottled most of its crop to make quality (rather than bulk) wines. This delicious white has a citric acidity woven with green apple, juicy apricot and spice.

Domaine Michel Coutoux | 2006 | PULIGNY-MONTRACHET

★★★ $ $ $ $ Michel Coutoux learned the secrets of crafting beautiful Burgundies from his father-in-law, winemaker Michel Niellon. One of the results, this unctuous Puligny-Montrachet is ripe with peaches and pears and has a nice bit of nuttiness on the finish.

Domaine Vincent Girardin Les Narvaux | 2005 | MEURSAULT

★★★ $ $ $ An elegant, gorgeous Meursault, this wine is aged primarily in new wood and never filtered, lending it flavors of fresh fruit and toasty oak. Apple and apricot aromas are rounded out with pear.

Fernand and Laurent Pillot | 2006 | CHASSAGNE-MONTRACHET

★★★ $ $ $ When Laurent Pillot took over the family business, he quickly transformed it from a grape-growing enterprise to an estate-bottling operation. One result is this impressive 2006, which smells of fresh flowers and tastes of crisp apples and citrus.

Joseph Drouhin White Clos des Mouches | 2005 | BEAUNE

★★★★ $ $ $ $ Talk about pedigree: This wine is made by one of the oldest families in Montrachet (they've owned the land since 1363). Buttery, fresh aromas of white flowers, toasted almonds and honey are followed by complex and powerful flavors of apricots and peaches. A hint of butterscotch on the finish is lightened by clean acidity.

Pascal Prunier-Bonheur Vieilles Vignes | 2005 |
AUXEY-DURESSES

★★ $ $ $ Pascal Prunier is a fifth-generation winemaker who works with old vines growing throughout several Côte de Beaune communes. Their fruit produces the rich apricot and peach notes of this 2005 white, whose luscious citrus flavor is touched with honey.

Thierry et Pascale Matrot Charmes | 2006 |
MEURSAULT PREMIER CRU

★ ★ ★ $ $ $ $ Charmes is not only the largest Premier Cru in Meursault, it's also reputed to produce the most pronounced wines. This lush example is a veritable tidal wave of peaches, full of mouthwatering acidity and accents of honey and apples.

Xavier Monnot Les Duresses | 2005 | MONTHÉLIE
★ ★ $ $ $ Monthélie, in the Côte de Beaune section of the Côte d'Or, is known mainly for reds; most of Monnot's bottlings, however, are white. This one is fragrant and elegant, with citrus and apple aromas bolstered by fleshy fruit and butter flavors and lemony acidity.

REDS

Alain & Julien Guillot Clos des Vignes du Maynes | 2006 |
BOURGOGNE

★ ★ $ $ The Guillots' vineyard has been organic since 1954, making it one of the first in France. This wine's bright, sour cherry flavor is lively and fresh, tinged with sweet spice and coriander.

Albert Bichot Domaine du Clos Frantin | 2005 |
CLOS DE VOUGEOT GRAND CRU

★ ★ ★ $ $ $ $ The Clos Frantin winery crafts an impressive Grand Cru, with cocoa and black licorice aromas draped over ripe cherry fruit. A very pretty wine, it doesn't lack for sophistication or intensity.

Chanson Père & Fils | 2005 | CHAMBOLLE-MUSIGNY
★ ★ ★ ★ $ $ $ $ From the small village of Chambolle-Musigny, home to two of the Côte d'Or's Grand Cru vineyards (Musigny and Bonnes Mares), comes this exquisitely complex and somewhat rustic wine. Ripe cherry fruit and vivid acidity define the palate, over which cherry cola, chalk and tobacco aromas hover. Delicious.

Château de Chamirey | 2005 | BOURGOGNE
★ ★ $ $ $ Though it hails from vineyards in historic Mercurey, this Pinot flaunts some New World flair, with cocoa and sweet spice layered nicely over bright raspberry and cassis flavors. The texture is juicy, turning silky on the long finish.

Domaine Bouchard Père & Fils Beaune du Château | 2005 |
BEAUNE PREMIER CRU

★ ★ ★ $ $ $ With its heady, perfumed aroma of cherry blossoms and black cherries, this wine is a testament to the superb 2005 vintage. More juicy black cherry bursts onto the palate before sweeping acidity comes pouring in, followed by penetrating chalky notes.

Domaine Henri Gouges Les Chênes Carteaux | 2005 |
NUITS-ST-GEORGES PREMIER CRU

★★★ $ $ $ $ Henri Gouges is one of the best producers of Nuits-St-Georges, turning out small amounts of carefully sculpted Pinot Noir. This bold wine reflects rugged elegance with floral, red currant and spice aromas, joined by tobacco, berries and mineral flavors.

Domaine Jessiaume Les Combottes | 2006 | POMMARD

★★ $ $ From an estate dating back to the 1850s and run by fifth-generation vinegrowers, this bottling is soft and perfumed, recalling summer cherries and chocolate with a hint of dust and cigar box. The cocoa and tobacco continue on the palate, and the finish lingers.

Domaine Michèle & Patrice Rion Clos des Argillières
| 2005 | NUITS-ST-GEORGES PREMIER CRU

★★★ $ $ $ $ In existence only since 1990, this small but steadily growing domaine offers a Pinot packed with spicy plum and blackberry flavors that turn dark and juicy on the palate. Those generous Nuits-St-Georges tannins appear, but are fine and nicely integrated.

news from a wine insider
burgundy by Daniel Johnnes, wine director for the Daniel Boulud restaurant group

Vintage Note

While demand for the highly rated 2005 Burgundies shows no sign of abating, the 2004 and 2006 vintages are also worth consideration. The 2004 whites are wonderfully mineral-laden, and the reds are evolving beautifully; both represent excellent value. Wines from the 2006 vintage are not as consistent. Top estates produced reds with great purity and expression, yet some lack mid-palate weight. The whites are a mixed bag as well: Some are fresh and richly flavored, others are heavy and alcoholic.

Winemakers to Watch

The quality of Burgundy's *négociants* (producers who buy grapes from growers) has greatly improved. Two boutique *négociants* worth seeking out are Pascal Marchand of Maison Moillard and Benjamin Leroux, winemaker at Comte Armand. Other great producers with *négociant* businesses include Lalou Bize Leroy (Maison Leroy), Jean-Nicolas Méo (Méo-Camuzet), Jacques Seysses (Dujac), Henri Boillot, Alix and Etienne de Montille (Deux Montille Soeur-Frère) as well as Drouhin, Bouchard and Jadot.

Jean-Marc Boillot Jarollières | 2005 | POMMARD PREMIER CRU
★★★ $ $ $ $ Once a winemaker for Olivier Leflaive, Jean-Marc Boillot now operates vineyards previously owned by his grandfather, Étienne Sauzet of Domaine Sauzet. His 2005 is rich, round and packed with berries; the concentration and acidity are in perfect harmony.

Joseph Drouhin | 2005 | GEVREY-CHAMBERTIN
★★★ $ $ $ The mega-merchant of Burgundy, Drouhin is best known for large-production bottlings, but this top-notch Pinot shows impressive structure and sophistication. Dusty plum and cocoa aromas lead to a palate that balances sweet spice with firm tannins.

Labouré-Roi Le Taillefer | 2006 | POMMARD
★★ $ $ $ Labouré-Roi is a familiar restaurant favorite; the winery uses 20 percent new oak to tame some of the inherent *animale* in this darkly ripe Pommard. Its cherry, currant and blackberry fruit offer great structure to this pleasantly spicy, medium-bodied wine.

Louis Latour | 2005 | SANTENAY
★★ $ $ Grown in marl- and limestone-rich soils in the Côte de Beaune's Santenay appellation, this Pinot Noir shows great pedigree; sweet blossoms and black cherry are evoked on the nose, and tart cherry flavors and vivid acidity bring freshness and balance.

Maison Champy Signature | 2005 | BOURGOGNE
★★★ $ From the oldest *négociant* in Burgundy, this wine couples pure, clean red cherry fruit with obvious Burgundian character; the result is a superb value. The cherry flavors are ripe, almost candied, on the palate, but the utterly dry wine remains fresh, with good length.

Olivier Leflaive Cuvée Margot | 2006 | BOURGOGNE
★★ $ $ Named for the owner's daughter, this tasty bottling delivers nice cherry and berry flavors tinged with flowers and sassafras. As a basic Burgundy, it's clean, slightly herbal and refreshingly tart.

Vincent Girardin Emotion de Terroirs Pinot Noir | 2005 | BOURGOGNE
★★ $ $ Despite the New World–looking label and unorthodox mention of grape variety, this is a traditional, serious Burgundy. Rustic, earthy and concentrated, it offers chocolate, licorice and violet aromas leading to an elegant, dark cherry palate.

Xavier Monnot Clos des Chênes | 2005 | VOLNAY PREMIER CRU
★★★ $ $ $ $ Made with grapes from a tiny two-acre parcel, this rich Volnay is marked by smoky, black cherry and currant aromas. Bold, ripe fruit flavors are layered with minerals and bracing acidity.

BURGUNDY

côte chalonnaise

The Côte Chalonnaise region is often overlooked, but true Burgundy aficionados know that great values can be found here. The villages of Mercurey and Givry produce delicious, well-priced reds, while the Chardonnays of Montagny provide lower-priced alternatives to the more popular vineyards to the north. In addition to Chardonnay, the village of Rully makes a small amount of sparkling wine, while Bouzeron offers Aligoté—Burgundy's "other" white grape.

côte chalonnaise recommendations

WHITES

Château de Chamirey | 2005 | MERCUREY
★★ $ $ $ Butter, lemon zest and floral aromas introduce this refreshing white. It offers more lemon on the palate, along with a little white pepper and a long finish full of citrus and minerals.

Jean-Marc Boillot St. Jacques | 2005 | RULLY
★★★ $ $ Boillot is considered a master of flavor extraction—especially with Pinot Noir grapes—and here he proves his skill with Chardonnay, too. This vanilla-scented beauty is kissed with peach, pear and nectarine fruit and has nicely integrated acidity.

Vincent Dureuil-Janthial Maizières | 2006 | RULLY
★★★ $ $ $ This is an excellent, off-the-beaten-track Chardonnay possessing serious depth. While it was aged partially in new oak, the wine is crisp and fruit-driven, with a distinctive lemon curd richness; it's both pretty and powerful at the same time.

Vincent Girardin Vieilles Vignes | 2006 | RULLY
★★ $ $ Grower/*négociant* Vincent Girardin always gives lesser-known appellations such as Rully the same care and attention as famous ones. This well-balanced white starts out as lush as cappuccino foam, then finishes with a squirt of limey acidity.

REDS

Besson Le Haut Colombier Rouge | 2005 | GIVRY
★★ $ $ Aromas of roses and spice announce this fruity, well-structured Givry. Its Pinot Noir fruit washes over the palate, offering chocolate and mocha nuances, fine tannins and a velvety texture.

Erker Les Bois Chevaux Cuvée Unique | 2003 | GIVRY
PREMIER CRU

★ ★ ★ $ $ If you close your eyes and sniff this wine, you might mistake it for Grenache. That's because the 30-year-old Pinot Noir vines that produced its grapes pack an intensity not common in most Givry. The delicious result brims with a mix of red fruit, spice and cocoa.

Vincent Dureuil Vieilles Vignes Rouge | 2005 | RULLY

★ ★ ★ $ $ $ The old-vine Pinot Noir grapes in this lovely red deliver cooked fruit aromas that are reminiscent of Zinfandel, but once in the mouth this wine has a luscious acidity that is all Pinot, with licorice spice, blueberry jam and a finish that goes on and on.

BURGUNDY

mâconnais

The Mâconnais differs from other Burgundian regions; with abundant sun and less risk of frost, it produces mostly simple, fresh whites, though some subregions have proven more ambitious in their endeavors. Pouilly-Fuissé is the region's most acclaimed appellation, as well as its most expensive, while St-Véran offers similar quality at a lower price. The best values can be found in wines with the Mâcon designation (listed here in ascending order of quality): Mâcon, Mâcon Supérieur, Mâcon-Villages or Mâcon followed by a particular village name, such as Mâcon-Viré.

mâconnais recommendations

Cave de Lugny Les Charmes Chardonnay | 2006 |
MÂCON-LUGNY

★ $ This is a consistent, widely distributed Chardonnay at a very agreeable price. Its assertive lemon-lime aroma follows through on the palate with refreshing citrus flavors and good depth.

Daniel et Martine Barraud La Verchère Vieilles Vignes
| 2006 | POUILLY-FUISSÉ

★ ★ ★ $ $ $ The grapes for this wine from up-and-coming young winemaker Daniel Barraud come from 40-to-50-year-old vines (hence the name *Vieilles Vignes*) on a lovely south-facing slope smack in front of Barraud's front door. A powerful white, it has a tart, lime nose but broadens on the palate into an unctuous, pear-flavored nectar.

Domaine Cordier Père et Fils | 2005 | MÂCON-FUISSÉ

★★ $ $ This well-structured dry Mâcon could compete with many more expensive Burgundies. Aromas of lemon meringue launch it on a sweet, seductive path; on the palate, though, it wraps its fruit in a robe of minerality and green apple acidity.

Domaine des Vignes du Maynes Aragonite | 2005 | MÂCON-CRUZILLE

★★ $ $ $ This barrel-fermented white from one of the first organic domaines in France (founded in 1954) is crafted by biodynamic champion Alain Guillot and his son, Julien. It has a cloudy appearance and an intense yeastiness, both of which complement its gripping acidity.

Domaine du Chalet Pouilly | 2005 | POUILLY-FUISSÉ

★★★ $ $ $ Rich, round and layered, this gorgeous example from the stellar 2005 vintage wavers between toasty/oaky and lemony/tart, and that tension is its charm. It hails from a small family-owned property that has been producing white wines from Pouilly-Fuissé and St-Véran for over 100 years.

Domaine Guillot-Broux Les Combettes | 2005 | MÂCON-CHARDONNAY

★★★ $ $ This sumptuous, unfiltered Chardonnay is crafted by biodynamic viticulturist Jean-Gérard Guillot, who grew up alongside his cousin Alain at the Domaine des Vignes du Maynes. Cloaked as it is in toasty oak, the wine needs to be open for a while to reveal itself fully. It's a powerhouse, worthy of cellaring.

Domaine Leflaive | 2006 | MÂCON-VERZÉ

★★★ $ $ $ In 2003, Ann-Claude Leflaive purchased several vineyards in the village of Verzé, venturing from her family's comfort zone in Puligny-Montrachet in the Côte d'Or. One result is this powerful and polished Mâconnais, with hints of lemon meringue and green apple lifted by steely acidity.

Domaine Vessigaud Vieilles Vignes | 2005 | POUILLY-FUISSÉ

★★★ $ $ $ Lucien Vessigaud's son, Pierre, maintains the family estate—founded in the 18th century—with an eye toward modern sustainable agriculture. Made with natural yeasts, this delicious, well-balanced, unfiltered Chardonnay is peachy, minerally and creamy.

Georges Duboeuf | 2006 | POUILLY-FUISSÉ

★ $ $ Beaujolais-master Duboeuf shows a deft hand with Mâconnais wine, too, in this creamy, immediately drinkable 2006. A clear, bright expression of Chardonnay without any ponderous oak, it's a good style for parties where versatility with food is key.

BURGUNDY

beaujolais

As Burgundy's southernmost region, Beaujolais is distinctly different from its neighbors to the north. To begin with, wines here are made exclusively with Gamay (instead of Pinot Noir), and the region has its own ranking system for quality. Beaujolais produces an abundance of mostly inexpensive, simple-but-satisfying red wines, as well as a number of high-quality bottles that can satisfy the palate of a Burgundy lover at a fraction of the cost. A handful of Chardonnay-based whites are also made here.

• **BEAUJOLAIS NOUVEAU** Designed for consumption within weeks of harvest, Beaujolais Nouveau is as light and simple as red wine gets. By law, it is released the third Thursday of every November, conveniently coinciding with the American holiday season.

• **BEAUJOLAIS** Wines made from grapes grown anywhere within the designated region earn the moniker "Beaujolais." These reds are marked by distinctive light, fruity flavors and are a bit more substantial than Beaujolais Nouveau.

• **BEAUJOLAIS-VILLAGES** The title of Beaujolais-Villages is given to any wine made from grapes grown within the 39 villages occupying the rolling hills at the center of the region. These wines are typically made with more care and precision, producing bright fruit flavors as well as an added depth of mineral and spice.

• **CRU BEAUJOLAIS** The region's greatest wines come from ten hillside villages in the northern part of Beaujolais. Called "Cru Beaujolais," these wines show an even heavier concentration of berry, mineral and spice flavors than Beaujolais-Villages, plus ample tannins, which allow them to age unlike other Beaujolais. These wines are so well regarded that many vintners don't even put "Beaujolais" on their Cru Beaujolais labels, instead listing just the name of the village where the grapes were grown: Brouilly, Chénas, Chiroubles, Côte de Brouilly, Fleurie, Juliénas, Morgon, Régnié, Moulin-à-Vent and St-Amour.

beaujolais recommendations

WHITES

Jean-Paul Brun Terres Dorées | 2006 | BEAUJOLAIS BLANC

★ ★ ★ $ $ All Beaujolais is made from Gamay grapes—except white Beaujolais. This one is made (like most Burgundies) from Chardonnay, and even without a bit of oak aging, it is rich, with pineapple flavors and a strong underpinning of chalky minerality. Terrific.

REDS

Château Cambon | 2007 | BEAUJOLAIS

★ $ $ Marcel Lapierre crafts this earthy, light-bodied Beaujolais without fining (i.e., clarification), filtering or adding any sulfur. It tastes entirely of the earth, from fresh soil to flowers and sweet raspberries.

Château de la Terrière Vieilles Vignes Cuvée Jules du Souzy | 2006 | BROUILLY

★ ★ $ $ Made from low-yielding vines averaging about 60 years in age, Jules du Souzy is Château de la Terrière's flagship bottling; it spends three months in oak, which lends the wine's deep flavors the structure to age well.

Château du Basty | 2006 | BEAUJOLAIS-VILLAGES LANTIGNIÉ

★ ★ $ $ Gilles Perroud is the 16th generation of his family to care for the 527-year-old Château du Basty estate in the tiny hamlet of Lantignié, near Morgon. And much like a Morgon, this wine is filled with dark, stony black raspberry flavor, delicious and lasting.

Georges Duboeuf | 2006 | BEAUJOLAIS-VILLAGES

★ $ The so-called "king of Beaujolais," Georges Duboeuf produces more than the simple Beaujolais Nouveau for which he is famous. This bottling shows floral scents, peppery black fruit and bright acidity that make it refreshing and eminently quaffable.

Jean-Claude Lapalu Cuvée Vieilles Vignes | 2006 | BROUILLY

★ ★ $ $ Jean-Claude Lapalu has barely five acres to his name and has been making wine only since 1996, but he's putting out very good Beaujolais. Take this old-vine Brouilly: It's dark and earthy, and filled with cherry and berry fruit.

Joseph Drouhin | 2006 | MOULIN-À-VENT

★ ★ $ $ Drouhin is best known for Chablis, but the producer crafted an impressively firm and meaty Moulin-à-Vent in 2006. The wine is earthy and granitic, with lots of black fruit and sweet spice, all the while maintaining the charm of a Gamay-based red.

Labouré-Roi Saint Armand | 2006 | **BEAUJOLAIS-VILLAGES**
★ $ Made by one of Burgundy's largest *négociants,* this is a well-made, affordable Beaujolais, full of fresh berries and bright acidity.

Marcel Lapierre | 2006 | **MORGON**
★★★ $ $ Rèvolutionary Beaujolais vintner Lapierre went bio-dynamic in 1981 and focused on making high-quality long-lived wines when much of the region was obsessed with Beaujolais Nouveau. His Morgon is a serious and worthwhile red, tannic and mineral-laden.

Potel-Aviron | 2005 | **JULIÉNAS**
★★★ $ $ Nicolas Potel, one of the great *négociants* of Burgundy, crafts this wine with Beaujolais native Stéphane Aviron. The gratifying result is more Burgundian in style than most Beaujolais ever is, with lean, pretty violet notes, sweet spice and chalk and cherry flavors.

loire valley

One of France's largest and most diverse wine regions, the fertile Loire Valley stretches some 300 miles along the Loire River. The wines made here range from dry, still reds, whites and rosés to elegant sparklers and sweet dessert nectars.

Loire Valley Grapes & Styles

The Loire Valley is home to a vast array of grapes. Of the whites, Muscadet, known locally as Melon de Bourgogne, makes crisp dry wines, while Chenin Blanc produces dry, sweet and sparkling wines. Chardonnay and Sauvignon Blanc are also grown in much of the valley, with the latter grape responsible for the well-known whites of Sancerre and Pouilly-Fumé. The valley's dominant red grape is Cabernet Franc, though Pinot Noir is also grown in the eastern part of the region. Blending is permitted in certain appellations, such as Valençay, where whites may be made from a combination of Sauvignon Blanc and Chardonnay.

Loire Valley Wine Labels

Loire Valley wines are identified by appellation, and since blending of grapes is rare, the appellation is usually enough to determine the variety. Wines made from grapes not tied to a region will list both the grape and the region name.

loire valley whites

The Loire Valley's broad range of white wines, from simple aperitifs to profoundly earthy wines designed for aging, are made from three primary grapes: Sauvignon Blanc, Chenin Blanc and Muscadet. Muscadet produces light, lively wines known for their ability to pair well with shellfish. Sauvignon Blanc yields similarly vibrant wines, with expressive citrus, mineral and herb notes. The wines from the distinctive Chenin Blanc grape vary greatly across the quality spectrum, but it is well worth seeking out the gems.

LOIRE VALLEY WHITES

chenin blanc

Chenin Blanc is the Loire Valley's most versatile grape, capable of producing some truly impressive and unusual wines. Styles can range from dry to sparkling or exquisitely sweet, but almost all are high in acidity, which gives them the ability to age beautifully. Though the Loire's most famous Chenin Blancs are probably the off-dry versions from the Vouvray appellation, these are often dull and uninspired, as are those from Montlouis across the river. Look to Savennières for higher-quality examples capable of long aging, as well as to Saumur and Anjou, where the best Chenin Blanc displays marvelous honey, citrus, truffle and smoky flavors.

chenin blanc recommendations

Domaine des Aubuisières Cuvée Silex | 2006 | VOUVRAY
★★★★ $ $ Silex is a flinty soil type found in Vouvray, and this luscious dry Vouvray from star winemaker Bernard Fouquet is sourced from his most siliceous vineyard sites. Hints of ripe pear and honey are checked by this spectacular wine's dusty minerality.

Domaine Laffourcade Clos la Royauté | 2006 | SAVENNIÈRES
★★ $ $ The sandy, rocky soils of the Savennières appellation are channeled in this sharp, mineral-laced white, which starts out with a welcoming perfume of red apples and wildflowers then turns more austere as it cleanses the palate with mouthwatering acidity.

Domaine Pichot Le Peu de la Moriette | 2006 | VOUVRAY
★ ★ **$ $** Wines from the 2006 vintage in the Loire are not for the cellar: It is considered a rich, drink-now vintage. This bold, off-dry white fits that mold with its lush pear fruit and assertive aromas of apricots and other stone fruits.

Marc Brédif | 2006 | VOUVRAY
★ ★ ★ **$ $** Owned by Loire Valley stalwart Baron de Ladoucette, Brédif delivers consistent value. This tightly wound white improves in the glass, releasing its honeysuckle and white flower aromas in time. The tenuous balance of appley sweetness and mineral dryness is textbook Chenin Blanc—delicious.

Nicolas Joly Clos de la Coulée de Serrant | 2005 |
SAVENNIÈRES-COULÉE DE SERRANT
★ ★ ★ **$ $ $ $** Biodynamic vintner/evangelist Nicolas Joly crafts this earthy Savennières from his famed Coulée de Serrant vineyard, one of the few single vineyards given its own appellation. This is a delightfully funky, golden-hued Chenin Blanc with aromas and flavors of toasted brioche and slow-baked apple, all enlivened by the wine's bold acidic grip.

Rémy Pannier Vallée des Jardins | 2006 | VOUVRAY
★ **$** Rémy Pannier is the single largest producer in the Loire Valley, owned by an alliance of more than 500 vinegrowers across the region. This clean, low-alcohol wine (11.5 percent) leans toward off-dry, with a honeyed texture and the flavor of pear nectar.

LOIRE VALLEY WHITES

melon de bourgogne/ muscadet

Basic Muscadets are relatively neutral white wines that are light-bodied with pleasant citrus flavors. Muscadets labeled *"sur lie"* (on lees), however, can achieve considerably more flavor intensity by remaining in contact with the "lees" (a sediment consisting of yeast cells, grape seeds, pulp, stem and skin fragments that is left behind after the fermentation process). The most interesting Muscadets hail from Sèvre-et-Maine and are at their best a year or two after vintage, though some well-made versions have the ability to age a decade or more.

muscadet recommendations

Château de la Ragotière (White Label) Muscadet sur Lie
| 2006 | SÈVRE-ET-MAINE

★★ $ Aging "on the lees" adds a layer of creaminess and complexity to this assertive 2006 Muscadet. Its briny flavors are augmented by grapefruit and green apple and bolstered by the region's classic high acidity.

Domaine de la Louvetrie Hermine d'Or Muscadet sur Lie
| 2007 | SÈVRE-ET-MAINE

★★★ $ Louvetrie is one of three properties owned by Joseph Landron, and one of several site-specific Muscadets he bottles. Sourced from old vines rooted in sandy soils, Hermine d'Or has a broad, melony richness on the palate, with a rather fruity aroma for Muscadet, and then unleashes a bracing dash of iodine on the finish.

Domaine de la Pépière Muscadet sur Lie | 2007 |
SÈVRE-ET-MAINE

★★★ $ Pépière is becoming a sought-after brand in restaurant circles, particularly as proprietor Marc Ollivier continues his ascent in the "natural wine" movement. This wine is slightly spritzy yet satisfying, whetting the appetite with its lemon-rind tartness and almost scouring the palate with its minerality.

Sauvion Château du Cléray Réserve Muscadet sur Lie
| 2007 | SÈVRE-ET-MAINE

★★★ $ Château du Cléray is the headquarters of the Sauvion family and essentially their top cru. Perhaps not for everyone, this Muscadet is lush yet bracing, sweet yet salty, and delivers a peculiar but fascinating mix of white peaches, beeswax and sea spray.

LOIRE VALLEY WHITES

sauvignon blanc

From Sancerre and Pouilly-Fumé, at the eastern reaches of the Loire Valley, come the finest Sauvignon Blancs the region has to offer. Filled with grapefruit, gooseberry and grass flavors, the wines typically possess a refreshing acidity plus a distinctive "gunflint" aroma. Sancerre tends to be fuller-bodied, while Pouilly-Fumé is lighter and more perfumed. Similar wines can be found in neighboring Quincy, Menetou-Salon and Reuilly.

sauvignon blanc recommendations

Château de Sancerre | 2006 | SANCERRE
★ ★ $ $ You can taste the limestone soils of Sancerre in this young wine. Yet unlike many austere Sancerres, this wraps its minerality in a silky sheet of ripe fruit with hints of lemon and honeydew melon.

de Ladoucette | 2005 | POUILLY-FUMÉ
★ ★ ★ $ $ $ The subtle aroma of this Pouilly-Fumé hints at peach, lime and herby grass; in the mouth, however, it explodes with broad richness balanced by refreshing citrus acidity. With a minerality that lingers from start to finish, this is a wine that is always delicious.

Domaine Guy Saget Domaine Saget | 2006 | POUILLY-FUMÉ
★ ★ $ $ Building from their original estate in Pouilly-sur-Loire, the Sagets have become big players in the Loire. From their home base comes this steely, mineral-rich wine with nice richness for the price.

Gérard Boulay Chavignol | 2006 | SANCERRE
★ ★ ★ ★ $ $ Most of Gérard Boulay's 20 acres of vines are on the chalky slopes of Chavignol, which have a similar soil content to Chablis' limestone-rich vineyards (said to contribute to the distinctly mineral flavor of that region's whites). Likewise, this full-bodied, citrusy Sancerre is wonderfully racy, teeming with acidity and minerals.

Lucien Crochet | 2006 | SANCERRE
★ ★ ★ $ $ This large estate run by the father-and-son team of Lucien and Gilles Crochet turns out elegant wines from vineyards throughout Sancerre. Their basic Sancerre is a clean and expressive Sauvignon Blanc, with assertive, pure floral aromas and a gripping acidity.

Olivier Girault Domaine de la Pucelle | 2006 | SANCERRE
★ ★ ★ $ $ This fruit-driven Sancerre has bold grapefruit aromas and a crisp but rounded texture. Winemaker Olivier Girault ages the wine on its lees for a bit, resulting in a softened, finely tuned wine.

Pascal Jolivet Sauvage Sauvignon Blanc | 2007 | SANCERRE
★ ★ ★ $ $ $ $ Sauvage is a rich, unfiltered Sancerre from a dynamic and prolific Sauvignon Blanc specialist. The wine spent 12 months aging on its lees, which gives it a nice yeasty heft; this is balanced by sharp acidity and pungent white grapefruit aromas.

Paul Thomas Chavignol Comtesses | 2006 | SANCERRE
★ ★ $ $ $ From a prized vineyard site within Sancerre comes this mineral-laden white. It shows the acidic tang of a good *chèvre* (for which the village is also famous) and a chalky, gripping style.

loire valley reds

Though it is a crucial blending grape in Bordeaux, Cabernet Franc performs even better in the Loire Valley. The grape's range is impressive, producing fruity, peppery wines meant to be enjoyed in their youth, as well as fuller-bodied, smoky, tannic reds suitable for considerable aging. The wines of Chinon and Saumur-Champigny are especially noteworthy. Pinot Noir, grown in the eastern part of the region, especially in Sancerre and Menetou-Salon, yields wines that tend to be light-bodied, with bright cherry flavors and high acidity. They're enjoyable, but rarely better than basic Burgundy. Gamay and other minor grapes are also grown in the Loire, though they are generally unremarkable.

loire valley red recommendations

Alphonse Mellot La Moussière | 2006 | SANCERRE
★★★★ $ $ $ $ This uncommonly deep and smoky Pinot Noir is made with grapes from a south-facing single-vineyard site. Very ripe and velvety, it's loaded with dark, black fruit flavors like currant and huckleberry, with a toasty edge lent by 10 to 18 months' aging in new oak. It's marvelous.

Catherine & Pierre Breton Clos Sénéchal | 2005 | BOURGUEIL
★★★ $ $ From a well-regarded (and biodynamic) single-vineyard site planted with 30-year-old vines, this earthy and tightly wound Cabernet Franc is a candidate for medium-range cellaring. It's got a fascinating mix of sweet and savory aromas, smelling of tart black cherries one minute and oregano and thyme the next.

Château Perray Jouannet | 2005 | ANJOU
★★ $ $ Here's a brightly fruity Cabernet Franc that puts a cheerful spin on this popular Loire Valley grape. Hailing from a property owned by Vignobles Laffourcade, which also has holdings in Savennières and Quarts de Chaume, it tastes of ripe red berries straight off the bush.

Domaine Bernard Baudry Clos Guillot | 2006 | CHINON
★★★★ $ $ $ Consistently one of the top-rated red wine producers in the Loire, Baudry sources this bottling from a prized old-vine site rooted in gravel and clay. True to its terroir, the wine tastes of the earth from which it springs, but also of so much more: black cherries, tar, roses and leather, too.

Domaine Desmoulins Le Carré du Prieur | 2007 |
CÔTE ROANNAISE

★ $ This light, chillable, berry-scented red is made from Gamay grapes grown in the far inland reaches of the Loire region, near Roanne, a stone's throw from Lyon and Beaujolais.

Domaine des Sablonnettes Les Copains d'Abord | 2006 |
VIN DE TABLE

★★ $ $ Crafted from the little-known Grolleau grape, this floral red from Anjou would be a good candidate to serve chilled: It has lots of cherry and berry fruit and a cracked black pepper bite, the overall effect light, refreshing and unusual.

Langlois-Château Les Montifault | 2006 | CHINON

★★ $ $ Aged only in stainless steel, this bright and aromatic Chinon brings out all the woodsy savor of Cabernet Franc: Think autumn leaves, campfires, even peat smoke. A terrific food wine, this would pair nicely with Thanksgiving turkey and cranberry sauce.

Paul Thomas | 2006 | SANCERRE

★★ $ $ This is a smoky, spicy, soil-expressive Pinot Noir from the steep, sloping vineyards of Chavignol in Sancerre. Light and berried, it's better suited to the picnic basket than the cellar.

Sébastien Bobinet Amatéüs Bobi | 2006 |
SAUMUR-CHAMPIGNY

★★★ $ $ $ Soft and supple wild raspberry aromas and a rich, round texture distinguish this nicely concentrated Cabernet Franc from boutique producer Sébastien Bobinet. For all of the wine's fruit and depth, the acidity comes on pleasingly strong in the finish, snapping the palate to attention.

rhône valley

At their best, the wines of the Rhône Valley have an unbridled power, spiciness and earthiness that make them unique among the fine wines of France. And yet, until only about 20 years ago, Rhône wines were largely dismissed as sturdy, second-class bumpkins. While many of the wines made here are indeed simple, vintners are crafting an increasing number of world-class reds that are just as profound as those from Burgundy or Bordeaux, yet with a distinctive, untamed character.

The Rhône Valley: An Overview

The Rhône River flows from the Swiss Alps down into France's Jura Mountains and on to the Mediterranean. The Rhône Valley wine region is divided into northern and southern parts, which differ greatly in terms of grapes, wine philosophies, soils and microclimates. The Rhône Valley ranks second in total wine production among major French regions, and while every style of wine is made here, reds represent nearly 90 percent of the region's AOC production.

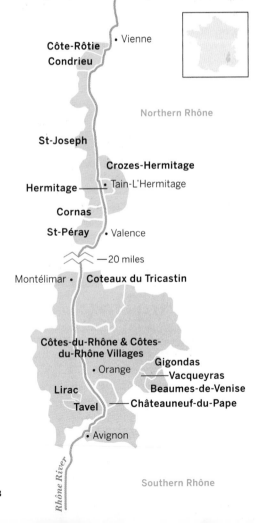

northern rhône

The northern Rhône is a narrow 50-mile or so stretch of terraced hills; some of the area's most sought-after wines hail from its steepest vineyards. Bookended by the appellations of Côte-Rôtie in the north and Cornas and St-Péray in the south, the northern Rhône lies at a crossroads between cooler Burgundy to the north and the sunny Mediterranean-influenced southern Rhône, and its wines reflect this geographical and climatic diversity.

Northern Rhône Grapes & Styles

Though the Viognier grape produces the the Rhône Valley's most celebrated white wines, two other grape varieties play supporting roles in the north: Marsanne and Roussanne. Viognier is synonymous with the white wines of Condrieu and the tiny neighboring appellation of Château Grillet. Brawny Marsanne is customarily blended with elegant Roussanne to create the full-bodied, nutty, baked pear– and apricot-scented whites of Hermitage, Crozes-Hermitage, St-Péray and St-Joseph. These wines are not especially high in acidity, yet many have the ability to age for a decade or more. The only red grape permitted in the production of northern Rhône red wines is Syrah, which in certain appellations was traditionally blended with a small amount of the region's aromatic white grapes—for example, up to 20 percent Viognier is permitted in Côte-Rôtie. Very few winemakers today, however, take this approach. Of the other appellation-specific wines, St-Joseph tends to be the lightest in body and the least tannic, followed in order of ascending strength by Crozes-Hermitage, Côte-Rôtie, Hermitage and, finally, Cornas. Known for their power and incredible longevity, the wines of Cornas must be made from Syrah alone, with no added white grapes. The total production of the northern Rhône is relatively small, accounting for less than 5 percent of all the wine made in the Rhône Valley; of that amount, well over half comes from Crozes-Hermitage.

northern rhône recommendations

WHITES

François Villard Les Contours de DePoncins Viognier

| 2006 | **VIN DE PAYS DES COLLINES RHODANIENNES**

★★★ **$ $ $** Former chef François Villard is a Condrieu expert, and this Viognier from his small northern Rhône estate is an amazing value: Hailing from a declassified parcel of young Condrieu vines that Villard is restoring to AOC status, it offers Condrieu's floral aromatics and honeyed heft at a much gentler price than most.

Jean-Luc Colombo La Redonne Blanc | 2006 |

CÔTES-DU-RHÔNE

★★ **$ $** While Jean-Luc Colombo is best known for powerful Cornas reds, he has holdings throughout the Rhône (and Provence) and makes whites and rosés as well. His lovely Viognier/Roussanne blend is pleasantly waxy with tropical fruit flavors.

star producers
northern rhône

Domaine Alain Voge

Alain Voge's Cornas and St-Péray wines have set quality benchmarks for some 50 years. Now at the helm here is Albéric Mazoye, who is maintaining the distinctive, terroir-driven character of Voge wines.

E. Guigal

The Rhône's most influential *négociant*, E. Guigal was the first to make single-vineyard "micro-crus" in Côte-Rôtie.

Jean-Luc Colombo

Often called the King of Cornas, Colombo is renowned for his intense, dark Cornas reds, but he also makes a wide range of high-quality Rhône wines.

Jean-Michel Gerin

Gerin's boundless energy and eye toward innovation and quality peg him as one of the region's most dynamic winemakers.

M. Chapoutier

Michel Chapoutier was an early pioneer of biodynamic viticulture; with vineyard holdings in every major Rhône appellation, he crafts an incredible array of wines.

Paul Jaboulet Aîné

From the legendary Hermitage La Chapelle to more modest bottlings, Jaboulet's wines are some of the Rhône Valley's most stunning and delicious.

Maison Alain Paret Lys de Volan | 2006 | CONDRIEU

★ ★ ★ **$ $ $** There may be no more seductive white wine than good Condrieu, and this bottling from a small northern Rhône farm is undeniably good. The peach and apricot aromas of Viognier grapes jump out of the glass, and though the wine is dry, its texture is unctuous.

M. Chapoutier Les Meysonniers | 2006 | CROZES-HERMITAGE

★ ★ ★ **$ $** Biodynamic dynamo Michel Chapoutier has a deft touch with reds and whites alike, as evidenced by this luscious Marsanne. Fermented in large vats, then aged on its lees for seven to eight months, Les Meysonniers is dripping with apple and peach flavors, with a stony savor holding the sweetness in check.

REDS

August Clape Cuvée Renaissance | 2005 | CORNAS

★ ★ ★ **$ $ $ $** This is wonderfully thick, darkly fruity Syrah from a Cornas icon. Clape farms about 27 acres, including some of the oldest plots in the appellation, though this bottling is from younger vines. The licorice and tar aromas are classic Cornas, which is known for its dark, brooding reds.

Delas Frères Seigneur de Maugiron | 2004 | CÔTE-RÔTIE

★ ★ ★ **$ $ $ $** Although Delas makes *négociant* wines, its best bottlings come from its estate-owned vineyards, including a small site in Côte-Rôtie from which this wine hails: It shows intense black fruit, cracked pepper and sausage flavors in a lush yet muscular package.

Domaine Alain Voge Vieilles Vignes | 2005 | CORNAS

★ ★ ★ **$ $ $ $** This tightly wound 2005, from a noted Cornas estate, will surely benefit from some time in the cellar. Yet while most Cornas wines are more burly than aromatic, this one has a pretty aroma of cassis and lavender and an elegant structure.

Domaine du Tunnel | 2006 | ST-JOSEPH

★ ★ ★ **$ $ $** Young Stéphane Robert started this small domaine in 1994, acquiring plots in Cornas, St-Joseph and St-Péray. This concentrated 2006 shows off the great vintage and the 80-year-old vines the wine is sourced from, with luscious notes of damson plum and black currant supported by silty tannins and judicious oak.

E. Guigal | 2005 | CROZES-HERMITAGE

★ ★ ★ **$ $** Here's a great value from the Rhône's premier house. The Guigals source fruit from vines over 30 years old for this meaty, well-structured Syrah. There's a smoky, almost charbroiled edge to its dark flavors, but tart acidity keeps the wine lively.

Jean-Luc Colombo Les Forots | 2006 | CÔTES-DU-RHÔNE
★ ★ $ $ An excellent substitute for Colombo's pricier Cornas bottlings, this bright and fragrant red displays textbook Syrah aromas of violet and black pepper and lush black fruit flavors.

Jean-Michel Gerin Les Grandes Places | 2005 | CÔTE-RÔTIE
★ ★ ★ $ $ $ $ Crafted from 100 percent Syrah and aged for 20 months in new oak, this is powerful stuff. The grapes come from Les Grandes Places vineyard on Côte-Rôtie's iron-rich slopes, and the wine mixes bright violet aromas with notes of roasted meat and tar.

M. Chapoutier Petite Ruche | 2005 | CROZES-HERMITAGE
★ ★ $ $ This straightforward northern Rhône Syrah is all about primary fruit and lively aromatics. It's fermented in cement and aged in large vats to preserve its black cherry freshness and spicy notes of sarsaparilla and nutmeg, finishing with a firm tannic bite.

Paul Jaboulet Aîné Les Jalets | 2006 | CROZES-HERMITAGE
★ ★ $ $ Bright and peppery, this crowd-pleasing Syrah is a candidate for by-the-case purchase. The quality of the 2006 vintage is evident in the wine's concentration and deep black fruit flavors.

RHÔNE VALLEY

southern rhône

About 30 miles south of the northern Rhône is where the milder, sun-kissed southern Rhône begins. Its rolling hills and wide-open vistas are home to vineyards that yield about 95 percent of the entire Rhône Valley's production.

Southern Rhône Grapes & Styles

There are 22 grape varieties permitted in the southern Rhône, but not all are allowed in each appellation. The main white grapes include Grenache Blanc, Clairette and Bourboulenc, plus classic northern Rhône varieties Marsanne, Roussanne and Viognier. They are typically blended and result in medium-bodied wines ranging in flavor from ripe peach and citrus to herbal and nutty. The southern Rhône's dark, fruity, earth-driven red wines can be made with ten grape varieties. Grenache is the principal one, and it is invariably blended with Cinsault, Syrah, Mourvèdre and/or Carignan. Rosés and good sweet wines are also made here.

Southern Rhône Wine Labels

As in the north, southern Rhône wines are labeled by appellation. Côtes-du-Rhône is the most basic, and can be used for any Rhône Valley wine, though most are from the south. Wines made in the dozens of designated villages that satisfy stricter requirements are labeled "Côtes-du-Rhône Villages." Eighteen villages that make wines of consistent quality have earned the right to add their name to the label, for example, Côtes-du-Rhône Villages Cairanne. The best villages—Châteauneuf-du-Pape, Gigondas, Tavel, Lirac and Vacqueyras—may use the village name alone. Satellite regions such as Côtes du Luberon, Côtes du Ventoux, Coteaux du Tricastin and Costières de Nîmes make wines similar in style and taste profile to basic Côtes-du-Rhône.

southern rhône recommendations

WHITES

Domaine de Lucéna Visan | 2006 |
CÔTES-DU-RHÔNE VILLAGES VISAN

★ $ Visan is just north of Rasteau and, like Rasteau, is one of a handful of communes allowed to be named on the label. This fresh, steely white is mostly Grenache Blanc, with notes of apple, pear and hay.

Domaine du Grand Tinel Blanc | 2006 |
CHÂTEAUNEUF-DU-PAPE

★★★ $ $ $ The large Domaine du Grand Tinel estate offers value and consistency in both red and white Châteauneuf. This floral, full-bodied white is straight-up delicious, like a drop of honey on the tongue. It finishes with the appellation's classic earthy, herbal edge.

E. Guigal | 2006 | CÔTES-DU-RHÔNE

★★★ $ The Guigals are Rhône royalty: They make wines of exceptional quality, and they make them in great quantities. This fantastic lower-level Viognier-based blend is a great value. It has a luscious, waxy texture and enticing aromas of acacia honey and apricot.

La Vieille Ferme | 2006 | CÔTES DU LUBERON

★★★ $ The Perrin family of Château de Beaucastel fame established this value brand, which delivers tasty, reliable wines from the Rhône and Languedoc. This big blend of Grenache Blanc, Bourboulenc, Ugni Blanc and Roussanne has hints of pineapple and mango.

Perrin Réserve | 2006 | CÔTES-DU-RHÔNE

★★ $ One of Perrin's well-priced brands, their eponymous label delivers consistent quality every vintage. This nicely structured blend of Grenache Blanc, Bourboulenc, Marsanne, Roussanne and Viognier is an exotic mix of honey, beeswax and honeydew melon flavors.

ROSÉS

Domaine de la Mordorée La Dame Rousse | 2007 | TAVEL

★★★ $ $ While most celebrated for its Châteauneuf-du-Pape, La Mordorée is based in Tavel and turns out consistently excellent rosé. Predominantly Grenache (60 percent), with Syrah, Cinsault, Mourvèdre, Bourboulenc and Clairette making up the remainder, this wine is a great mix of watermelon fruitiness and wild herb aromatics.

La Vieille Ferme | 2006 | CÔTES DU VENTOUX

★★ $ This leans into light red wine territory, loaded as it is with deep strawberry color and flavor. The fruit is juicy and ripe and there's even a hint of tannin lending grip, making it a bold choice for a summer afternoon of grilling.

Les Lauzeraies | 2007 | TAVEL

★ $ Here's another gutsy, dark-hued rosé, with loads of fruit, from watermelon to strawberry to red cherry. A solid effort from a large cooperative winery in Tavel, the wine shows real power.

Paul Jaboulet Aîné Parallèle "45" | 2007 | CÔTES-DU-RHÔNE

★★ $ Proof that Jaboulet does everything well, here's a clean, soft, fruit-driven rosé with a delicate pink hue and light appley fruit. It combines Grenache, Cinsault and Syrah and is marked more by its supreme freshness than its spiciness.

REDS

Camille Cayran La Réserve | 2005 |
CÔTES-DU-RHÔNE VILLAGES CAIRANNE

★ $ Founded in 1929, the Cave de Cairanne cooperative recently created the Camille Cayran line for its higher-tier wines sold exclusively through restaurants and wine shops. This crisp, juicy red blend is refreshingly rustic and would be nice with a chill.

Château Grande Cassagne G.S. | 2006 |
COSTIÈRES DE NÎMES

★★ $ With climate and soils similar to neighboring Côtes-du-Rhône, Costières de Nîmes can produce wines that are delightfully close to the Rhône's offerings. This one shows currants, blackberry and lavender aromas, and spice, tobacco and soft tannins on the palate.

Château La Nerthe | 2004 | CHÂTEAUNEUF-DU-PAPE

★ ★ ★ ★ $ $ $ This is marvelous Châteauneuf from one of the area's most historic estates. The fruit is syrup-ripe, the oak toasty, the tannins fine but firm. There's a healthy dose of spicy Mourvèdre in the blend, lending notes of black olive and lavender.

Domaine Brusset Les Hauts de Montmirail | 2005 | GIGONDAS

★ ★ ★ $ $ $ Sourced from a rocky, terraced vineyard in the Dentelles de Montmirail mountain foothills, this wonderfully spicy and meaty Gigondas offers good weight and aromatic complexity for the price. It blends Grenache, Mourvèdre and Syrah aged in French oak.

Domaine de Beaurenard Rasteau | 2005 | CÔTES-DU-RHÔNE VILLAGES RASTEAU

★ ★ $ $ Beaurenard is a noted Châteauneuf producer, and this spicy Rasteau bottling has the pedigree without the price tag. A Grenache/Syrah blend, it shows gutsy notes of roasted tomato savor.

star producers
southern rhône

Château La Nerthe

Château La Nerthe is one of Châteauneuf's oldest estates; today, it produces modern and elegant whites and reds under the direction of Alain Dugas.

Domaine du Grand Tinel

One of the Rhône's most undervalued producers, Grand Tinel is the fruitful merger of two wine families that date back 400 years; it's known for big, Grenache-centric reds.

Domaine du Pesquier

Guy Boutière has been the driving force behind the Domaine du Pesquier's stellar Grenache-based Gigondas wines for nearly two decades.

Domaine La Garrigue

The Bernard family's rich, full-bodied and spicy wines come from 60-year-old vines grown in soil that seems to be composed entirely of rocks.

Domaine La Millière

Domaine La Millière is said to have some of the best soil in Châteauneuf-du-Pape for growing Grenache, and winemaker Michel Arnaud's examples are first-rate.

E. Guigal

While Guigal is most lauded for its superb single-vineyard Côte-Rôties, the family-owned firm makes great, affordable southern Rhône wines, too.

Domaine de Cassan | 2005 | GIGONDAS

★ ★ ★ $ $ Located in the mountains above Gigondas, Domaine de Cassan specializes in wines from the appellation as well as from Beaumes de Venise. This dark and spicy Gigondas is truly a wine of place, herbal, mouthwatering and full of savory scrubland aromas.

Domaine de la Renjarde Massif d'Uchaux | 2004 | CÔTES-DU-RHÔNE VILLAGES

★ ★ $ $ Think of this village-designated red as "baby" Châteauneuf-du-Pape: It's a velvety, earthy, licorice-scented mouthful of Grenache, Syrah, Cinsault, Mourvèdre and Carignan from the Châteauneuf-neighboring commune of Massif d'Uchaux.

Domaine de Piaugier | 2005 | GIGONDAS

★ ★ ★ $ $ Located in Sablet, next door to Gigondas, Domaine de Piaugier is known for Sablet-designated Côtes-du-Rhône as well as for Gigondas. This is a powerful yet perfumed example, delicious and packed with dark berry fruit and spice-rack aromatics.

Domaine du Galet des Papes Tradition | 2005 | CHÂTEAUNEUF-DU-PAPE

★ ★ ★ $ $ $ Hints of menthol, herbs and maraschino cherry start off this medium-bodied red with an aromatic bang. The wine is clean, crisp and lush, not as massive as most Châteauneuf but instead bright and fresh, almost Pinot Noir-ish in scale.

Domaine du Grand Tinel Cuvée Alexis Establet | 2005 | CHÂTEAUNEUF-DU-PAPE

★ ★ ★ ★ $ $ $ Sourced from 100-year-old vines, this is spectacularly viscous, brackish-dark Châteauneuf brimming with licorice and black currant flavor. Predominantly Grenache (90 percent) plus a bit of Syrah, it has soft and sweet tannins, bright and herbal aromas and a huge concentration.

Domaine du Pesquier | 2005 | GIGONDAS

★ ★ ★ $ $ Syrah's currant, berry and licorice flavors dominate this ripe, concentrated Gigondas. Winemaker Guy Boutière blends 75 percent Grenache, 20 percent Syrah and 5 percent Mourvèdre and avoids excess oak. The result is a big, gamey, varietally expressive red.

Domaine Font de Michelle Cuvée Etienne Gonnet | 2004 | CHÂTEAUNEUF-DU-PAPE

★ ★ ★ $ $ $ This is the top wine from Font de Michelle, a muscular bottling with a touch of heat. Sourced from vines between 75 and 110 years old, the mix of Grenache, Syrah and Mourvèdre teems with black cherry and licorice flavors and sweet tannins.

Domaine Font Sarade | 2006 | VACQUEYRAS

★★ $ $ Whereas most Vacqueyras is Grenache-dominated, Font Sarade's Bernard Burle blends Grenache equally with Syrah to create this rich, deeply fruity expression of an often rustic and hard-edged wine. It's a great mix of supple, sweet fruit and exotic spice.

Domaine La Garrigue | 2005 | VACQUEYRAS

★★★ $ $ A terrific, consistent value from a well-known name in the Vacqueyras region, this Grenache-based blend includes a touch of Syrah and offers good body, deep black cherry fruit and a flinty, mineral-driven finish. It's a pure expression of the stony soils of the region, unadorned by oak.

Domaine La Lorentine | 2006 | LIRAC

★★ $ $ Southwest of Châteauneuf-du-Pape, the little-traveled Lirac appellation produces some appealingly rustic and affordable wines. This tangy red is one of them, a kitchen-sink blend of Grenache, Cinsault, Mourvèdre, Carignan and Syrah.

Domaine La Millière | 2006 | CHÂTEAUNEUF-DU-PAPE

★★★ $ $ $ La Millière's vines are all situated in the Châteauneuf-du-Pape subzone of Mont Redon-Cabrières, where the terroir features a mix of sand, limestone and the smooth, polished stones called *galets.* It is considered an ideal place for Grenache, and this mouth-watering, spicy and floral red is dominated by that variety.

Domaine la Soumade Cuvée Prestige | 2006 | CÔTES-DU-RHÔNE VILLAGES RASTEAU

★★ $ $ $ This is a gutsy but polished Rasteau from dynamic producer André Romero, who ages a portion of the wine (about 20 percent) in barrel to lend it a slight oaky veneer. Composed of 80 percent Grenache with a balance of Syrah and Mourvèdre, it has a chocolate-like richness yet is brightly acidic.

Domaine Le Couroulu | 2005 | VACQUEYRAS

★★★ $ $ Vacqueyras is often billed as the affordable alternative to Châteauneuf, and this is especially true of the reds from Le Couroulu. Combining a majority of Grenache with Syrah, Mourvèdre and Cinsault, this dense beauty balances its blackberry sweetness with savory notes of black olives.

Domaine Les Genestas | 2006 | CÔTES-DU-RHÔNE VILLAGES

★★ $ $ Flavors of stewed plums and dates give this wine some bass notes to complement its volcanic spiciness. A blend of the southern Rhône stalwarts Grenache, Syrah and Mourvèdre, it's produced at a cooperative winery located just south of Tavel.

J. Vidal-Fleury | 2004 | CHÂTEAUNEUF-DU-PAPE

★★ $ $ $ This *négociant* house, with roots in the Rhône going back to the 18th century, produces a range of wines. If you like rusticity, you'll love this earthy, savory Châteauneuf—it's a bottled evocation of the fragrant southern French scrubland known as the *garrigue*.

La Font du Vent Confidentia | 2005 |
CÔTES-DU-RHÔNE VILLAGES

★★ $ $ The Gonnet family, producers of Châteauneuf-du-Pape at Font de Michelle, acquired the 50-acre Font du Vent property near Tavel in 2002. Their Confidentia is a supple Grenache-Syrah blend with a woodsy mix of wild berry fruit and black pepper bite.

L'Anglore Cuvée des Traverses | 2007 | CÔTES-DU-RHÔNE

★★ $ $ From a small organic estate near Tavel, this blend of Syrah, Mourvèdre and Grenache is full of lavender and violet aromas. On the palate it's toasty and supple, with cocoa-powder tannins.

Maison Bouachon Les Rabassières | 2006 | CÔTES-DU-RHÔNE

★★ $ $ The cooperage-turned-winery Maison Bouachon has holdings throughout the Rhône. This Grenache-Syrah-Mourvèdre blend is from Plan de Dieu, north of Châteauneuf, and brims with the black fruit, spice and herbal edge of an authentic Mediterranean red.

Perrin Réserve | 2006 | CÔTES-DU-RHÔNE

★ $ This bold, rustic blend of Grenache, Syrah, Mourvèdre and Cinsault is a big wine for the money. It's slick and deep, with a rich blueberry flavor overlaid with some cracked black pepper.

southern france

A staggering amount of the wine made in France comes from the huge swath of land encompassing Languedoc, Roussillon, Provence and the Southwest. Though Greeks are thought to have made wine in Provence long before the Romans, in modern times this area was, until recently, known largely for the quantity, not the quality, of its wine. During the 1990s, however, a growing global demand for affordable wines brought renewed attention to the south, where bold vintners with a disregard for AOC rules were experimenting with nonnative grapes. Today, this is France's go-to region for inexpensive wines of dependable quality.

Southern France: An Overview

France's storied south, *le Midi,* encompasses the regions of Languedoc, Roussillon and Provence (the first two are often referred to as a single hyphenated entity, Languedoc-Roussillon, or just Languedoc). This part of France is blessed with so much Mediterranean sunlight that it's possible to make wines of every imaginable style here. The lands of the French Southwest, *le Sud-Ouest,* are under the combined influences of the Atlantic and the Pyrenees mountains.

SOUTHERN FRANCE

languedoc-roussillon

In addition to being France's most prolific region, producing by some estimates more wine than the entire U.S., Languedoc-Roussillon has also become the most dynamic. In the last decade, vintners here have aggressively pursued quality winemaking, often by ignoring rigid government regulations on grape growing and vinification processes. The resulting wines are widely regarded as some of the finest ever from the region, even though they must still be classified as merely Vin de Pays or Vin de Table.

Languedoc Grapes & Styles

The formidable Languedoc grows a wide range of grapes, some indigenous to the region, others (such as Cabernet Sauvignon) from different French regions. Red grapes dominate, especially Carignan, which is capable of delicious berry- and spice-flavored wines; excellent examples can be found in Corbières. Syrah, Grenache and Mourvèdre are blended to create the hearty, often rustic wines of Minervois and Fitou, as well as those of the Roussillon appellation Collioure near Spain. Cabernet Sauvignon and Merlot—imported from Bordeaux and increasingly planted here—are used mostly for inexpensive wines destined for export (the wines from Cabernet champion Mas de Daumas Gassac are a notable exception). White varieties Grenache Blanc, Maccabéo, Muscat, Picpoul Blanc and Rolle create fresh, interesting wines, while Viognier yields richer, more complex whites similar in some cases to examples from the northern Rhône, yet at a fraction of the cost. Chardonnays from Limoux are worth exploring, too. The Languedoc is also famed for its dessert wines (see p. 276).

Languedoc Wine Labels

Languedoc labels list region and sometimes grape. Most of the region's simplest wines are designated "Vin de Pays d'Oc," meaning they can be made from grapes grown any-where in Languedoc. Vins de Pays made in specific areas will indicate this on their labels and are subject to greater restrictions. The appellations Languedoc (including the area known until 2007 as Coteaux du Languedoc) and Côtes du Roussillon are umbrellas for smaller ones. Within them, the appellations Minervois, Fitou and Corbières often show distinct characteristics, as do wines from Faugères, St-Chinian, Montpeyroux, Pic-St-Loup and Collioure.

languedoc recommendations

WHITES

Arrogant Frog Lily Pad White | 2006 | **LANGUEDOC**
★ **$** The jovial, self-deprecating label sets the tone for this easy-breezy white. It's a blend of Chardonnay and Viognier with aromas of peach, citrus and pear that reiterate themselves nicely on the palate.

Domaine de Belle Mare Picpoul de Pinet | 2006 |
COTEAUX DU LANGUEDOC
★ ★ **$** The Picpoul grape has been growing on the banks of Langue-doc's Lake Thau since antiquity and still yields lovely wines. This well-balanced sample offers peaches, citrus, almond and minerals.

Domaines Barons de Rothschild (Lafite) Aussières Blanc
| 2006 | **VIN DE PAYS D'OC**
★ ★ **$ $** This limited-production Chardonnay comes from a cool vineyard site that enjoyed mild conditions in 2006, producing a lovely wine with orange and tangerine notes and aromas of acacia blossom.

Laroche Mas la Chevalière Blanc | 2004 | **VIN DE PAYS D'OC**
★ ★ **$ $** Chablis impresario Michel Laroche purchased this estate in 1995, and today melds northern French grapes with their Mediterra-nean counterparts. This plump, affordable, oak-aged white combines 90 percent Chardonnay with an aromatic dollop of Viognier.

Le Grand Noir Viognier | 2006 | VIN DE PAYS D'OC

★ $ This pronounced, fruity and floral Viognier hails from the Minervois region. The wine's palate is reminiscent of peach jam bordering on marmalade—intense but well done—and the finish is long.

Mas de Daumas Gassac White | 2007 | VIN DE PAYS DE L'HÉRAULT

★ ★ ★ $ $ $ Wow. This wine boasts all the complexity and flavor of a Châteauneuf-du-Pape blanc. Its juicy apple and citrus zest aromas lead to lemon peel flavors, mouthwatering acidity, nuances of mineral and stone and a crisp, clean finish.

ROSÉS

Château de Jau Le Jaja de Jau Rosé | 2006 | CÔTES DU ROUSSILLON

★ $ Château de Jau's Jaja wines—*Jaja* is a French slang word for light, everyday wine—are exactly that: light in price and perfect for everyday enjoyment, paired with food or on their own. Expect ripe fresh berries, a touch of spice and mouthwatering refreshment from this Syrah-Grenache blend.

Château de Pennautier Rosé | 2007 | CABARDÈS

★ $ This blend of equal parts Côt (Malbec), Grenache and Syrah has everything you want in a rosé: power that's finessed, berry fruit balanced with bright acidity and just enough tannin to make it fit for pairing with food of any weight.

Domaine Salvat Rosé | 2007 | CÔTES DU ROUSSILLON

★ $ $ Though quantity has long trumped quality in this part of France, the Salvats have dedicated decades to making fine wines. This rosé is a great example, packed with wild berry and cherry flavors and spicy notes that last well into the finish.

REDS

Clos des Camuzeilles La Grangette | 2003 | FITOU

★ ★ ★ $ $ $ Old vines are said to produce more concentrated wines, and La Grangette truly lives up to the hype. It's a heady bottling with briar fruit and coffee aromas and a smooth, full-bodied palate redolent of earth, blackberry, blueberry and cedar.

Cuvée Mythique Réserve | 2005 | CORBIÈRES

★ ★ $ $ This tasty blend comes from the Val d'Orbieu growers' association of southern France. A potent blackberry- and plum-scented red, it's mouthwatering and spicy, with ripe dark fruit, fennel and coffee notes.

Domaine de Nidolères La Justine | 2006 |
CÔTES DU ROUSSILLON

★★★ $ $ The Grenache Noir, Syrah and Carignan in La Justine come from clay-rich, stony, sandy soils, resulting in a bold and beautiful wine with earthy depth and a heady bouquet of violets, coffee, mocha and berries.

Domaine des 2 Ânes L'Enclos | 2005 | **CORBIÈRES**

★★ $ $ A hillside vineyard that enjoys ample sunshine and minimal rain produced the full-flavored grapes for this southern French red blend. The wine displays a lovely earthiness, with notes of coffee, mushroom, black cherries and spice.

Domaine Rimbert Travers de Marceau | 2006 | **ST-CHINIAN**

★ $ $ Jean-Marie Rimbert controls the yields of his old vines through exhaustive pruning, and that's the key to producing wines like this spicy, concentrated red, which boasts fresh cherries and nice acidity.

Domaines Barons de Rothschild (Lafite) Aussières Rouge
| 2006 | **VIN DE PAYS D'OC**

★★ $ $ Château d'Aussières' winemaking history dates to the Roman period, but their mixing of Languedoc and Bordeaux varieties is rather modern. A blend of Cabernet, Grenache, Merlot and Syrah, this bright cherry- and berry-flavored red has hints of spice and herbs.

Domaine St-Antonin Les Jardins | 2006 | **FAUGÈRES**

★ $ From the highlands of the Languedoc comes this bright and fruity wine. It smells of cherries, raspberries and a whiff of violets and has a soft, slightly chalky palate reminiscent of violet candy.

Hecht & Bannier | 2003 | **FAUGÈRES**

★★ $ $ $ The high-altitude schist slopes of Faugères are home to this spicy, earth-scented red. The wine's blackberry fruit spills onto the palate, with chocolate and mocha notes playing a supporting role, and firm tannins providing structure.

Le Loup Blanc La Mère Grand | 2004 | **MINERVOIS**

★★ $ $ Hailing from vines ranging between 20 and 100 years in age, La Mère Grand shows pleasant aromas of lavender and raspberries and flavors of berries, spice and coffee.

Les Camuzeilles Carignan | 2005 |
VIN DE PAYS DE LA VALLÉE DU PARADIS

★★ $ $ Made entirely from old-vine Carignan, this rustic red offers a nice balance of smoky black fruit, spice and violet aromas. The palate is layered with more floral spice and has an earthy, mineral finish.

Les Verrières de Montagnac Clos des Soutyères | 2005 |
COTEAUX DU LANGUEDOC

★ ★ ★ $ $ $ The vintners at Les Verrières de Montagnac describe the terroir of this wine as "gentle and violent." These dueling forces give birth to a wine of heady fig and stewed prune notes, rounded out by cocoa, spice-box and tobacco and a luscious texture.

Les Vignerons de la Méditerranée Les Deux Rives | 2006 |
CORBIÈRES

★ $ A number of good-value wines come from the Pyrenean foot-hills, and this mouthwatering red is one of them. Its raspberry and cherry aromas are highlighted by bright fruit, spice and a bit of oak.

Mas Foulaquier Les Tonillières Pic St-Loup | 2005 |
COTEAUX DU LANGUEDOC

★ ★ ★ $ $ The Pic St-Loup region has one of the best reputations in the Languedoc and it's easy to see why. This blend delivers amazing depth, starting with gorgeous spicy-earth aromas and finishing with plush blackberry, cassis, coffee and chocolate.

Prieuré de St-Jean de Bébian | 2005 |
COTEAUX DU LANGUEDOC

★ ★ ★ $ $ $ Critics applauded this château's 2001 vintage, some declaring it equal to or better than Rhône Valley offerings. The encore is delivered in the 2005 vintage, boasting raspberry and cherry aromas that are complemented on the palate by coffee and tobacco.

SOUTHERN FRANCE

provence

Provence is home to one of the world's oldest winemaking traditions, but over the years it became associated with simple, bulk production. Today, however, thanks to technology and winemaking expertise from other parts of France and abroad, Provençal wines have never been better.

Provence Grapes & Styles

Provence's best-known wines are its lovely, dry rosés. Typically made from a blend of Cinsault, Grenache and Mourvèdre, they are meant to be consumed young and with food. Those from Bandol are considered the finest, but many rosés from Côtes de Provence and Coteaux d'Aix-en-Provence are also beautifully crafted. Provence's bright,

citrusy whites are usually blends of local grapes Bourboulenc, Rolle, Clairette, Grenache Blanc and/or Ugni Blanc;
the best come from the seaside village of Cassis. Bandol's
mineral-laden whites are full-bodied, as are its more famous,
robust reds made primarily from Mourvèdre. Grenache,
Carignan, Cabernet, Cinsault and Syrah are also planted
throughout Provence, though the best examples are from
Les Baux de Provence and Coteaux d'Aix-en-Provence.

provence recommendations

WHITES

Château de Pibarnon Blanc | 2007 | BANDOL
★★ $ $ $ The grapes for this refreshing white blend are grown on
north-facing slopes, which slows their ripening under the warm Provençal sun. The resulting wine is filled with stone fruit and flower aromas and has a weightier palate than expected, rounded and plump.

Henri Milan Le Grand Blanc | VIN DE TABLE
★★ $ $ $ Labeled as a simple table wine (*vin de table*) and there-
fore not allowed to carry a vintage date, this sweet-salty white combines Grenache Blanc, Rolle, Roussanne, Chardonnay and Muscat to
lavish effect. It's floral and peachy but finishes with a briny tang.

Routas Coquelicot | 2006 | VIN DE PAYS DU VAR
★★ $ $ *Coquelicot* means "poppy" in French, here referring to the
fields of wild poppies that grow near Routas's vines in Provence's Coteaux Varois region. This Viognier-based white is fragrant with acacia
and stone fruits and nicely balances its waxy texture with acidity.

ROSÉS

Bieler Père et Fils Sabine Rosé | 2007 |
COTEAUX D'AIX-EN-PROVENCE
★★★ $ Charles Bieler, of California's irreverent Three Thieves
wines, is the mind behind this delicious, classically styled Provençal
rosé. Mostly Syrah, blended with Grenache, it has notes of ripe, sun-
kissed strawberries and is an utterly thirst-quenching summer wine.

Château Miraval | 2006 | CÔTES DE PROVENCE
★★★ $ $ A chalky clay soil is the origin of this mouthwatering
blend of old-vine Cinsault and Grenache. It's a good value, with heady
spice aromas and a palate brimming with ripe pear, red fruit and a kiss
of vanilla on the finish.

Les Domaniers | 2006 | CÔTES DE PROVENCE
★ ★ $ $ An offshoot of rosé specialist Domaines Ott, Les Domaniers creates this vibrant wine from Grenache, Cinsault and Syrah. It has spice and tropical citrus on the nose, dried cherry on the palate and bright acidity.

Mas de la Dame Rosé du Mas | 2007 | LES BAUX DE PROVENCE
★ ★ $ Organically grown on the well-drained soils of the Alpilles mountains and cooled by the mistral's fierce winds, the grapes that go into this lovely dry rosé produce sweet, concentrated cherry and berry aromas and flavors and a nice, long finish.

REDS

Château de Pibarnon | 2005 | BANDOL
★ ★ ★ $ $ $ Made from 95 percent Mourvèdre, this is a substantial red for the region, with black fruit and cassis flavors and hints of eucalyptus. While it's approachable now, the meaty structure and refined tannins will carry nicely in the cellar.

Henri Milan Domaine Milan St. Rémy de Provence | 2005 |
LES BAUX DE PROVENCE
★ ★ $ $ Henri Milan has been practicing sustainable organic farming for more than a decade; like all of his wines, this powerful red is terroir-driven. Its raspberry and black pepper aromas lead to pungent spice flavors and a finish of dark red fruit.

Jules Reserve | 2004 | CÔTES DE PROVENCE
★ ★ $ $ This substantial red pours on some serious tannins; marrying smoky fruit and black spice, it begs for grilled steak or barbecue. Its flavors are of darkest currants, woven with dampened earth and autumn leaves.

SOUTHERN FRANCE
the southwest

The French region known as the Southwest borders the rugged Pyrenees near Spain and is outshined by its formidable neighbor to the northwest, Bordeaux. As a result, its wines remain little known in the U.S. Three appellations are worth exploring, however: Bergerac, for its Bordeaux-like finesse; Cahors, for its prestigious reds of massive ruggedness; and Monbazillac, for its Sauternes-like sweet wines that cost a fraction of the famed sweet wines of Bordeaux.

The Southwest Grapes & Styles

The red wines of Bergerac are made with the same grapes as those in Bordeaux—Cabernet, Merlot, Malbec and Cabernet Franc. The heady, full-bodied reds of Cahors are based on the Auxerrois grape (known elsewhere as Malbec or Côt). In Madiran, vintners use the Tannat grape to craft wines that are even darker, fuller-bodied and more tannic. The hearty wines from the Basque country are made from a blend of difficult-to-pronounce local grapes. Jurançon is a full-bodied, spicy white wine produced from Petit and Gros Manseng grapes in two styles: dry (labeled "Jurançon Sec") and sweet. Monbazillac and Gaillac are similar wines, with both dry and sweet versions. Vins de Pays des Côtes de Gascogne are light-to-medium-bodied wines from local and international varieties.

southwest recommendations

WHITES

Charles Hours Clos Uroulat Cuvée Marie | 2006 |
JURANÇON SEC

★★★ $ $ Since buying the Clos Uroulat estate in 1983, Charles Hours has turned it into one of the wine-producing stars of southwest France. His Cuvée Marie is bone-dry, light and crisp, and it ages spectacularly, gaining smoky, mineral depth.

Domaine Cauhapé Chant des Vignes | 2007 | JURANÇON SEC

★★ $ $ Domaine Cauhapé, producer of stunning dessert wines, makes a great foray into dry whites with this fresh and flavorful wine. Made from the Gros Manseng grape, it's full-bodied with floral and zesty citrus notes and lingering stone fruit on the finish.

Domaine Duffour Blanc | 2007 | CÔTES DE GASCOGNE

★★ $ A trio of humble grapes—Colombard, Ugni Blanc and Gros Manseng—shine in this refreshing, melon-tinged white. Citrus notes and a dry, herbal finish make it great with light foods or as an aperitif.

Union de Producteurs Plaimont Colombelle | 2007 |
VIN DE PAYS DES CÔTES DE GASCOGNE

★★ $ The often dull Colombard grape excels here, lending lovely apple and stone fruit flavors to this refreshing medium-bodied white blend. It's rounded out with minerals, citrus and nice floral aromas.

Château Bouscassé Vieilles Vignes | 2003 | MADIRAN

★ ★ ★ $ $ $ Château Bouscassé is a sibling to superstar winery Château Montus, also in southwest France; both are owned by Alain Brumont. Made from 100 percent old-vine Tannat, this wine shows impressive power and structure, with layer upon layer of chewy black fruit and Christmas spice, and a minutes-long finish.

Château Haut Lavigne | 2006 | CÔTES DE DURAS

★ ★ $ The diminutive Château Haut Lavigne has only 4.5 hectares of vines producing red grapes; these provide the Merlot, Cabernet Franc and Cabernet Sauvignon for this earthy, spicy blend, whose black-berry fruit and supple tannins end in a surprisingly fresh finish.

Château Lagrézette Cru d'Exception | 2003 | CAHORS

★ ★ $ $ $ Malbec may inspire thoughts of Argentina, but it owes its existence to Cahors (where it originated). This Malbec-based red brims with chocolate and cherry aromas—like Black Forest cake—with hints of coconut. The silky palate supplies lots of dark black fruit and more chocolate.

Château Montus Prestige | 2003 | MADIRAN

★ ★ ★ $ $ $ $ Wines rendered from the Tannat grape are darkly in-tense; Château Montus makes one of the best, with richly layered dark fruit, a full body and waves of ripe tannin. Prestige is massive, inky stuff, best left in the cellar for a few years or enjoyed with equally big-flavored foods.

Clos Siguier | 2005 | CAHORS

★ ★ ★ $ A terrific value, this delicious Malbec boasts compelling, complex aromas. Herbs, damp leaves, forest floor and spice all wrap around a core of blackberry, cherry, currant and plum. The palate is filled with more black fruit and tinged with licorice, but remains fresh.

Le Duras par Robert and Bernard Plageoles | 2005 | GAILLAC

★ ★ $ $ Robert and Bernard Plageoles show particular dedication to Gaillac's native grapes. This wine, made from the region's long-standing Duras variety, has fruit-forward cherry flavors and nice earth and spice sophistication, along with a good balance of black fruit and pepper on the palate.

italy

Although Italy has been making wine for millennia, its viticulture seems more dynamic now than it has in centuries. Today, the country with the third most acreage under vine is the world's leading exporter, and fine wine has become a defining hallmark of Italian culture.

Lombardy

Trentino–Alto Adige

Valle d'Aosta

Friuli–Venezia Giulia

Veneto

• Milan

Piedmont

Venice

• Genoa

Emilia-Romagna

Liguria

Florence •

Adriatic Sea

Le Marche

Tuscany

Umbria

Abruzzo

Lazio

Rome ☆

Molise

Campania

Apulia

Naples •

Sardinia

Basilicata

Tyrrhenian Sea

Calabria

Palermo

Pantelleria

Sicily

▦ Principal Wine Region

Italy: An Overview

Unlike its wine-producing neighbors France and Spain, Italy grows vines in almost every corner of its territory. Italian vintners manage to succeed throughout their country's varied topography and climatic zones by utilizing a wide array of grapes and winemaking styles. As a result, Italy contains more than 300 DOC and DOCG designations (see Italian Wine Labels, below). Two regions, however, stand out above the rest: Piedmont in the northwest, where the Nebbiolo grape yields famously rich, long-lived Barolo and slightly lighter Barbaresco; and Tuscany, home of the cherry-scented Sangiovese grape, responsible for two of Italy's most recognized wines—Chianti and Brunello di Montalcino. Still, from the mineral-laden whites of Friuli and Trentino–Alto Adige to Umbria's dark, sultry Sagrantino di Montefalco and the powerful reds of Sicily, Italy produces wines for all tastes, budgets and seasons.

Italian Wine Labels

Italian wines are traditionally labeled by their place of origin, though some labels may list the grape if it defines a region, such as Montepulciano d'Abruzzo, made from the Montepulciano grape in the Abruzzo region. Grape names are used most commonly in the northeast regions of Alto Adige and Friuli–Venezia Giulia. Italy's regulatory system is the *Denominazione di Origine Controllata* (DOC), which delineates basic areas and standards; more rigorous standards apply to wines with the DOCG (*Denominazione di Origine Controllata e Garantita*) imprimatur. For much of the system's history, wines not adhering to DOC or DOCG standards were given the humble title *Vino da Tavola* (table wine). In 1992, the *Indicazione Geografica Tipica* (IGT) classification was created for the growing number of superb wines being vinified with unapproved grape varieties and unorthodox techniques. The term "Classico" on a wine label indicates a prestigious subregion.

piedmont

Located in northwestern Italy in the foothills of the Alps, Piedmont is home to the Nebbiolo grape, which produces some of the world's most outstanding wines. Chief among them is Barolo and, to a lesser extent, Barbaresco—though both draw comparisons to Burgundy for their elegance and ability to age. The region is also known for light, fruity everyday wines, such as Barbera and Dolcetto, and the popular sparkling white Asti.

piedmont whites

Piedmont's reputation is based firmly upon its reds, but there are still a handful of interesting whites from the region worth seeking out. Gavi di Gavi, from the Cortese grape, is perhaps Piedmont's most famous still white, though Arneis, particularly those from the subregion of Roero, are more substantial and more compelling. Chardonnays here can be wonderfully balanced. Sweeter sparkling wines are also prevalent, with the well-known, though rarely exciting, Asti Spumante leading the way. The superior Moscato d'Asti (see p. 259) is unusually delicate and wonderfully fragrant.

piedmont white recommendations

Broglia La Meirana | 2006 | GAVI DI GAVI
★★ $ $ The flagship wine of Broglia—one of Gavi's top producers—this appley, razor-sharp white would be a great choice for shellfish.

Deltetto San Michele | 2007 | ROERO ARNEIS
★★★ $ $ This is a consistently excellent wine from a single vineyard in the village of Canale. It's partially fermented in small French oak *barriques* to lend creaminess to its otherwise bright, citrusy frame.

Marco Porello Camestri | 2007 | ROERO ARNEIS
★★★ $ $ Classic white-flower aromatics and a firm spine of citrusy acidity distinguish this deeply flavorful Arneis from the multitude of light whites produced in Roero. Porello is an emerging young producer showing great consistency from year to year.

Picollo Ernesto | 2007 | GAVI DI GAVI
★ ★ $ A great value and a pure, clean expression of the Gavi area's Cortese grape, this quenching, simple white has a chalky minerality that reflects Gavi's limestone soils; the aroma is like a dewy pine forest in early morning.

Villa Sparina | 2006 | GAVI DI GAVI
★ ★ $ $ Consistently one of the top-ranked Gavis from a luxurious estate in Monterotondo—where the Moccagatta family has a top-notch restaurant and hotel on the property—this brims with ripe peach, sweet pear and lemony citrus flavors.

piedmont reds

The Nebbiolo grape is responsible for Piedmont's greatest red wines: Barolo and Barbaresco. Also called "Spanna," Nebbiolo produces the less familiar wines of Gattinara, Ghemme and Langhe as well. The region's most prolific grape, though, is Barbera, a highly acidic chameleon that, depending on where it is grown, can yield anything from a powerful, ageworthy wine to a young, light red. Dolcetto produces a large amount of the region's simpler reds. Varieties such as Cabernet, Pinot Noir and Syrah are also grown here, but they generally aren't worth seeking out.

PIEDMONT REDS

barolo & barbaresco

These two renowned reds are among the greatest wines of Italy and the world. Although both are Nebbiolo-based, Barolo tends to be heartier and more intensely aromatic, while Barbaresco is typically lighter and more subtle. While both improve dramatically with years of aging, regulations require Barolo to be aged three years, two in barrel, before release, whereas softer Barbaresco must be aged only two years, one in barrel. Traditionally, these wines require at least a decade to soften, but many vintners today apply modern techniques that enable their wines to mature earlier. This has caused a rift with the more traditionalist winemakers who believe the wine is worth waiting for.

barolo & barbaresco recommendations

Ceretto Bricco Rocche Brunate | 2004 | **BAROLO**
★★★ $ $ $ $ Ceretto's wines are typically tightly wound and require many years of bottle age; this Barolo, though, is always one of the winery's more early-drinking bottlings. Cedary, smoky and loaded with brambly berry fruit, it's got an opulent, oaky shimmer.

Damilano Lecinquevigne | 2003 | **BAROLO**
★★ $ $ $ A hint of licorice and cherry announces this supple Barolo, which contains grapes from five different vineyards. It's a good example of the drink-now style produced in the superhot 2003 vintage.

Francesco Rinaldi & Figli Cannubbio | 2004 | **BAROLO**
★★★ $ $ $ $ Many believe that 2004 is the best of a recent run of great vintages in Barolo. This wine shows the Nebbiolo grape at its most leathery and earthy, with firm tannins and mouthwatering acidity.

star producers
barolo & barbaresco

Ceretto
Brothers Bruno and Marcello Ceretto began their "reign of terroir" in the late 1960s, buying the best Barolo and Barbaresco crus. Their single-vineyard wines are the stuff of legend.

Gaja
Barbaresco phenom Angelo Gaja, the first to use small French oak *barriques*, has been making stunningly beautiful wines since JFK was in office.

Giuseppe e Figlio Mascarello
Mauro Mascarello (Giuseppe's son) toes the hard line as one of the most traditionalist producers in Barolo, and his

Monprivato stands shoulder-to-shoulder with wines from France's best châteaux.

Massolino
The Massolino brothers have established their family's hillside estate as one of the best producers of magnificent single-vineyard Barolos.

Pio Cesare
Pio Boffa eschews the single-vineyard trend by masterfully blending grapes from carefully selected sites.

Vietti
Luca Currado carries on his family's custom of making beautifully focused wines that offer both quality and value.

Gaja | 2004 | **BARBARESCO**

★★★★ $ $ $ $ Anyone who loves great wine needs to try Gaja Barbaresco at least once, so why not one of the best vintages ever? Mocha, licorice and dried porcini aromas give way to a polished and balanced mix of sweet and savory flavors. This is liquid silk.

Giuseppe e Figlio Mascarello Monprivato | 2003 | **BAROLO**

★★★★ $ $ $ $ Traditionalist Mascarello's Barolo is usually too austere to drink young, but thanks to the heat of 2003, this is a rounder, sweeter take on the producer's iconic, Burgundy-style red. Dried cherry and rose petal aromas lead to a soft-textured mouthful of bright red berry fruit.

Massolino | 2004 | **BAROLO**

★★★ $ $ $ $ Although Massolino, known for their finely tuned Barolos, produce more opulent (and costly) single-vineyard wines, this spicy and perfumed "base" Barolo is delicious, old-school Neb-biolo and offers great bang for the buck in this expensive region.

Pio Cesare Il Bricco | 2003 | **BARBARESCO**

★★★ $ $ $ $ This luminous, powerful red hails from the Il Bricco vineyard, which—unusual for the Piedmont region—is wholly owned by the Pio Cesare estate. A luxurious, modern Barbaresco, it's fragrant and balanced (in spite of its hot vintage) and kissed with sweet oak.

Vietti Castiglione | 2004 | **BAROLO**

★★★★ $ $ $ At about $45 a bottle, here's an amazing value in an ageworthy Barolo. If you buy a case of this cedary, brooding red and cellar it, when you open a bottle in 2020 (or you can sneak some before then), you can brag about what a great deal it was.

PIEDMONT REDS

barbera & dolcetto

If Barolo and Barbaresco are Piedmont's noble wines, Barbera and Dolcetto are the wines of the people. Though often produced in large quantities and served soon after bottling, these wines can manifest themselves in many ways, from smooth, crowd-pleasing Dolcettos to more complex, aromatic Barberas. Dolcetto, in particular, is important to Piedmont vintners, as it allows them to create marketable, young wines while they give their Nebbiolo-based wines time to age properly.

barbera & dolcetto recommendations

Abbona Papà Celso | 2005 | DOLCETTO DI DOGLIANI

★★★ $ $ Papà Celso, made from grapes grown in a high-altitude vineyard in Dogliani, is named for the father of the Abbona winery's proprietor. Like most Dolcettos here, this delicious example is deeply concentrated and intensely fruity, almost purple in color.

Accornero Bricco Battista | 2005 | BARBERA DEL MONFERRATO

★★★ $ $ $ North of the Barolo/Barbaresco corridor, the Monferrato zone is known for its intense Barberas. This superluxurious, inky, concentrated bottling is massive yet balanced by brisk acidity.

Ca'Viola Vilot | 2006 | DOLCETTO D'ALBA

★★★ $ $ Beppe Caviola is one of Italy's well-known "flying wine-makers," and one of his specialties is chunky, inky, cocoa-rich Dolcetto. From his eponymous estate comes this purple-hued giant, starting out with gobs of fruit and finishing with a tarry savor.

Cogno Vigna del Mandorlo | 2006 | DOLCETTO D'ALBA

★★ $ $ $ Dolcetto is sometimes compared to Beaujolais, at least when it's made in this more classic, brightly acidic style. The plummy, violet-scented fruit in this wine is offset by acidity and soft tannins.

Damilano | 2005 | BARBERA D'ALBA

★★ $ $ This is Barbera done in the more gutsy, acid-driven traditional style: It's not about superconcentrated fruit or heavy oak, just bright, brambly red fruit and a tasty, earthy, forest-floor funk.

Pertinace | 2005 | BARBERA D'ALBA

★★ $ A terrific value from an exceptional vintage—and a pure expression of the Barbera grape from a historic cooperative winery—this is rich and silky with lots of concentrated fruit.

Poderi Luigi Einaudi Vigna Tecc | 2006 | DOLCETTO DI DOGLIANI

★★★ $ $ Dogliani is thought by some to be the birthplace of Dolcetto and one of the best growing zones in Piedmont for the grape. Here, the region produces a typically chunky, tarry, superpowered take on the variety, with a touch of scrubland savor.

Vietti Tre Vigne | 2005 | BARBERA D'ALBA

★★★ $ $ In the best of ways, this is the Toyota Corolla of Italian red wine: stalwart, reliable, economical juice that you can trust vintage after vintage. There's a great mix of ripe red fruit and stony savor in this rich yet vibrantly acidic bottling.

other piedmont reds

The Piedmont region hosts a significant number of international grapes, including Cabernet, Merlot and Syrah, all from neighboring France. These grapes are ideal for blending with local varieties, though many native grapes are just as intriguing on their own. Wines from indigenous grapes range from the sweet and effervescent Freisa to the fruity and floral Ruchè. There are also some interesting Nebbiolo-based wines from Gattinara, Ghemme and Langhe, as well as Nebbiolo d'Alba, which can somewhat mimic the characteristics of Barolo at a fraction of the cost.

other piedmont red recommendations

Antoniolo | 2004 | GATTINARA
★ ★ ★ $ $ $ Antoniolo's reds have the refinement and complexity of good red Burgundy. This benchmark Gattinara, from the exceptional 2004 vintage, is an aromatic mix of dried cherry, black tea and leathery notes—everything you want from the Nebbiolo grape.

Cantalupo Agamium | 2004 | COLLINE NOVARESI
★ ★ $ $ Cantalupo anchors the Ghemme appellation in northern Piedmont. And while Ghemme wines are their headliners, Agamium is an affordable, entry-level Nebbiolo (here called Spanna) and a plush take on the often-biting grape, with scents of tar and roses.

Conterno Fantino Monprà | 2003 | LANGHE ROSSO
★ ★ ★ $ $ $ You've heard of Super-Tuscans? Well, this is a super-Piedmontese: a meaty slab of a wine containing 50 percent Nebbiolo, 40 percent Barbera and 10 percent Cabernet Sauvignon. After 18 months' oak aging, it is a toasty, syrupy mouthful.

Filippo Gallino | 2004 | ROERO SUPERIORE
★ ★ $ $ The Roero DOCG is just north of Barolo, and it's not just a pumping station for simple white Arneis; the real Roero stars are reds from the Nebbiolo grape. This lean, spicy, berry-scented beauty is an affordable Barolo alternative.

Podere Rocche dei Manzoni Bricco Manzoni | 2001 | LANGHE
★ ★ ★ ★ $ $ $ This voluptuous marriage of opposites is a blend of 80 percent Nebbiolo and 20 percent Barbera. The Nebbiolo imparts tarry tannic structure and aromatic uplift, while the Barbera lends plush red fruit and deep color. Try it, and you'll be wowed.

other northern italian regions

Northeastern Italy's most productive region is Veneto, where popular, though inconsistent, wines such as red Valpolicella and Bardolino and white Soave and Pinot Grigio are produced. Throughout northeastern Italy, winemakers focused on quality are creating some truly excellent and unique wines using a variety of indigenous grapes not grown in any of the larger regions.

• TRENTINO–ALTO ADIGE & FRIULI–VENEZIA GIULIA Trentino–Alto Adige—actually two separate regions often grouped together due to their close proximity—is located in northeastern Italy bordering Austria and is predominantly German-speaking in the north. The wines here also have a distinctly German accent, produced from grapes including Gewürztraminer (also known as Traminer), Sylvaner and Müller-Thurgau. Friuli–Venezia Giulia boasts a vast assortment of unusual grape varieties such as Refosco, Tazzelenghe, Schioppettino and the recently revived Pignolo. Though Friuli is more famous for whites, its subregion Colli Orientali del Friuli is a prominent producer of reds. Even the seemingly desolate hill region of Carso makes a handful of noteworthy wines.

• VENETO Hidden beneath Veneto's reputation as Italy's largest source of insipid bulk wine is a subculture of quality vintners dedicated to crafting wines of the highest caliber. The Soave and Valpolicella zones are responsible for most of the region's best bottlings, especially the hilly Classico regions. Another important wine of note is the popular sparkling white Prosecco (see p. 259).

• LOMBARDY The best-known region here is Franciacorta, where Italy's finest sparkling wines are made (see p. 259). Lombardy also encompasses Valtellina, near the Swiss border, where the well-regarded Sforzato wine is made from the Chiavennasca (Nebbiolo) grape.

other northern italian whites

White wine lovers will find many inspired choices in Italy's northern regions. In Trentino–Alto Adige there are German-influenced wines such as Weissburgunder (Pinot Bianco), Müller-Thurgau, Sylvaner and the weighty, incredibly aromatic Gewürztraminer, as well as more common varieties such as Chardonnay, Pinot Grigio and Sauvignon (Blanc). Veneto offers the Garganega-based Soave, much of which is poorly crafted. The best Soaves hail from the Classico zones spanning the hills outside Verona. Indigenous white grape varieties from the Friuli region include Friulano, Ribolla Gialla and Picolit, yet the region is perhaps more renowned for its stunning Pinot Grigio, Pinot Bianco and Sauvignon. The white Prosecco grape flourishes in Veneto, where it is used to produce a refreshingly light sparkling wine of the same name.

other northern italian white recommendations

Bastianich Tocai Friulano | 2007 | **COLLI ORIENTALI DEL FRIULI**
★ ★ ★ $ $ Restaurateur-winemaker Joseph Bastianich produces this fleshy and aromatic white, which tastes of peaches and pears and has the typical mineral edge of the Tocai grape. This is a great value from an excellent vintage.

Ca' del Bosco Chardonnay | 2004 | **TERRE DI FRANCIACORTA**
★ ★ ★ $ $ $ $ From one of Italy's top sparkling wine producers comes this luxurious Chardonnay made in a distinctly modern style and aged ten months in new oak barrels. There's plenty of good acid and minerality to balance the richness, and the oak influence and alcohol are both well moderated.

Castello di Spessa Ribolla Gialla | 2006 | **COLLIO**
★ ★ ★ $ $ $ Although many Friulian winemakers choose to vinify and age the Ribolla grape in oak barrels, Castello di Spessa presents it in a shimmering, steel-fermented style. Crisp green apple fruit flavors and a refreshing citrusy acidity mark this precise take on a unique indigenous grape variety.

Collavini Villa Canlungo Pinot Grigio | 2007 | COLLIO
★★ $ $ An example of how Pinot Grigio, particularly from Friuli, can have some viscosity and weight on the palate, this wine has the classic apple-almond flavor buttressed by a firm backbone of acidity.

Elena Walch Kastelaz Gewürztraminer | 2006 | ALTO ADIGE
★★★★ $ $ This single-vineyard wine is a shining example of Gewürztraminer as grown in Italy's Alto Adige. (The Elena Walch winery is even located in Tramin, the village where the grape is thought to have originated.) Beautiful, rich flavors of white peach and apricot are balanced by refreshing acidity in this superlative wine.

Grosjean Petite Arvine | 2006 | VALLE D'AOSTA
★★ $ $ From a tiny producer in the Alpine heights of the Valle d'Aosta comes this steely, mineral-rich white. It has delicate aromas of wildflowers, a glistening appearance, and the crisp, tart flavor of green apples.

Kuenhof Sylvaner | 2005 | ALTO ADIGE
★★ $ $ $ This gripping white is crafted at a small farmstead in the South Tyrol, a region that's geographically part of Italy but Austrian in spirit. While Sylvaner is not quite as aromatically exotic as Riesling, this wine has a great, clean wet-stone minerality.

Lechthaler Pinot Grigio | 2007 | TRENTINO
★ $ $ Here's an excellent party white from the cool Alpine climes of northeast Italy; it's solid and versatile, with a stony edge and plump apple-pear fruit.

Muzic Tocai Friulano | 2006 | COLLIO
★★★ $ $ Friuli's native Tocai grape is a genetic mutation of herby Sauvignon Blanc, and in this flinty and crystalline white you get a clear sense of the Sauvignon connection. Nicely structured, it's grassy, herbal and deliciously snappy.

Prà | 2006 | SOAVE CLASSICO
★★★ $ A deep golden color and a honeyed texture lend this wine a luxurious sheen. Graziano Prà is known for extracting richness and aroma out of the sometimes-reticent Garganega grape, and his wines are some of the deepest Soaves available.

Roccolo Grassi La Broia | 2005 | SOAVE SUPERIORE
★★★ $ $ Young winemaker Marco Sartori makes luxurious Soave whites to go along with his similarly polished reds from Valpolicella. This potent Soave brims with melon and apple flavors. The texture is viscous and rich, with a nice mineral bite on the finish.

Scarbolo Ramato XL Pinot Grigio | 2006 | **FRIULI GRAVE**
★ ★ ★ $ $ *Ramato* means "coppery" in Italian, and in this case refers to the copper-pink hue of this rich, round Pinot Grigio. It is fermented for a short period with its skins in the traditional Friulian manner, which yields a remarkably full-flavored wine.

Schiopetto Pinot Grigio | 2006 | **COLLIO**
★ ★ ★ $ $ $ This is gold-standard Pinot Grigio from a Friulian legend. Stainless steel–fermented, it's crisp, clean and mineral-laced, with a more powerful structure than is typical from the grape, enlivened by hints of chalk and green apple.

Vie di Romans Flors di Uis | 2006 | **ISONZO DEL FRIULI**
★ ★ ★ ★ $ $ $ A marvelous combination of floral, complex aromas and a honeyed texture, this is a fascinating blend: 55 percent Malvasia Istriana, 20 percent Riesling and 25 percent Tocai Friulano. There's no oak aging, but plenty of palate-coating viscosity and a clean finish.

other northern italian reds

Valpolicella suffers from the same reputation as its white counterpart Soave in the northern regions: Its huge popularity is due in no small part to low-quality mass production. Carefully crafted Valpolicellas, made primarily from the Corvina grape, can, however, be bright, floral and inspired. Such wines often come from the Classico zone and are labeled "Superiore." Two additional types of Valpolicella that deserve attention are Amarone and Ripasso. Amarone is a rich wine made from grapes that traditionally have been air-dried for several months prior to pressing, which intensifies the flavor of the grapes; Recioto is a sweet version of Amarone (see p. 276). Ripasso seeks a middle ground by infusing Valpolicella wine with the leftover pressed grapes of Amarone. Other varieties indigenous to the northern regions include rustic Refosco; sharp, tannic Pignolo and Schioppettino; softer Lagrein; and the highly acidic Tazzelenghe (translated locally as "tongue cutter"). Cabernet Sauvignon is making its presence known here today, while long-established Merlot, Cabernet Franc and Carmenère tend to be more peppery and herbal in northern Italy than in other countries.

other northern italian red recommendations

Caldaro Saltner Pinot Nero | 2006 | ALTO ADIGE

★★ $ $ Here's a light, fragrant Pinot Noir from one of Alto Adige's many excellent cooperative wineries. A leathery note lends savor to the Bing cherry fruit, and the overall feel is crisp and focused.

Caves Cooperatives de Donnas Donnas | 2005 | VALLE D'AOSTA

★★ $ $ This is a light, smoky, delicately perfumed red from the Alpine slopes of the Valle d'Aosta, in Italy's extreme northwest. Mouthwatering acidity and hints of leather and tar announce it as a wine made from Nebbiolo grapes (here called Picotendro).

Foradori | 2006 | TEROLDEGO ROTALIANO

★★★ $ $ Winemaker Elisabetta Foradori is the standard-bearer of the Teroldego grape, which she grows in the gravelly soils of the Adige River basin. Purple-black and berry-scented, this wine is a delicious chunk of dark-toned fruit that finishes clean and relatively light.

Franz Gojer-Glögglhof Lagrein | 2006 | ALTO ADIGE

★★★ $ $ $ Artisanal producer Franz Gojer is a reliable source for deep, inky, velvety reds from the Lagrein grape. This succulent effort is a push-pull of sweet-savory sensations, with hints of cocoa, black fruits and roasted meat.

Masi Costasera | 2004 | AMARONE DELLA VALPOLICELLA CLASSICO

★★★ $ $ $ One of the tricky things about Amarone is that it can often be bruisingly alcoholic and overly sweet. This nicely moderated wine is neither—and commendable for it. It's got the toffee/chocolate Amarone deliciousness without any cloying heft.

Nicolis Seccal Ripasso | 2005 | VALPOLICELLA CLASSICO SUPERIORE

★★ $ $ Typical of many Valpolicellas, this wine was given added weight and complexity through the addition of a small amount of dried-grape wine. There's a dark, charred quality to the black fruit flavors here, but the style is ultimately smooth and medium-bodied.

Nino Negri Fracia | 2004 | VALTELLINA SUPERIORE

★★★ $ $ $ This is a smoky, leathery red from a historic winery in the Valtellina, the borderland region in the northernmost reaches of Lombardy. It's crafted from single-vineyard Nebbiolo (here called Chiavennasca), with a dollop of French oak lending sweetness.

Roccolo Grassi | 2004 | **VALPOLICELLA SUPERIORE**
★ ★ ★ ★ **$ $ $** This velvety red acquires added weight and complexity by the inclusion of a small amount of dried-grape wine in its blend (permitted under appellation rules). Notes of cocoa, black currant and dark spice characterize this Valpolicella of uncommon richness.

San Leonardo | 2003 | **TRENTINO**
★ ★ ★ ★ **$ $ $ $** This under-the-radar gem from Trentino is a collector's item: The noble Guerrieri Gonzaga family crafts their elegant blend of Cabernet, Merlot and Cabernet Franc in a balanced, aromatic style. It's an Italian Bordeaux blend that drinks like real Bordeaux.

Tenuta Ca'Bolani Refosco Aquileia | 2006 | **FRIULI**
★ ★ **$** Keep an eye out for Friuli's native Refosco grape, a variety enjoying a resurgence for its dark, satisfying spiciness. Hints of blackberry, tar and violet on the nose are followed by a silky mouthfeel.

news from a wine insider
italy by David Lynch, New York–based author of *Vino Italiano*

Most Significant Trends
Italian wines have inspired great enthusiasm among American wine drinkers in recent years: In 2006, the value of Italian wine exports to the U.S. exceeded $1 billion and rose even higher in 2007. Price increases have not dampened the enthusiasm, particularly for top Barolos and Brunellos from the heralded 2004 vintage.

Regions Making News
Two of Italy's most innovative regions today are Montefalco in Umbria and Maremma in Tuscany. Investment has been pouring into Montefalco's vineyards, where plantings of Sagrantino have grown fourfold between 2001 and 2007 and new wineries like Perticaia have raised the region's profile. There are notable developments in Maremma, from producers like entrepreneur Claudio Tipa (who's been running Bolgheri stalwart Grattamacco since 2002) and his Colle Massari estate, which produces Super-Tuscan blends such as Rigoleto. Also worth noting here is the creation of Rocca di Frassinello, a joint venture between Paolo Panerai (owner of Castellare di Castellina in Chianti) and Eric de Rothschild of Château Lafite in Bordeaux.

tuscany

Tuscany lies at the heart of Italy's wine heritage. Home to the versatile Sangiovese grape, Tuscany produces what could be called Italy's most popular wine, Chianti, as well as one of its most esteemed, Brunello di Montalcino. In addition, Tuscany's creative vintners make many outstanding blends, such as the modern-style Super-Tuscans classified under the IGT designation (see page 79).

tuscany whites

Although Tuscany is famous for its reds, the region does produce a decent amount of white wine, most of it based on the bland Trebbiano grape and somewhat overpriced. Two of Tuscany's whites, however, are definitely worth seeking out: Vernaccia from San Gimignano, which is light and crisp on its own, but has more body when blended with Chardonnay; and Vermentino, a wine full of mineral and lime flavors.

tuscany white recommendations

Agricola Querciabella Batàr | 2005 | TUSCANY
★★★★ $ $ $ $ Crafted by a winery that is both organic and biodynamic, this luscious, toasty, nectarlike blend of 50 percent Pinot Bianco and 50 percent Chardonnay is one of Italy's most serious, structured whites. It will stand up to aging and could be paired with rich poultry and game dishes.

Antinori Tenuta Guado al Tasso Vermentino | 2007 | BOLGHERI
★★ $ $ A clean and crisp white for summer drinking, this zesty, well-priced coastal wine is from Antinori's legendary Bolgheri estate. Its perfume is reminiscent of the wild sage, fennel and eucalyptus that aromatize the Mediterranean scrub.

Lunae Vermentino | 2007 | COLLI DI LUNI
★★ $ $ The Colli di Luni are coastal hills that extend from the northwest corner of Tuscany up into neighboring Liguria. So it's not surprising that this aromatic, herbaceous, supercrisp Mediterranean Vermentino tastes of sea air and cries out for *zuppa di pesce*.

Montenidoli Fiore | 2006 | **VERNACCIA DI SAN GIMIGNANO**
★★★★ $ $ Practically a one-woman show, Elisabetta Fagiuoli crafts several delicious, complex Vernaccias at the landmark organic Montenidoli winery; her magnificent Fiore has a golden color, strong acidity and a yeasty quality from aging on its lees before bottling.

Mormoraia | 2006 | **VERNACCIA DI SAN GIMIGNANO**
★★ $ $ Hints of apple and honey and lots of acidity characterize this unoaked wine. It's a bright, fruity, expressive Vernaccia from one of the most highly regarded producers in San Gimignano.

tuscany reds

Tuscany's much-loved red wines are almost entirely based on the distinctive Sangiovese grape. Though the variety's chief characteristics include high acidity and bright fruit flavors, the wines it produces range from light and simple to bold and complex. There are also many excellent Tuscan blends crafted with other varieties, including relative new-comers Cabernet, Merlot and Syrah, all of which are grown in the regions of Bolgheri and Maremma. Other grapes native to the region, such as Canaiolo, Mammolo and Col-orino, are used mainly in blends, particularly in Chianti.

TUSCANY REDS

chianti

Less than 25 years ago, regulations required Chianti pro-ducers to blend Sangiovese with several indigenous red and white grape varieties and to age their wines in large, old casks. Today, while examples of the old-fashioned style still exist, most wineries are crafting modern wines from 100 percent Sangiovese, or adding up to 20 percent Caber-net, Merlot or native grapes like Canaiolo and Colorino. Generic "Chianti," which is easy to identify because there is no subregion listed on the label, is the simplest. Wines labeled "Riserva" require at least two years of oak aging, and are more concentrated and powerful as a result. Chi-anti contains eight subregions, which are noted on labels; Chianti Classico and Chianti Rùfina are the finest.

chianti recommendations

Agricola Querciabella | 2005 | CHIANTI CLASSICO

★★★ $ $ $ Quite ripe, round and color-saturated for a non-Riserva Chianti, this raspberry-scented red from the village of Greve is a great wine for the price. It's worth buying by the case to enjoy some upmarket everyday drinking at home.

Antinori Marchese Antinori Riserva | 2003 | CHIANTI CLASSICO

★★★ $ $ $ This is the benchmark "white-label" Riserva from the venerable Florentine Antinori wine family, who in the heat wave of 2003 turned out this saturated powerhouse. It's got a charred meat savor to counterbalance its sweetly ripe black cherry fruit.

Castello d'Albola | 2005 | CHIANTI CLASSICO

★★ $ $ This traditional Chianti skews more brick-red in color and more rustic in flavor than many modern bottlings. Indeed, a dried-porcini savor roots the wine in the thickly wooded hills of Chianti.

Castello di Ama | 2005 | CHIANTI CLASSICO

★★★★ $ $ $ $ Although 2005 was an exceedingly wet vintage, Ama focused all its resources and produced this tremendous Riserva-level wine. Sourced from some of the highest-elevation vineyards in Chianti Classico, it's a tightly wound red with a dense core of smoldering, stony flavor. This was made for cellaring.

Castello di Meleto | 2004 | CHIANTI CLASSICO

★★ $ $ This is a polished style of Chianti (thanks to a brief aging period in small oak barrels) with smooth, sweet tannins and aromas of blackberry jam on toast. Soft and inviting, it has more than enough foresty flavor to identify it as Sangiovese.

Fattoria di Rodáno Viacosta Riserva | 2001 | CHIANTI CLASSICO

★★★ $ $ $ Dark and smoky, this deep and structured Riserva-level Chianti would be ideal with well-charred *bistecca alla fiorentina*. Unlike many Chiantis, which incorporate Cabernet or Merlot, it's crafted from 100 percent Sangiovese grapes.

Fattoria Poggiopiano | 2006 | CHIANTI CLASSICO

★★★ $ $ The youngish Poggiopiano winery (their first release was 1993) crafts Chianti from Sangiovese grown on the rocky slopes of San Casciano Val di Pesa. This seductive 2006 was aged partially in large oak casks and partially in small French oak *barriques* for a delicate oak influence; the texture is crisp and gripping.

Fèlsina Berardenga | 2005 | **CHIANTI CLASSICO**

★ ★ ★ $ $ Here's a textbook expression of the Sangiovese grape from one of Chianti Classico's most celebrated estates. It's a crisp, woodsy red with a Pinot Noir-ish delicacy and perfume, great for game birds or other hunter's fare.

Il Molino di Grace Riserva | 2004 | **CHIANTI CLASSICO**

★ ★ ★ $ $ $ American entrepreneur Frank Grace has received high marks for his wines from a small property on the celebrated south-facing slopes of Panzano. This silken Riserva from the estate has fine, sweet tannins and good weight without being ponderous.

Isole e Olena | 2005 | **CHIANTI CLASSICO**

★ ★ ★ ★ $ $ Another superb effort (in a difficult vintage) from one of Chianti Classico's most reliable producers, Isole e Olena Chianti is a model of elegance and aromatics, with terrific black currant and black cherry fruit and a soft, inviting texture.

star producers
chianti

Agricola Querciabella

Under the direction of Sebastiano Castiglioni, Querciabella has become one of Chianti's greatest producers; it's also strictly biodynamic.

Antinori

There's not enough room here to sing the praises of Italy's most dynamic winemaker, Marchesi Piero Antinori. Think Robert Mondavi, but Italian.

Castello di Ama

Winemaker Marco Pallanti and his wife and partner, Lorenza Sebasti, tend one of Chianti Classico's best estates, and are champions of improving the appellation's quality standards.

Fattoria di Rodáno

Located in the heart of the Chianti Classico district, Fattoria di Rodáno has 250 acres under vine and is a terrific source for complex, classically made Chianti.

Il Molino di Grace

American Frank Grace opened this winery to rave reviews only a decade ago, but the estate has grown grapes for 350 years.

Isole e Olena

Paolo de Marchi, owner and winemaker of this fine estate, is a maestro of Sangiovese as well as Cabernet; he bottles the latter under his Collezione De Marchi label.

Lilliano Ruspoli | 2006 | CHIANTI CLASSICO
★★★ $ $ The 2006 vintage is highly regarded among Chianti producers, and this wine, from the Castellina in Chianti area, is broader and lusher than others. Most noteworthy is the sweet, inviting aroma of crushed red berries swimming in their juice.

Monsanto Il Poggio Riserva | 2000 | CHIANTI CLASSICO
★★★ $ $ $ One whiff of this old-school Chianti will send you directly to the cypress-studded Tuscan hills, preferably someplace where there's a grill sizzling with steaks. Cedary and well aged, it's like grilled meat in a glass.

San Fabiano | 2006 | CHIANTI
★★ $ A terrific quaffer from a noble estate outside Arezzo, this wine has a classic, traditional Chianti profile (read: notes of leather, wood smoke, dried cherry). The lively acidity makes it great for an outdoor summer gathering.

San Leonino | 2004 | CHIANTI CLASSICO
★★ $ $ A touch of toasty sweetness from oak frames this otherwise spicy and dark-toned Chianti. San Leonino is one of three Tuscan estates owned by Tenimenti Angelini, and the wines are typically slick and made in a modern style.

TUSCANY REDS

montalcino

Brunello di Montalcino is made with 100 percent Sangiovese (called Brunello in Montalcino) and is Tuscany's crowning achievement in wine. Bold and tannic, Brunello requires at least four years of aging before release (five if "Riserva"). A lighter, less costly version of Brunello can be found in Rosso di Montalcino (a.k.a. "Baby Brunello"). These wines require only one year of aging before release and are usually offered at a fraction of the cost of Brunello.

montalcino recommendations

Camigliano | 2003 | BRUNELLO DI MONTALCINO
★★★ $ $ $ $ From the superhot and superripe 2003 vintage comes this pumped-up Brunello, redolent of molasses and tar and blessed with a lush, viscous texture. It's toasty, polished and ready to drink immediately.

Capanna | 2003 | BRUNELLO DI MONTALCINO
★★★★ $ $ $ Due to Capanna's traditionalist winemaking methods, not even the intense heat of 2003 could make this wine anything but lean, finely tuned and evocatively aromatic. Truly impressive, this is a rustic yet refined Brunello.

Caparzo | 2005 | ROSSO DI MONTALCINO
★★ $ $ Here's a smooth and glossy Rosso with a cherry kirsch edge and fine, silty tannins. Caparzo wines always have a soft, sweet feel but stop short of going overboard on the oak.

Castello Banfi Poggio alle Mura | 2001 |
BRUNELLO DI MONTALCINO
★★★ $ $ $ $ Named for the medieval fortress that dominates this sprawling estate on the south-facing slopes of Montalcino, Castello Banfi has long been a leading name in Montalcino. Here, they have turned out a single-vineyard powerhouse wine with rich, black, mulberry fruit hemmed in by coffee-ground tannins.

Col d'Orcia | 2003 | BRUNELLO DI MONTALCINO
★★★ $ $ $ This is big, broad-shouldered Sangiovese from one of Montalcino's larger estates, presided over by Count Cinzano (of the famed vermouth) and headquartered in the southwestern corner of the DOCG zone. Because of the vintage, the tannins are softer than normal and the black raspberry fruit is more forward.

Conti Costanti | 2003 | BRUNELLO DI MONTALCINO
★★★★ $ $ $ $ Although Costanti's vineyards face southeast, the producer handled the heat of 2003 deftly, managing to eschew the overblown style of many Brunellos from that vintage for a leaner, more perfumed one. This wine is ripe and sweet but manages to remain supremely elegant.

Fuligni | 2003 | BRUNELLO DI MONTALCINO
★★★ $ $ $ $ From a vineyard on the northern slope of the Montalcino hill, this is another well-proportioned wine from the superripe 2003 vintage. Aged half in 500-liter French oak and half in larger Slavonian barrels, it has sweet, crushed-velvet tannins and perfumy black cherry aromatics.

Il Poggione | 2005 | ROSSO DI MONTALCINO
★★★★ $ $ This gorgeously balanced black cherry– and licorice-scented Rosso nicely captures the brightness of the Sangiovese grape and the woodsy, aromatic terroir of the Montalcino region. A firm backbone of cleansing acidity gives it an electric charge on the palate, perfectly balancing bold fruit flavors.

TUSCANY REDS

montepulciano, carmignano, morellino di scansano

Though the wines of Montepulciano are produced less than 30 miles from Montalcino, the two wines are markedly different. Vino Nobile wines from Montepulciano are made primarily with Prugnolo Gentile (the local name for the Sangiovese grape) and have a minimum aging requirement of two years (three for "Riservas"). Like Rosso di Montalcino, Rosso di Montepulciano requires much less aging—only six months—and is lighter, ready to drink upon release and much less expensive. Carmignano wines are made of Sangiovese grapes blended with Canaiolo Nero and Cabernet Sauvignon and/or Cabernet Franc; they have lower acidity and firmer tannins than typical Chianti Classico. Morellino di Scansano (the "little cherry of Scansano") is a charming, mainly Sangiovese-based wine that has improved considerably in recent years.

montepulciano recommendations

Avignonesi | 2005 | **VINO NOBILE DI MONTEPULCIANO**
★★ $ $ This is an amazingly consistent and well-priced Vino Nobile from the leading house in the appellation, founded in 1974 by the dynamic Falvo brothers. A combination of Prugnolo Gentile grapes with a splash of Canaiolo Nero and a dash of Mammolo results in a wine with violet aromas, cherry fruit and firm tannins.

Crociani | 2005 | **ROSSO DI MONTEPULCIANO**
★★ $ $ With lots of the same flavors as "big brother" Brunello yet at a fraction of the cost, Rosso di Montepulciano wines from the superb 2005 vintage offer great quality and value. This deep, rustic Rosso has tense acidity and pleasingly earthy funk.

Fattoria del Cerro | 2005 | **VINO NOBILE DI MONTEPULCIANO**
★★★ $ $ This is a silky-smooth, modern, oaky red that nevertheless manages to speak to its Tuscan roots: The cedary, varnishy, smoky qualities of Sangiovese and its traditional blending partners, Mammolo and Canaiolo Nero, sing clearly in this luxe red, which makes a good match for grilled meats or a medium-aged cheese.

Poliziano | 2004 | **VINO NOBILE DI MONTEPULCIANO**

★★★ $ $ $ Federico Carletti's 300-acre estate is an elite producer of Vino Nobile, turning out dark, polished reds. This 2004 has a dense, sappy texture and big tannins, with delicious jammy, toasty flavors.

Salcheto | 2003 | **VINO NOBILE DI MONTEPULCIANO**

★★★ $ $ $ The small Salcheto estate delivers a consistently elegant, aromatic Vino Nobile, eschewing excess extract and oak in favor of a more Pinot Noir-ish expression. Telltale aromas of wood char and black cherry peg this as an authentic 100 percent Sangiovese wine.

Valdipiatta | 2004 | **VINO NOBILE DI MONTEPULCIANO**

★★★ $ $ While this powerful Vino Nobile is made with the traditional grapes (85 percent Sangiovese, 15 percent Canaiolo Nero), it is given a modern sheen by way of time in French oak *barriques*. The chocolaty richness of the wine is nicely balanced by earth flavors.

carmignano & morellino di scansano recommendations

Capezzana | 2005 | **BARCO REALE DI CARMIGNANO**

★★★ $ One of Italy's greatest values, this Sangiovese-based stunner should be snapped up by the case. A touch of Cabernet lends inky color and cassis fruit to the savory, smoky base; this is real character at a party-wine price.

Piaggia Il Sasso | 2006 | **CARMIGNANO**

★★★ $ $ $ The small Piaggia estate, founded in 1990, farms 15 acres in the heart of Carmignano, and, true to the region's roots (Carmignano was the first Tuscan appellation to incorporate "French" grapes), blends Cabernet Sauvignon and Merlot with Sangiovese to create an elegant yet fruit-saturated wine.

Poggio Argentiera Capatosta | 2006 |
MORELLINO DI SCANSANO

★★ $ $ $ This sweet, plump Sangiovese from southern Tuscany is aged in small barrels of French Allier oak, resulting in a dark and sappy powerhouse. Sangiovese can often have sharper angles, but this hot-climate coastal expression is voluptuous.

Val delle Rose | 2004 | **MORELLINO DI SCANSANO**

★★ $ $ Smooth and sweet in the manner of southern Tuscan Sangiovese, this consistent and widely available red is a luscious offering from a great vintage. It's versatile and fruit-driven—a great candidate for party quaffing.

TUSCANY REDS

super-tuscans

Before the creation of the IGT (*Indicazione Geografica Tipica*) classification in 1992, any Italian wine not produced under the strict guidelines of the DOC or DOCG was relegated to the lowly category of *Vino da Tavola,* or table wine. Meanwhile, inventive vintners were experimenting with different grapes, blending Sangiovese with Cabernet Sauvignon, Syrah and/or Merlot—grapes untraditional to the region—to produce the superb wines that became known as the Super-Tuscans. Once the IGT designation was in place, vintners could finally market their wines as their quality merited, adding regional and compositional information to their labels. Of course, such freedom and popularity has led to a proliferation of Super-Tuscan wines, some better than others. Still, Super-Tuscans—typically powerful, concentrated and expensive—remain some of the most sought after and finely crafted exports Italy has to offer. Famous Super-Tuscans include Masseto, Solaia and Sassicaia, the last of which was granted its own DOC appellation in the late '90s, the only Italian wine from a single estate to achieve such an honor.

super-tuscan recommendations

Antinori Tenuta Guado al Tasso | 2005 | **BOLGHERI SUPERIORE**
★★★ $ $ $ $ This blend of Cabernet, Merlot and Syrah is relatively restrained despite its heat-wave vintage. It displays a hint of leather from the Syrah and an overall personality that's earthy and dense.

Argiano Non Confunditur | 2005 | **TUSCANY**
★★★★ $ $ Super-Tuscans are usually quite costly, so when you find a cheaper one that delivers the goods like this does, it's time to buy by the case. This delicious blend of Cabernet (40 percent) with 20 percent each of Sangiovese, Merlot and Syrah is an affordable luxury.

Barone Ricasoli Casalferro | 2003 | **TUSCANY**
★★★ $ $ $ Rich as motor oil, with a hint of black pepper and eucalyptus, this wine was once 100 percent Sangiovese but now includes a softening, sweetening, blackening dollop of Merlot.

Brancaia Ilatraia | 2005 | MAREMMA
★★★ $ $ $ The Widmer family of Chianti fame has expanded their Brancaia brand to the warm, wide-open Maremma region of southern Tuscany, where they produce this lip-smacking powerhouse of Cabernet Sauvignon, Sangiovese and Petit Verdot.

Ca'Marcanda Magari | 2005 | TUSCANY
★★★★ $ $ $ $ A sublime and smoky blend of Merlot, Cabernet Sauvignon and Cabernet Franc, this Bordeaux-style blend has the scorched-earth blackness of a big-name Pomerol. It's luxurious but with a sense of proportion.

Castello Banfi Colvecchio Syrah | 2004 | SANT'ANTIMO
★★ $ $ $ The vanilla sheen of new French oak is there, but it doesn't overpower the violet scent and meaty flavor of this Syrah. This is one of many excellent Syrahs emerging from the Montalcino area.

Cesani Luenzo | 2003 | TUSCANY
★★★ $ $ $ With Super-Tuscans, you expect dense color, generous oak and intensity. This wine, based on Sangiovese from the San Gimignano region, has it all, but stops just short of being over-the-top. It's well priced for the category, too.

I Greppi Greppicante | 2005 | BOLGHERI
★★★ $ $ This newish project is headed by Alessandro Landini of Chianti's Fattoria Viticcio. Made from 60 percent Cabernet Sauvignon, 30 percent Merlot and 10 percent Cabernet Franc, it offers concentrated dark fruit flavors for a fair price.

Il Pino di Biserno | 2005 | TUSCANY
★★★ $ $ $ $ This is like a Pomerol from Tuscany, courtesy of Piero and Lodovico Antinori and French consultant Michel Rolland. Made from Bordeaux grapes, it is wonderfully earthy, sappy and decadent in the manner of most modern Super-Tuscans.

La Mozza Aragone | 2005 | MAREMMA
★★★★ $ $ $ $ A superb wine, this uniquely Mediterranean blend of Sangiovese, Alicante and Syrah is leaner and more perfumed than the typical Super-Tuscan blockbuster; there's an herbal edge to the aromas and firm acidity supporting its mass of red fruit.

Le Macchiole | 2004 | MESSORIO
★★★ $ $ $ $ One of Tuscany's elite Merlots, right up there with Ornellaia's Masseto, this midnight-black monolith belongs next to a well-marbled slab of porterhouse. It's an incredibly fruity wine, but a smoky, river-gravel earthiness lends it gravitas.

Rocca di Frassinello Le Sughere di Frassinello | 2005 |
MAREMMA

★★★★ $ $ $ This is the second wine from a relatively new—the first vintage was 2003—southern Tuscan project of publisher and vintner Paolo Panerai (Castellare di Castellina) and Baron Eric de Rothschild (Domaines Barons de Rothschild). Made with grapes from vineyards surrounded by cork forests, it's a deliciously smoky and velvety mix of Sangiovese, Merlot and Cabernet.

Ruffino Romitorio di Santedame | 2003 | TUSCANY

★★★ $ $ $ $ Produced at Ruffino's Santedame Estate near Castellina in Chianti Classico, this unique red features Tuscany's indigenous Colorino grape, blended with 40 percent Merlot. Like most 2003s, it is superripe, with intense huckleberry fruit and a tarry, coffee-ground savor.

Tenuta di Arceno Arcanum I | 2004 | TUSCANY

★★★ $ $ $ $ This estate, owned by California wine legend Jess Jackson, is located in the hills of Chianti. In addition to producing solid, well-made Chiantis, Arceno crafts luxurious, sweetly oaky Super-Tuscans, including this massive, showy example based primarily on Cabernet Franc.

Tenuta Monteti Caburnio | 2005 | TUSCANY

★★ $ $ Located in the Maremma region of southern Tuscany, up-and-coming Tenuta Monteti enlisted über-consultant Carlo Ferrini to craft this Cabernet Sauvignon–Alicante–Merlot blend. While dry, it's a succulent hot cocoa of a wine, toasty and viscous.

other central italian regions

Beyond Tuscany and its many treasures lie other central Italian regions whose wines and winemaking traditions are well worth exploring. The most notable of these regions is Abruzzo. Responsible for the lion's share of Montepulciano production in Italy, Abruzzo is known for its spicy, robust and affordable reds. Other central Italian offerings range from the earthy, smoky Rosso Conero of Le Marche to the popular (if admittedly unremarkable) and slightly sparkling red Lambrusco of Emilia-Romagna.

• **EMILIA-ROMAGNA** Much better known for its culinary contributions, Emilia-Romagna still produces some interesting wines. The most popular is fizzy red Lambrusco, but whites from Chardonnay and the distinctive Albana grape are also produced here, as are reds from Sangiovese, Barbera and Cabernet.

• **LE MARCHE** The underestimated region of Le Marche produces both reds and whites, but its signature wine is the distinctively rich white made from the Verdicchio grape. Two interesting reds particular to the region are the bold, full-bodied Rosso Conero and Rosso Piceno.

• **ABRUZZO** Unlike the dull Trebbiano grown in other regions, the white Trebbiano d'Abruzzo is crisp and lovely. The Montepulciano grape is crafted here into a dark and spicy wine (no relation to Tuscany's Sangiovese-based Montepulciano, which is named after a town). Wines from Abruzzo tend to be well priced and present excellent value.

• **UMBRIA** Red wines of note from Umbria include the Sagrantino-based wines of Montefalco and the Sangiovese-based wines hailing from Torgiano. Orvieto is the region's most important white wine. Simple, less interesting examples are made from the Trebbiano grape alone; those blended with the lively Grechetto grape are far better.

• **LAZIO** The region surrounding Rome provides the capital with one of its simpler pleasures—the lightly sparkling white Frascati. Made from a Trebbiano and Malvasia blend, most versions of this wine offer delicate, citrusy refreshment.

other central italian whites

Like many Italian wines, Le Marche's Verdicchio was once a simple, mass-produced commodity with little character. Today, as winemakers focus their attention and resources on the variety, more and more interesting expressions are being crafted. Trebbiano d'Abruzzo is another central Italian white wine making a name for itself internationally. The low-acid Albana grape shines particularly brightly in the Emilia-Romagna region, where it yields a variety of styles, both dry and sweet.

other central italian white recommendations

Bisci | 2007 | VERDICCHIO DI MATELICA

★★★ $ $ Matelica, which is situated near Le Marche's border with Umbria, is a lesser-known growing zone for the Verdicchio grape. This steel-fermented version bristles with mouthwatering, crisp acidity, which upholds pronounced green apple flavors and a refreshing core of minerals.

Falesco Ferentano | 2006 | LAZIO

★★★ $ $ The obscure Roscetto grape grows in Rome's suburbs, where it seems to have languished until Falesco's Cotarella brothers took a shine to it. Highly aromatic, this wine boasts pineapple and banana fruit plus a hint of vanilla in the nose and a boatload of honeyed, mouth-filling fruit. Beautifully balanced and nuanced, it's a great value.

Fattoria San Lorenzo Vigna di Gino | 2006 |
VERDICCHIO DEI CASTELLI DI JESI

★★ $ This Verdicchio is made by allowing some contact between juice and skins during fermentation, creating a deep golden color and a rich, round texture. Peach-scented, it has some of the exotic aromas and waxy texture of a good Viognier.

Moncaro Verde Ca'Ruptae | 2006 |
VERDICCHIO DEI CASTELLI DI JESI CLASSICO SUPERIORE

★★ $ A clean, fresh and classic expression of the Marche region's Verdicchio grape, this wine has a bright green apple flavor followed by a touch of almondy bitterness on the finish. Extended lees contact lends it a creamy feel.

Nicodemi | 2005 | TREBBIANO D'ABRUZZO

★★ $ Grown in the hills near Teramo in northeastern Abruzzo, this is a fleshy, pear-scented Trebbiano with lots of weight in spite of being made with no oak. Ripe, fruity and substantial, it's much more than just a quaffing white.

Poggio Calvelli La Carraia | 2006 | ORVIETO CLASSICO

★★★ $ $ One of the richest, most expressive Orvietos around, this honeyed white combines Grechetto with Chardonnay and Trebbiano. Its pear and apple flavors are creamy, thanks to a short rest in oak.

Tenuta di Salviano | 2006 | ORVIETO CLASSICO

★★★ $ The inclusion of 20 percent Sauvignon Blanc and aging in neutral cement vats yield this fresher, more aromatic take on Orvieto Classico. The region's tufaceous soils impart an appealing chalkiness.

other central italian reds

The Marche region produces two notable Sangiovese-Montepulciano blends: Rossos Conero and Piceno. Emilia-Romagna, sometimes called the birthplace of Sangiovese, makes a fine, if underappreciated, version of the grape. Umbria's Sagrantino di Montefalco is dark and complex, though small production can lead to high prices. Probably the most popular wine from Italy's other central regions is Montepulciano d'Abruzzo: Typically a simple wine with nice berry flavors, it can also be remarkably robust and tannic.

other central italian red recommendations

Antonelli | 2003 | SAGRANTINO DI MONTEFALCO
★ ★ ★ $ $ $ This wine is made by a great small-scale producer of Sagrantino in the syrupy, palate-coating style. A potent winter red, it has an intensity due in part to the hot 2003 vintage, but Antonelli always coaxes luscious extract from the rich Sagrantino grape.

Arnaldo Caprai Venticinque Anni | 2004 |
SAGRANTINO DI MONTEFALCO
★ ★ ★ ★ $ $ $ $ The 2004 vintage was one of the best in Montefalco, and this benchmark reserve wine from Arnaldo Caprai beautifully displays Sagrantino's characteristic burly structure. Dark-hued, with flavors of black fruits and spices, it will age 10 to 20 years easily.

Binomio | 2003 | MONTEPULCIANO D'ABRUZZO
★ ★ ★ $ $ $ Binomio is a collaboration between Abruzzo's Fattoria La Valentina and Veneto Soave producer Stefano Inama. From high-altitude vineyards near Pescara, their Montepulciano is a powerhouse—a huge yet soft-textured wine that's ink-black in color.

Capestrano | 2006 | MONTEPULCIANO D'ABRUZZO
★ ★ $ Fermented and aged entirely in stainless steel to preserve its fruitiness, this great-value wine is ideal for barbecues: Its lush fruit and soft, velvety tannins will embrace all manner of grilled meats.

Cocci Grifoni Il Grifone | 2003 | OFFIDA ROSSO
★ ★ ★ $ $ The flagship red of the Cocci estate outside Ascoli Piceno in the southern Marche, this blend of 75 percent Montepulciano and 25 percent Cabernet Sauvignon is deep and velvety, with great color and ripeness; its toasty edge comes from 20 months of oak aging.

Còlpetrone | 2004 | SAGRANTINO DI MONTEFALCO

★★ $ $ This is a jammy, rich, decadent red, with such a big blast of tannin that it almost requires a well-marbled steak to tame it. Through the use of new oak, Còlpetrone has given the black, spicy fruit of the Sagrantino grape a luxurious vanilla-scented gloss.

Drei Donà Vigneti delle Rosenere | 2006 |
SANGIOVESE DI ROMAGNA

★★ $ Some in the Bologna area of Emilia-Romagna believe Sangiovese originated on their side of the Apennines, not in Tuscany. This is an elegant Romagnan take on the grape, full of black cherry fruit.

Emidio Pepe | 2001 | MONTEPULCIANO D'ABRUZZO

★★★ $ $ $ A cult favorite from an organic farm where grapes are still foot-trod and all wines are hand-decanted into new bottles before release, this Montepulciano d'Abruzzo offers a combination of soft tannins and deep black fruit flavors that makes it drinkable now, but will enable it to age like a red Burgundy.

Lamborghini Trescone | 2004 | UMBRIA

★★ $ $ Given the car-making family involved, it's not surprising that most of the wines from this estate near Umbria's Lake Trasimeno are sleek and expensive. Trescone is a well-priced alternative; a blend of Sangiovese, Ciliegiolo and Merlot, it's bright with nice fruit flavors.

Marchetti | 2005 | ROSSO CONERO

★★ $ $ Maurizio Marchetti's small estate near Ancona is well regarded for its consistent, fruity, nicely balanced Rosso Coneros. His inclusion of 10 percent Sangiovese to the base of Montepulciano (contrary to the 100 percent Montepulciano trend in Conero today) lends this medium-bodied wine spice and acidity.

Masciarelli Marina Cvetic | 2004 |
MONTEPULCIANO D'ABRUZZO

★★★ $ $ $ This richly concentrated Montepulciano is a solid value, considering the depth of flavor it offers. It's a big, well-rounded mouthful of blackberry fruit, almost cassislike in its viscosity. In a word: ultrasmooth.

Poderi dal Nespoli Prugneto | 2005 |
SANGIOVESE DI ROMAGNA

★★★ $ $ Another well-made Sangiovese from the hills outside Bologna, this is a woodsy, brightly aromatic take on the variety. The tart red berry fruit and forest-floor aromas suggest Tuscany, but this Sangiovese is from the other side of the Apennine mountains.

southern italy

A word often used when describing southern Italy's current wine scene is "exciting." In truth, certain regions, such as Campania and Sicily, are producing excellent wines, among them Sicily's well-priced Nero d'Avola and Campania's red Aglianico and white Falanghina. However, the sunny, hot region as a whole is still in the process of transforming itself from a bulk producer to a land of quality vintners.

• **APULIA** Still known mainly for its mass production of wines that will never reach an international market, Apulia (or Puglia in Italian) is home to an increasing number of high-quality red wines. Look for the spicy reds from Salice Salentino and Copertino, made from the dark-skinned Negroamaro grape, as well as the fruity Primitivo, which tastes similar to a California Zinfandel.

• **BASILICATA** With the menacingly named Monte Vulture volcano looming in the background, the vineyards of the Basilicata region produce Aglianico-based reds that echo the inherent volcanic soils. Aromatic and spicy, the more tannic versions of this variety require years of aging.

• **CALABRIA** This region, which is located in the "toe" of Italy's boot, is responsible for much low-quality wine. The lone exception is the Gaglioppo-based red wine of Cirò, lightly tannic and flush with berry.

• **CAMPANIA** Campania is the highlight of southern Italian winemaking. The Aglianico-based red Taurasi, which requires a minimum of three years of aging, has earned much well-deserved acclaim since achieving DOCG status in 1993. Both the quality and quantity of Falanghina, the main white in the region, are on the rise, while the two other whites particular to Campania, Fiano di Avellino and floral Greco di Tufo, also deserve recognition.

• **SICILY & SARDINIA** Easily two of southern Italy's most up-and-coming regions, Sicily and Sardinia have benefited greatly from winemakers' commitment to cultivating grapes indigenous to the region. While a growing number of international varieties such as Cabernet, Syrah and Merlot are made here as well, vintners continue to celebrate their native grapes. Sicily's whites, usually made from Catarratto and often blended with Inzolia, can be bright, citrusy and quite good. The white Vermentino of Sardinia is a standout, as are the spicy reds Cannonau (Grenache) and Carignano (Carignane). Meanwhile, the increasingly popular Nero d'Avola is making great strides in solidifying Sicily's reputation as a producer of world-class reds.

southern italian whites

In defiance of their warm climate, southern Italian vintners produce wonderfully light and crisp white wines, such as Falanghina, Fiano di Avellino and Greco di Tufo from Campania and Vermentino from Sardinia.

southern italian white recommendations

Cantine Pala Crabilis | 2006 | **VERMENTINO DI SARDEGNA**
★★★ $ $ A great-value wine, this Mediterranean white clearly reflects its Sardinian origin, with aromas of scrubland and a slight sea-air salinity. Its flavors of green herbs and mint are delivered on a raft of racy acidity.

Ceuso di Melia Scurati Bianco | 2006 | **SICILY**
★★ $ $ A winery near Trapani in western Sicily produces this clean, refreshing white with lots of character. In it, mineral-tinged local grapes Grecanico and Grillo are given a creamy, melony boost with a dose of Chardonnay.

De Conciliis Donnaluna | 2007 | **FIANO DI AVELLINO**
★★★ $ $ Campania's Fiano grape was known to the ancient Romans as *Vitis apiana* because its sweet juice attracted bees (*api*). This modern take on the grape, made in southern Campania, tastes like it was made by bees: Though dry, it has a rich, aromatic honey quality.

Di Giovanna Grillo | 2006 | **SICILY**
★★ $ $ Grillo is one of several Sicilian white grapes that once went anonymously into Marsala wines but is now vinified on its own. This bright Grillo-based bottling starts out with a hint of tropical fruit, then finishes with a shellfish-friendly mineral bite.

Feudo Principi di Butera Insolia | 2006 | SICILY

★ ★ $ Another of Sicily's light, floral, brightly fruity native white grapes, Insolia is the star of this simple, unoaked white, which would be terrific with swordfish *involtini* or some other Sicilian seafood.

Pietracupa | 2006 | FIANO DI AVELLINO

★ ★ $ $ $ Brisk and clean, this white offers a delicate wildflower honey aroma, along with a whiff of the well-forested hinterlands of central Campania. Unadorned by oak, its acidity has the zing and grip of grapefruit juice.

Santadi Cala Silente | 2007 | VERMENTINO DI SARDEGNA

★ ★ ★ $ $ The name of this wine means "silent cove," referring to the inlet in southwestern Sardinia that its vines overlook. A consistently great value from one of the leading names in southern Italian wine, it's a rich and viscous (yet completely dry) white, with lots of green herb and muskmelon flavors.

Terredora di Paolo Irpinia Falanghina | 2007 | CAMPANIA

★ ★ $ $ The Falanghina grape has been part of winemaking since the days of the Greeks in Campania. This chalky, gripping modern example offers a hint of kiwi and white grapefruit on the nose, with plenty of citrus fruit and acidity on the palate.

southern italian reds

There is certainly no shortage of unique red wines to sample from the regions of southern Italy. Running the gamut from soft and simple quaffers to bold and spicy wines suitable for long aging, they are often made from indigenous grapes rarely seen elsewhere.

southern italian red recommendations

Appollonio Divoto | 2000 | COPERTINO ROSSO RISERVA

★ ★ $ $ Copertino wines are the Negroamaro-based cousins of Apulia's better-known Salice Salentino wines, and this one drinks like liquid chocolate. Here, the tarry, smoky edge of Negroamaro is softened and sweetened with 30 percent Montepulciano.

Argiolas Costera | 2006 | CANNONAU DI SARDEGNA

★ ★ $ $ Hints of eucalyptus and licorice distinguish this lush southern Italian red, a Cannonau (a.k.a. Grenache) that delivers lots of flavor in a medium-bodied package. It's made by Argiolas, one of Sardinia's best-known producers, whose winemaking history dates to 1918.

Cantele | 2003 | SALICE SALENTINO RISERVA

★★ $ The cooperative Cantele winery in southern Apulia has a huge, consistent, well-priced lineup of wines. This Negroamaro-based red from the famed town of Salice Salentino is superripe and simply satisfying, like fruity milk chocolate.

Cantine Lonardo | 2001 | TAURASI

★★★★ $ $ $ Here's a superb example of southern Italy's most important appellation wine (Taurasi), made from the region's most important red grape (Aglianico). Tarry, spicy and tannic, this is a cellar-worthy red from a producer who only began bottling in 1998.

Castello Monaci Maru Negroamaro | 2006 | SALENTO

★★ $ $ Negroamaro, which translates as "black and bitter," is the key grape in southern Apulia's Salice Salentino wines, among others. This is one of many interesting single-variety bottlings, showing off the grape's huckleberry fruit and lavender fragrance.

Contini 'Inu | 2004 | CANNONAU DI SARDEGNA

★★ $ $ $ Cannonau, or Grenache, is a grape (and a wine) on the rise in Italy: It has a floral, perfumy aroma reminiscent of Pinot Noir, but a darker, more luscious fruit component makes it more hedonistic on the palate. Contini 'Inu offers an herbal, concentrated example.

Conti Zecca Nero | 2003 | ROSSO DEL SALENTO

★★★ $ $ $ Unlike many southern Italian reds, this blend of 70 percent Negroamaro and 30 percent Cabernet Sauvignon has good acidity balancing its deep core of particularly ripe fruit. Exotic, spicy and soft-textured, it hails from the Lecce province of southern Apulia.

Elena Fucci Titolo | 2005 | AGLIANICO DEL VULTURE

★★★ $ $ $ The tiny, family-run Elena Fucci winery burst onto the scene a few years ago and produces this deliciously modern (meaning rich and oaky) take on the Aglianico grape. Its savage, smoky edge is derived from the volcanic soils of the Vulture volcano in Basilicata.

Feudi di San Gregorio | 2004 | TAURASI

★★★ $ $ $ The fierce tannins of the Aglianico grape surface briefly on the finish of this massive wine, which otherwise keeps its bite buried under a down comforter of rich, toasty purple fruit. This is a polished, fruit-driven Taurasi wine.

Feudo Principi di Butera Iperion | 2006 | SICILY

★★ $ $ An exceptionally soft, ripe Sicilian red, this wine combines Nero d'Avola with Cabernet and Merlot. The fruit has a warm-pie-on-the-windowsill quality, toasty and satisfying.

Layer Cake Primitivo | 2006 | APULIA
★★ $ $ Created by Californian winemaker Jayson Woodbridge, the Layer Cake brand features bottlings from four different countries. This Primitivo is very fruity, with a dark purple hue, ripe flavors and a texture so viscous it's almost like chocolate frosting.

Masseria Altemura Sasseo Primitivo | 2005 | SALENTO
★★ $ Soft, sweet tannins, low acid and ripe fruit are Primitivo hallmarks, and this fits the profile without tasting too jammy or "cooked." There's a cassislike richness to its texture and a hint of black pepper.

Ocone Diomede | 2003 | AGLIANICO DEL TABURNO
★★ $ $ $ This burly, smoky, unfiltered red hails from high-altitude, biodynamically farmed vineyards near Monte Taburno, a volcano in northern Campania. Made from 100 percent Aglianico, the wine has a dark, brooding intensity.

Paternoster Synthesi | 2005 | AGLIANICO DEL VULTURE
★★★★ $ $ $ Yet another Italian wine grown in proximity to a volcano (in this case, Monte Vulture in Basilicata), Synthesi is a manifestation of its wild, wonderful terroir: It smells like an extinguished campfire, and its acidity and tannin give it a feral grip. Notes of dried sausage and herbs lend mouthwatering savor.

Planeta La Segreta | 2006 | SICILY
★★ $ $ This distinctive, widely available, easy-drinking red is based on Sicily's Nero d'Avola grape but includes small percentages of Syrah, Merlot and Cabernet Franc. It's silky, spicy and velvet-soft.

Re Manfredi | 2004 | AGLIANICO DEL VULTURE
★★★ $ $ $ A rather luscious take on the normally sharp-elbowed Aglianico grape, this consistently excellent bottling finishes with a dry, black-tea edge, but on entry it's all warm, sweet cherry pie—a nice mix of lush fruit and savory spice.

Valle dell'Acate Il Frappato | 2007 | SICILY
★★★ $ $ Frappato is a berry-scented grape native to southeastern Sicily. It's usually blended with Nero d'Avola, but here it is featured alone. The result has terrific *frutti di bosco* (forest fruit) aromas and a crisp, light touch.

Vestini Campagnano Pallagrello Nero | 2004 |
TERRE DEL VOLTURNO
★★★ $ $ $ $ This gorgeous, dark, peppery red—with incredibly powerful yet balanced tannins—is the best example out there of the obscure Pallagrello Nero, a grape native to Campania.

spain

Spain's march to the forefront of European winemaking over the past 20 years has been breathtaking. Until a decade ago, most wine drinkers were familiar with only two of the country's regions: Rioja and Ribera del Duero. Today, the robust, high-alcohol, New World–style wines from Spain's sunny Mediterranean climes showcase a new side to Spanish winemaking and have fueled the industry's remarkable resurgence.

Bay of Biscay

Rías Baixas
Bierzo
Rioja
Navarra
Somontano
Catalonia
Toro
Ribera del Duero
Barcelona
Priorat
Penedès
Rueda
Calatayud
Madrid ☆
Utiel-Requena
PORTUGAL
SPAIN
Valencia
Ribera del Guadiana
La Mancha
Valdepeñas
Jumilla
Alicante
Mediterranean Sea
• Seville
Jerez
Málaga
Atlantic Ocean

Principal Wine Region

Spain: An Overview

Spain's mountain ranges divide the country into distinct viticultural areas. Crisp, dry, seafood-friendly Albariño-based whites hail from the cool Atlantic region of Rías Baixas, while farther east, Rueda produces whites that are zippier. Catalonia, in the northeast, is home to fine sparkling Cavas as well as still wines from Penedès and the full-bodied reds of Priorat. Luxurious reds come from along the Duero River in Ribera del Duero, while Bierzo is known for denser reds. Toro and Jumilla earn praise for their powerful red wines, and winemakers in Spain's great central plain continue their conversion from bulk to fine wine production. Jerez is famous for its sweet and dry fortified wines (see p. 265).

Spanish Wine Labels

Spain's *Denominación de Origen* (DO) board determines a region's permitted grapes, harvest limits and vinification techniques, and regulates wine labels. Spanish labels typically list region and some give the grape variety used. Terms such as *Joven, Crianza* or *Reserva* indicate the length of time spent in oak barrels (see Rioja, below).

rioja

Rioja is often called the Bordeaux of Spain for its celebrated, ageworthy red wines. However, many of these traditional wines lacked fruitiness as a result of spending long periods of time aging in small American oak barrels. Contemporary tastes are driving winemakers to vinify and age their wines differently, favoring bottle age over barrel (and subtler French oak over American), yielding wines with pronounced fruit flavors augmented by sweet spice and Rioja's signature vanilla notes. Rioja whites, too, are now made in a fresher style (though some older-style whites are excellent). Look also for Rioja's dry, flavorful *rosados* (rosés).

Rioja Grapes & Styles

If one grape is synonymous with Rioja, it is Tempranillo. Traditionally, it is blended with Garnacha (Grenache), Graciano and Mazuelo (Carignane), then aged in American oak, which imparts spice and vanilla flavors. Cabernet is allowed in certain vineyards, and many vintners experiment with it. All Rioja reds are accorded designations based on aging in barrel and bottle: *Joven* wines spend little or no time in oak barrels; *Crianza* reds must be aged two years, one in barrel. *Reservas* require three years total, one in oak; *Gran Reservas,* five years total, two in oak. A growing number of vintners here, however, are now using subtler French oak barrels and aging their wines for shorter lengths of time. Sometimes referred to as *alta expresión* (high expression), these wines are characterized by fresh, bold flavors. Rioja's *rosado* wines are dry, with orange and berry flavors. The region's whites are refreshing wines with apple and citrus flavors; they are traditionally made from Viura and Malvasia, although since the 2007 vintage, grapes such as Chardonnay, Sauvignon Blanc and Verdejo are also permitted. A few vintners still make traditional, long-aged whites.

rioja recommendations

WHITES

Cune Monopole | 2006 |
★★★ $ $ Made by the venerable winery La Cuné, founded in 1879, Monopole is an outstanding white with a round, waxy, succulent texture and a stone fruit sweetness balanced by a chalky bite.

Marqués de Cáceres | 2006 |
★★ $ Clean, rich appley fruit and a hint of yeastiness characterize this bright white. Its screw-cap closure makes perfect sense, as this wine is all about freshness and immediacy.

R. López de Heredia Viña Gravonia | 1998 |
★★★★ $ $ For those seeking something completely different, this well-aged white from one of Rioja's traditionalist producers hums with dramatic tension. The acid is youthful and lively, while the flavors and aromas are more mature, with Sherry-like notes. It's a sublimely funky white that would be fantastic with cheese.

ROSÉS

El Coto | 2007 |
★ ★ $ The beautifully precise shade of pink is one of the reasons to like this dry rosé. Another is the vibrant fruity flavor, with hints of watermelon, raspberry and strawberry.

Muga Rosado | 2007 |
★ ★ ★ ★ $ One of the world's great rosés, this beautifully made blend of Garnacha, Viura and Tempranillo is wonderfully spicy, hinting at paprika and pink peppercorns; perfect summertime refreshment.

REDS

Allende | 2004 |
★ ★ ★ ★ $ $ $ Aged only 14 months in barrel, this Rioja is modern, but moderated. Lusciously dark and ripe, it is well balanced with acidity, while its toasty oak is seamlessly integrated into a powerful yet elegant mix of plum and currant flavors.

Baron de Ley Reserva | 2003 |
★ ★ $ $ This is a very modern style of Reserva, with its cherry and berry fruit framed by a healthy dose of sweet American oak. Extremely soft, nearly nonexistent tannins make it a red to drink now.

Faustino I Gran Reserva | 1996 |
★ ★ ★ $ $ $ Here's a sound, mature red wine at a very fair price (around $35). A savory yet brightly fruit-flavored take on Tempranillo, it offers hints of eucalyptus, herbs and cigar box. As a Rioja Gran Reserva, it's aged a minimum of five years before release.

Marqués de Cáceres Crianza | 2004 |
★ ★ ★ $ From Rioja's highly rated 2004 vintage comes this excellent, complex Crianza. With tobacco and tar notes accenting vivid red cherry fruit, it's ripe yet full of bracing acidity; a terrific value.

Marqués de Murrieta Reserva | 2004 |
★ ★ ★ $ $ The grapes for this pillowy Reserva hail from Murrieta's Ygay estate on the southern fringes of Rioja Alta, where temperatures climb higher than in other Rioja subzones. You can taste the sun in this lush, brambly red, which has a long, smoky finish.

R. López de Heredia Viña Bosconia Reserva | 2000 |
★ ★ ★ ★ $ $ $ Reserva-level Riojas like this may be one of the best deals in wine: For around $40 you get a beautifully aged red with all its attendant complexities: hints of herbs, meat, dried fruits, pepper. Smooth yet rustic, it spent five years in barrels before being bottled.

Sierra Cantabria Crianza | 2004 |

★★★ $ $ Aromas of crushed red berries leap out of this smooth, fruity Crianza. With 14 months in oak, only 40 percent of it new, the overall effect of wood is minimal, making this a lively, relatively un-adorned Tempranillo.

Vega del Río Crianza | 2003 |

★★ $ After a touch of bottle age, this medium-bodied, lightly oaked Crianza is starting to show some mature aromas of varnish, leather and mulch. The tannins are soft and sweet, but the acidity is bright.

Viña Real Reserva | 2001 |

★★★★ $ $ $ Viña Real is one of the brands produced by the huge CVNE group, a.k.a. La Cuné, whose winemaking experience dates back to the 19th century. Even so, this Reserva is fairly modern in style—showing a bit of sweet, new oak—but beautifully balanced, with tart acidity and a hint of cigar-box savor.

star producers
rioja

Allende

Traditionalists may protest the innovations of winemaker Miguel Angel de Gregorio, but his modern-style wines are undeniably great.

Faustino

Faustino exports more Gran Reserva bottles than any other Rioja producer—at prices that are very fair.

Marqués de Murrieta

Winemaker V. Dalmau Cebrián-Sagarriga's dynamic *alta expresión* wines represent, ironically, a return to a style that was fashionable before the commercial taste profile of Rioja emerged in the 1960s.

Muga

Muga may be considered part of Rioja's old guard, but current winemaker Jorge Muga has an eye toward the future, as evidenced by his "super-Rioja," Torre Muga.

R. López de Heredia

Winemaker Maria José López de Heredia's traditionally made wines stand apart—and stand the test of time.

Viña Real

This veteran brand was developed by the CVNE group (Compañía Vinicola del Norte de España) in the 1940s; today, its acclaimed wines are crafted in a state-of-the-art winery.

ribera del duero

For decades Ribera del Duero was known for a single producer: Vega Sicilia, whose legendary Unico (a Tempranillo-Cabernet blend) is famous for its longevity—and its exorbitant price. Not until Alejandro Fernández's Pesquera—a tremendous bargain by comparison—debuted about a quarter century ago, however, did interest in the region increase significantly. Today Ribera del Duero makes some of Spain's best and most expensive wines.

Ribera del Duero Grapes & Styles

Ribera del Duero reds are mostly made from Tinto Fino, a local variant of Tempranillo. Bordeaux's Cabernet, Merlot and Malbec are now permitted in the denomination. Garnacha is used in the production of *rosados*.

ribera del duero recommendations

Bodegas Aalto | 2005 |
★★★★ $ $ $ $ Winemaker Mariano García (formerly of the legendary Vega Sicilia winery) co-founded Bodegas Aalto in the late 1990s and helped fashion this outstanding, deep red, made from old-vine Tinto Fino (Tempranillo) grapes. A hint of coconut lies like icing over the wine's rich huckleberry fruit flavors.

Condado de Haza | 2005 |
★★★ $ $ $ Alejandro Fernández secured this large estate in the late 1980s to create affordable alternatives to his legendary Pesquera reds. This powerful wine, which could be drunk now or cellared for a decade, brims with blackberry, tobacco and sweet American oak.

O. Fournier Urban | 2005 |
★★ $ Freshness and finesse distinguish this aromatic and unusually light Ribera, which is a nice departure from the region's full-bodied reds. High-altitude vineyards provide the acid-rich, red berry fruit.

Valdubón Reserva | 2002 |
★★★ $ $ A fine effort in a difficult vintage, this dark and stormy expression of Tempranillo tastes of blackberries and dark cocoa, with well-integrated oak and soft tannins. You can hardly beat the price (about $25) for such a luxurious Reserva.

catalonia

Although Codorníu's José Raventós put the sparkling Cavas of Penedès (see p. 260) on the map in the early 1870s, only recently have the region's still wines merited attention. Thanks to the efforts of vintners like Miguel Torres and René Barbier, Catalonia now produces an eclectic range of wines.

Catalonia Grapes & Styles

Catalonia is largely planted with Garnacha (Grenache), which, along with Cariñena (Carignane), composes the heart of Priorat's full-bodied reds and is the basis of reds from most subregions. Monastrell and Tempranillo are also grown here, as are international grapes Cabernet, Merlot and Syrah. Garnacha Blanca is responsible for the region's nut-flavored whites. Local grapes Macabeo, Parellada and Xarel-lo are used in many generic wines and Cavas.

catalonia recommendations

WHITES

Albet i Noya Clàssic Xarel-lo | 2007 | PENEDÈS
★ $ This fiercely acidic white is made from Spain's native Xarel-lo grape (the primary grape in Cava production). Extremely chalky and sharp, it truly channels the limestone-based soils it comes from.

Can Feixes Blanc Selecció | 2006 | PENEDÈS
★★ $ $ A still wine from a Cava producer, this steel-fermented white includes Macabeo and Parellada along with a fattening dollop of Chardonnay, making for a clean and refreshing aperitif.

Clos d'Agon Blanco | 2006 | CATALONIA
★★★ $ $ $ $ This rich, oak-fermented blend is distinctly Mediterranean, made in vineyards just a few kilometers from the sea in northeastern Spain, near the French border. The wine is exotically aromatic, combining Viognier, Roussanne and a bit of Marsanne.

Parés Baltà Electio | 2006 | PENEDÈS
★★★ $ $ $ Here's an unabashedly modern white from a traditional grape. In this highly unusual yet supremely delicious bottling, Cava blending grape Xarel-lo is barrel-fermented to lend a toasty edge to its characteristic green apple fruit and brisk acid.

René Barbier Mediterranean White | NV | **CATALONIA**
★ $ An appealingly fresh white from Spanish giant Freixenet, this brims with tropical fruit balanced by vivacious acidity. It's crafted from local grapes Xarel-lo, Macabeo and Parellada.

ROSÉS

Fra Guerau | 2007 | **MONTSANT**
★★ $ Fruit-driven with a lovely dark shade of pink, this Merlot-based blend of Garnacha and Syrah possesses big, bold, luscious flavors.

Parés Baltà Radix | 2005 | **PENEDÈS**
★★★ $ $ $ While this is more of a light red than a true *rosado,* its producers consider it the latter and recommend serving it chilled. It's a tangy, peppery quaffer made from 100 percent Syrah, delicious and refreshing if not exactly pink.

REDS

Cellers Unió Perlat | 2005 | **MONTSANT**
★★ $ $ This 100 percent Garnacha wine comes from the ascendant Montsant appellation, which is located near the more famous Priorat DO. Pretty, fruity and aromatic (in a mentholated Mediterranean way), the wine is ripe and sunny without being overly sweet.

Costers de Mas Igneus | 2001 | **PRIORAT**
★★★ $ $ $ $ Composed of four parts Garnacha and one part Cariñena, this concentrated red has lots of fruit intensity, with notes of blueberry and prune. Hints of damp earth and roasted meat give it a compelling balance between sweet and savory.

Escoda-Sanahuja Les Paradetes | 2005 | **CONCA DE BARBERÀ**
★★ $ $ Conca de Barberà is a relatively obscure appellation in Tarragona, near Penedès. This crisp, medium-bodied red blends the local Sumoll grape with Garnacha, resulting in lots of spicy black fruit flavor and a hint of Mediterranean scrub.

Melis | 2005 | **PRIORAT**
★★★ $ $ $ $ A monolithic, incredibly delicious wine from a newish property owned by Victor Gallegos, the general manager of California's Sea Smoke Vineyards, this massive Priorat red combines a majority of Garnacha with Cariñena, Syrah and Cabernet.

Olvena | 2004 | **SOMONTANO**
★★ $ From a DO in northeastern Spain, this internationally styled red blends Tempranillo with Cabernet and Merlot. It's familiar and unfamiliar at the same time, plump and fruity but darkly spicy, too.

other spanish regions

In a country with more land under vine than any other on the planet, Spain is blessed with dozens of unique wine-making regions in every part of its severe, mountainous landscape. The country's finest white wines come from the northwest coastal region of Rías Baixas. Rueda is known for well-made, inexpensive whites, and Toro for its bold reds. Other robust reds come from Bierzo to the west. Navarra, a longtime producer of dry *rosados,* is now an emerging red wine region. The quality of Somontano's bold, polished reds is also on the rise. While all of these regions are evolving, perhaps the most interesting development is the transformation of regions formerly known only for crude, bulk wines into producers of terrific value wines. Search out bottlings from these regions: Jumilla, Yecla, Valdepeñas and Alicante, as well as Vinos de Madrid, La Mancha, Ribera del Guadiana and Utiel-Requena.

Other Spanish Grapes & Styles

Spain is undeniably a country of red grapes—most of them hearty. La Mancha, Vinos de Madrid, Valdepeñas and Ribera del Guadiana produce many graceful, full-bodied wines made with the standard Spanish mix of grapes. Garnacha dominates in Navarra but is sometimes blended with Tempranillo, Cabernet Sauvignon and Merlot. The region's dry *rosados* are considered Spain's best. Vintners in Somontano make smooth, earthy reds from Moristel. Toro reds are similar to Ribera del Duero, though more concentrated and less elegant. Wines from Bierzo are even fuller-bodied, made from the Mencía grape. Monastrell (Mourvèdre in French) rules in eastern regions, joined by Garnacha and the funky Bobal grape—a blend that results in black, brooding reds. Albariño is the basis for the excellent whites of Rías Baixas. Rueda's whites are made mainly from the Verdejo grape, often supported by Sauvignon Blanc.

other spanish recommendations

WHITES

Buil & Giné Nosis | 2007 | RUEDA
★★ $ $ The Priorat-based Buil & Giné winery sources the grapes for this lush, round, melony Verdejo from 35-year-old vines in Rueda. Aromas of cantaloupe and peach carry through on the fleshy palate, ultimately washed by a nice blast of acidity.

Martín Códax Burgáns Albariño | 2007 | RÍAS BAIXAS
★★ $ Grown in granitic soils near Mount Burgans in Galicia, this is a modern-style bottling from benchmark Albariño producer Martín Códax, and a great introduction to the grape. Plump, fruity and focused, this vintage boasts stone fruit flavors and a mineral bite.

Naia | 2007 | RUEDA
★★★ $ Ripe and powerful flavors of pear and green apple are seared onto the palate by this wine's fiery acidity, tempered by herbal notes. Overall, this delicious, 100 percent Verdejo white is an intriguing mix of power and refreshment at a great price.

Pazo de Señorans Albariño | 2007 | RÍAS BAIXAS
★★★ $ $ Though fermented in stainless steel, this expressive white is held on its lees (yeasty post-fermentation sediment) for a brief period to lend a lovely depth and complexity. There's a pearlike richness to the wine, but good acidity and a pronounced minerality keep it electric and aromatic.

Rafael Palacios As Sortes Val do Bibei | 2006 | VALDEORRAS
★★ $ $ $ The Valdeorras appellation is a little pocket in eastern Galicia that grows the high-acid, aromatic Godello grape (also found in neighboring Bierzo). This 100 percent Godello white, with its penetrating citrus peel aromas, is fermented in large oak vats to round out its otherwise sharp edges.

Txomin Etxaniz | 2007 | GETARIAKO TXAKOLINA
★★ $ $ First, the pronunciation: Cho-MEEN Etch-AH-neez. Second, a warning: This isn't a wine for the meek. Ferociously, tongue-curlingly acidic, this delicious Basque white shows briny, sea-air aromas.

Vionta Albariño | 2006 | RÍAS BAIXAS
★★ $ $ Vionta is one of a number of estates that comprise the Heredad Collection, a group of small wineries owned by Cava giant Freixenet. Their chalky, citrusy Albariño features Granny Smith apple flavors, lime-accented acidity and a touch of herbaceousness.

ROSÉS

Artazu Artazuri Rosé | 2007 | NAVARRA

★★★ $ Crafted by Juan Carlos Lopez de la Calle, owner and wine-maker at Rioja cult estate Artadi, this gutsy, wonderful rosé comes from high-altitude vineyards in Navarra. It's made from Garnacha, which delivers a mix of ripe berry fruit and Mediterranean herbs.

Casa de la Ermita | 2007 | JUMILLA

★★ $ This is a big, bold, dark pink rosé from Spain's Mediterranean coast. A combination of Monastrell and a splash of Garnacha, it shows spicy, peppery aromas with flavors of lush watermelon and berry.

REDS

Bodegas Borsao Monte Oton | 2007 | CAMPO DE BORJA

★★ $ This incredibly well-priced 100 percent Garnacha comes from grapes grown in the shadow of the Moncayo mountain range in north-eastern Spain. A silky-smooth, licorice-scented red, it has an enliven-ing acidity that smacks of the whitish chalk of the region's soils.

Casa de la Ermita Monasterio de Santa Ana Monastrell
| 2006 | JUMILLA

★★ $ Pure Monastrell, Monasterio de Santa Ana is a warm-climate red that's focused, not flabby. A hint of lavender roots it in the Medi-terranean, and nice acidity and spiciness keep it lively.

Descendientes de José Palacios Pétalos | 2006 | BIERZO

★★★ $ $ From the steep, slate-rich slopes of Bierzo in northwest Spain, star winemaker Alvaro Palacios and his cousin, Ricardo, craft this spicy, eucalyptus-scented red from 100 percent Mencía, a grape thought to be related to Cabernet Franc.

El Burro Kickass Garnacha | 2006 | CARIÑENA

★★★ $ A superb value imported by the Virginia-based Well Oiled Wine Co., El Burro's Garnacha is a fresh, lightly oaked red loaded with perfumy aromas and soft, sappy red cherry fruit flavors.

Finca Coronado | 2004 | VINO DE LA TIERRA DE CASTILLA

★★ $ $ $ This blend of Cabernet, Tempranillo, Syrah, Merlot and Petit Verdot hails from the sandy soils of La Mancha. Plush and con-centrated, it shows sweet notes of plum and black raspberry.

Juan Gil | 2005 | JUMILLA

★★★ $ $ Jumilla is a region on the rise, particularly for the Monas-trell grape. This beautifully made, powerful bottling is a lusty, unique mix of black currant, black olive and coffee-ground flavors.

Osborne Solaz Shiraz/Tempranillo | 2005 |
VINO DE LA TIERRA DE CASTILLA

★ **$** From the arid plains south of Madrid comes this blend of two grapes that can handle the heat: Tempranillo and Shiraz. It has a deep, purplish color, sweet black currant fruit and ultra-soft tannins.

Tres Barcos | 2004 | TORO

★★★ **$** Sourced from 25-to-40-year-old vines rooted in sandy, stony soils, this wine starts out coffeeish and lush and finishes with a bright, floral lilt. It's an excellent value, made of 100 percent Tinta de Toro grapes (a.k.a. Tempranillo), from the up-and-coming Toro region.

Volver | 2005 | LA MANCHA

★★ **$ $** In spite of its considerable alcohol (14.5 percent), this wine manages to stay well balanced. Made from old-vine Tempranillo grown on the vast, dry plains of south-central Spain, it yields ample chocolate and fruit flavors for a fair price—a La Mancha hallmark.

---

news from a wine insider

spain by Victor de la Serna, deputy editor, *El Mundo*, Madrid

In the News

The most notable winery sale of 2008 took place between the Eguren brothers of Rioja and LVMH, the French luxury group that owns Dom Pérignon. The brothers sold their Toro-based winery, Numanthia-Termes, for an estimated 25 million euros exactly one year after its 2004 Termanthia was awarded 100 points by *The Wine Advocate*. Meanwhile, the Egurens have built a new winery in Toro named Dominio de Eguren.

In other news, Spain's Minister for the Environment, Cristina Narbona, caused an uproar when she announced that wine producers must use returnable, reusable wine bottles in the near future. Wineries claim that this imposes a terrible financial burden; the final decision has been postponed.

Notable New/Old Varieties

In recent years, Spanish vintners have been rediscovering and vigorously relaunching many of their native grapes. Interesting indigenous varieties on the rise include the fresh and pungent Prieto Picudo in northwest León, the aromatic and floral Sumoll in Catalonia and the tannic, richly colored Bobal in east-central Spain.

portugal

Portugal holds the title for the world's most recognized fortified wine: Port (and to a lesser extent, Madeira). Over the last decade, however, producers of dry wines have been making inroads in the international market, crafting fresh, beautiful wines from Portugal's unique and abundant collection of indigenous grapes.

Atlantic Ocean

Vinho Verde

Porto

Douro

Bairrada

Dão

Beiras

Estremadura

Ribatejo

Bucelas

☆ Lisbon

Borba

Evora

Terras do Sado

Alentejo

Algarve

Principal Wine Region

Portugal: An Overview

For decades Portugal's non-Port wine production was dominated by large cooperatives that prioritized quantity over quality. This began to change in 1986 when Portugal entered the European Union and an influx of outside investment enabled producers to vastly improve their wines. Results have been particularly dramatic in the Douro—home of the country's famed fortified Port wines—where vintners began making great quality strides with their refined dry reds. While traditional Douro Ports and the new generation of dry red wines are indeed wildly different, they do share a similar flavor profile, since they are typically crafted with the same grape varieties. Other regions of note in this small yet geographically diverse country include Alentejo and Dão, where structured, spicy reds are produced. Look to Estremadura, Ribatejo and Terras do Sado near Lisbon for great-value reds made from international and local varieties.

Portuguese Grapes & Styles

Though relatively small in size, Portugal is home to many diverse regions where dozens of indigenous grape varieties thrive. Though largely unknown to most wine drinkers, Vinho Verde should be named the official white wine of summer. It is one of the most refreshing whites made anywhere, thanks to its bracing acidity, slight effervescence and low alcohol. Fuller-bodied examples are made from Alvarinho (called Albariño in Spain) and Loureiro grapes, which are often identified on the label. Whites from other regions such as Alentejo, Dão, Douro, Bairrada and Bucelas are worth seeking out, too. Not surprisingly, Cabernet, Merlot and Syrah have been planted in Portugal, but the country's most compelling reds remain wines made from local varieties such as Baga, Touriga Franca, Touriga Nacional and Tinta Roriz, appearing in blends or on their own. Baga is especially important in Bairrada, where winemakers use it to make dry and tannic red wines with pronounced berry flavors.

Portuguese Wine Labels

Most Portuguese wines are labeled by region and adhere to requirements set up by the country's governing body, the *Denominação de Origem Controlada* (DOC). Wines labeled "Reserva" must be at least half a percent higher in alcohol than the DOC-established minimum. Wines labeled by variety must be made from at least 85 percent of that grape.

portuguese whites

Portugal's enviably long Atlantic coastline yields a lovely range of fish-friendly white wines, from the north's simple, tart Vinho Verde to the long-lived, relatively full-bodied whites from Alentejo in the south.

portuguese white recommendations

Andreza | 2005 | VINHO VERDE
★ $ $ Given its appellation of Vinho Verde (literally, "green wine"), this wine is surprisingly golden in color. Blending honey and nut flavors with a nice minerality and a subtle natural fizz, it brings to mind a Blanc de Blancs Champagne.

Casa de Santar Branco | 2006 | DÃO
★ $ The largest private estate in central Portugal's mountainous Dão region, Casa de Santar boasts a 400-year winemaking history and lovely wines such as this one, with its waxy aromas cut by fragrant minerality and finishing with refreshing candied dried lemon nuances.

Casa de Santa Vitória | 2006 | ALENTEJANO
★ $ The Portuguese and French grapes in this big, briny wine are harvested from young vineyards in southern Portugal. On the nose, maritime aromas waft into zesty, lemony-citrus flavors that have a lovely cleansing effect on the palate.

Castello D'Alba | 2006 | DOURO
★ ★ $ With a wild, invigorating aroma, this flinty wine shows notes of stone fruit and peaches, with a hint of the refreshing acidity to come. Good minerality leads to a spicy, white-pepper finish.

Herdade dos Grous Branco | 2007 | ALENTEJANO
★ $ $ Here's a crisp, juicy white seemingly made with seafood in mind: Granny Smith apple and citrus flavors combine with flinty minerality and a dash of spice.

José Maria da Fonseca Twin Vines | 2007 | VINHO VERDE
★ $ The Soares Franco family named this chalky white wine in honor of the newest member of its eighth generation (a pair of twin girls). Its creamy apple fruit and fresh citrus flavors are uplifted by a slight natural carbonation.

Marquês de Borba Branco | 2006 | ALENTEJO
★ $ From J.P. Ramos, one of Portugal's most renowned winemakers, comes this mineral-laden wine showing notes of grass and the tropical flavors of kiwi and passion fruit.

Quinta do Alqueve Fernão Pires | 2006 | RIBATEJO
★ ★ $ Twenty years ago, a small family farm was converted to the meticulously maintained vineyard from which this wine hails. It bursts with the flavors of juicy, ripe peach and apple, beautifully balanced by bright acidity and minerality.

portuguese reds

Although interest in Portugal's red wines is growing, even most of those from the acclaimed Douro region remain underappreciated. There are many wines to consider here: The simpler examples have a charming rustic quality and a unique array of flavors, while others have the complexity and grace of some of the world's best reds.

portuguese red recommendations

Adegaborba.pt Reserva | 2004 | ALENTEJO
★ $ With notes of cinnamon, clove, fruitcake, candied citrus and ginger abounding in the mouth, this three-month-barrel-aged wine is like Christmas in a glass. Despite it all, the wine is still remarkably dry.

Adega Coop Borba Reserva | 2003 | ALENTEJO
★ $ Harvested from old-growth vines, this earthy red shows notes of stewed fruit, sweet spice, plum and tobacco leading to a soft finish. An eye-catching label made of thinly sliced cork (harvested from locally grown trees) is the crowning touch.

Adriano Ramos Pinto | 2005 | DOURO
★ ★ $ Renowned Port house Ramos Pinto was founded in 1880 by Adriano Ramos Pinto, who is this unfortified table wine's namesake. It has notes of plum and blackberry mingled with milk chocolate and sweet oak flavors and finishes with soft tannins.

Altano | 2005 | DOURO

★ $ Known for Vintage Ports, Altano's Symington family only began producing unfortified wine in 1999. This nice rendition, made from Tinta Roriz and Touriga Franca (grapes typically used in Port), has notes of blackberry, raspberry and sweet oak with soft tannins.

Andreza | 2003 | DOURO

★★ $ $ From the small village of Peso da Régua in the heart of the Douro comes this pleasantly complex wine that is all at once floral, spicy, meaty and fruity with big blackberry and black cherry flavors.

Casa de Santar Reserva | 2004 | DÃO

★★ $ $ Made from grapes harvested solely from Casa de Santar's estate vineyards and aged for 10 to 12 months in new French oak barrels, this wine is wonderfully spicy, with notes of dried sausage. Plum, blackberry and black cherry fruit also shine through.

news from a wine insider

portugal by Jamie Goode, UK-based wine journalist

Most Significant Trends

Portugal's exceptional 2007 vintage is expected to yield some of the country's best wines yet. With the growing expertise of a new generation of vintners and a rise in export sales, the country's wine industry is making big strides.

Regions to Watch

Interesting wines are now made throughout Portugal, yet the Douro is responsible for the great majority of the country's finest. While the region's dry red table wine category barely existed a couple of years ago, today there are more than two dozen exemplary producers.

The other two up-and-coming regions, Dão and Alentejo, continue to make more impressive wines each year.

Wine Country Travel

Portugal is finally making the most of its scenic wine regions, most notably the stunning Douro Valley, where two luxury hotels opened in 2007: Aquapura, a boutique hotel and spa near Peso da Régua; and Quinta da Romaneira, a restored working winery and hotel on the banks of the Douro. Visitors to the Alentejo region should check out the new country-house hotel and spa at Herdade da Malhadinha Nova.

Castello D'Alba | 2005 | DOURO
★ ★ $ Crafted by award-winning winemaker Rui Madeira in the remote eastern corner of the Douro, this delicious wine shows flavors of raspberry and cherry complemented by dark chocolate and spice.

Dom Martinho | 2005 | ALENTEJANO
★ ★ ★ $ $ This beautifully balanced wine is made under the watchful eye of Bordeaux's Rothschild family, who in 1992 took over an estate once owned by Portugal's royal family. The wine blends notes of tart cherry, sweet spice and coffee bean, topped with bright acidity.

Herdade dos Grous Tinto | 2006 | ALENTEJANO
★ ★ $ $ Crafted exclusively from three indigenous grapes, this wine uses its fine tannins to mouthwatering effect. A whiff of cocoa leads into a fruity blend of red cherry, blackberry and plum, enriched with a hint of dried linguiça (Portuguese sausage).

Marquês de Borba Tinto | 2006 | ALENTEJO
★ ★ $ $ Marquês de Borba producer J. Portugal Ramos stands behind the uniqueness of his native country's grapes. This pleasingly plush, mouthfilling wine is made with Aragonês and Trincadeira, grapes that give spicy floral aromas and blackberry and plum flavors.

Quinta da Alorna Reserva | 2004 | RIBATEJANO
★ ★ ★ $ $ Quinta da Alorna's vineyard, first planted in 1723, grows Merlot and Cabernet Sauvignon, along with several native varieties. Among the latter, local grape Touriga Nacional pairs up with Cabernet in this terrific, opulent wine, which has a big, delightful texture bursting with mint, black fruit and licorice flavors.

Quinta de Ventozelo Tinto | 2004 | DOURO
★ $ $ Until 1999, this 200-year-old vineyard produced Port wine in bulk for export. Their winemakers have since developed several signature wines, including this nice raisin-flavored blend of native grapes.

Quinta do Carmo Reserva | 2004 | ALENTEJANO
★ ★ ★ $ $ $ Produced on the same estate as Dom Martinho and also overseen by the famed Rothschilds, this wine is beautiful and complex. Bright cherry aromas lead into ripe black fruit, soft vanilla, clove and pepper, then to a juicy finish with fine tannins.

Quinta do Portal Grande Reserva | 2003 | DOURO
★ ★ ★ $ $ $ Famous for its Vintage Ports, Quinta do Portal hasn't released an unfortified Reserva since 2000. This delicious wine has raisin and dried fruit aromas followed by black cherry, black currant and plum flavors, all upheld by moderate tannins on the finish.

germany

No one in Europe makes wine quite like the Germans do. Germany's vintners produce mostly fruit-driven, high-acid, unoaked white wines that are low in alcohol. Not incidentally, these are also some of the most delicious white wines made anywhere.

Principal Wine Region

Germany: An Overview

Many of Germany's most lauded wines are made under the most challenging of circumstances. The country's vineyards are situated at the northernmost extreme of where grapes can typically ripen. Yet Germany's relatively frigid climate yields some of the world's most extraordinary wines. Many of the best vineyards cling to steep, south-facing slopes along the river valleys of the Rhine and Mosel, and the Mosel's tributaries Saar and Ruwer. It is here that the noble Riesling grape thrives. Rieslings from the Mosel tend to be delicate and mineral-laden; those from the Rheingau are usually drier and fuller-bodied. The hilly terrain of the Rheinhessen yields many low-quality sweet wines, the sort that have besmirched Germany's reputation for years and fueled the common perception that all German wines are sweet (though the region does yield some wonderful wines, particularly from the subregion Rheinterrassen). The relatively warmer Pfalz (Palatinate), Nahe and Baden regions produce lusher Rieslings, as well as a range of wines from other varieties such as Gewürztraminer, Grauburgunder (Pinot Gris) and Weissburgunder (Pinot Blanc).

German Grapes & Styles

Unlike most other Old World countries, Germany is famous for its white wines. The Riesling grape arguably performs better here than anywhere else, thriving in spite of the cold and producing wines of rare delicacy and refinement. Thanks to high levels of residual sugar tempered by equally high acidity, Germany's best Rieslings achieve impressive balance and a range that extends from crisp and dry to concentrated sweet nectars, with many styles in between.

Germany's second most planted grape is Müller-Thurgau, although with the exception of some compelling wines from Franken (Franconia), it is used mostly for dull blends. Germany's other grapes of note include Gewürztraminer, Grauburgunder (Pinot Gris) and Weissburgunder (Pinot Blanc), which excel in the regions of Baden and Pfalz. Centuries of tradition—culled, of course, from experimentation—have given German winemakers an acute understanding of their country's terroir, helping them transform often hard-to-ripen red grapes such as Spätburgunder (Pinot Noir) and Dornfelder into respectable wines.

German Wine Labels

Charming but often difficult to decipher, Germany's Gothic-script labels usually include the winery, region, village and sometimes the vineyard where the grapes were grown, as well as the lot and cask numbers. Grapes are mentioned, though in regions like the Rheingau, Riesling is assumed.

German wines carry an official designation of "quality." The first "quality" category is *Qualitätswein bestimmter Anbaugebiete* (QbA), often simply called "Qualitätswein." This guarantees that the grapes came from a particular region and reached a mandated level of ripeness at harvest. *Qualitätswein mit Prädikat* (QmP) wines are held to higher standards; they are ranked by grape ripeness at harvest, from *Kabinett* to *Spätlese, Auslese, Beerenauslese* (BA) and *Trockenbeerenauslese* (TBA) in ascending order of ripeness. In theory, riper grapes yield sweeter wines. Yet in practice, sweetness depends more on the balance between acidity and sugar or how much natural grape sugar was allowed to ferment into alcohol. Therefore, depending on how a wine is made, a Kabinett wine can taste sweeter than even an Auslese. Some wineries put *trocken* (dry) or *halbtrocken* (off-dry) on labels to indicate that the wine is dry. "Spätlese trocken," for example, means the wine is dry and made from grapes picked at Spätlese levels of ripeness.

In an effort to simplify German wine labeling, an additional designation system was established in 2000. Two terms, "Classic" and "Selection," now denote wines that are high in quality and dry. Classic wines are almost always made with a single grape variety and bear the name of the producer but not the vineyard. Selection wines are higher in quality; they must be made from hand-harvested grapes and list both the producer's name and the vineyard.

riesling

Riesling rivals Chardonnay for the title of noblest white grape. Full of citrus and peach flavors, vibrant acidity and a distinct minerality, Rieslings achieve a full range of styles from dry to off-dry, and youthfully fresh to aged and concentrated. Some of the best can age for decades, a process that brings out appealing smoky, steely aromas. Dessert wines made from Riesling (see p. 271) are capable of very long aging, which highlights their intense, sweet flavors.

riesling recommendations

Bassermann-Jordan Forster Jesuitengarten First Growth | 2006 | PFALZ

★ ★ ★ $ $ $ Made with carefully selected grapes that were grown in volcanic soils, this has a touch of apricot and quince, but is unmistakably minerally and flinty throughout, especially on the dry finish, which is reminiscent of chalk dust—and surprisingly delicious.

Blue Fish Original | 2007 | PFALZ

★ $ Clean, stony and salty, this dry Riesling comes in a screw-cap bottle. Crafted by a cooperative winery in the Pfalz township of Niederkirchen, it's an inexpensive party pour with legitimate character.

Carl Ehrhard Rüdesheimer Kabinett Feinherb | 2005 | RHEINGAU

★ ★ $ $ With its big flavors of apple and slightly smoky flint aroma, this wine is nicely balanced and well priced. Fresh, with a hint of sweetness, it offers abundant green apple and pear flavors supported by pronounced minerals.

C.H. Berres Erdener Treppchen Auslese *** | 2006 | MOSEL-SAAR-RUWER

★ ★ ★ ★ $ $ $ $ This stellar Riesling even boasts stars on its label (they indicate an outstanding barrel selection), so it's little wonder the wine is so ripe and richly layered, showing all the textbook aromas of nectarine and apricot, tinged with petrol.

Clean Slate | 2007 | MOSEL

★ $ From Seattle's Click Wine Group and its German partner, Moselland, the largest vineyard owner in the Mosel, this wine is exactly what it advertises: clean and from slate soils, with zesty grapefruit nuances and juicy acidity.

Dönnhoff Schlossböckelheimer Felsenberg Spätlese
| 2006 | NAHE

★★★ $ $ $ As this superb white from a benchmark producer shows, the pleasure of good Spätlese has its contradictions: It starts out rich and syrupy, bursting with peach-apricot fruit, but just when you think it could be cloying, it snaps back with a citrusy jolt of acid.

Dr. Bürklin-Wolf Bürklin Estate | 2007 | PFALZ

★ $ $ This entry-level wine from one of the top estates of the sunny Pfalz region has a nice, waxy apple aroma, with bracing lemon-lime acidity. The green apple flavor has real bite, with a touch of tropical mango and bit of tannin on the finish.

Dr. Loosen Erdener Treppchen Auslese | 2006 |
MOSEL-SAAR-RUWER

★★★ $ $ This fully ripe Riesling, made from the grapes of 120-year-old vines, pours on sweet fruit flavors so big and unctuous it's like slurping apricot and quince preserves. Generous acidity keeps it impressively balanced throughout the long finish.

Georg Breuer Charm | 2006 | RHEINGAU

★★ $ $ The sweet-tart palate of this seductive Riesling combines flavors of juicy green apple with lovely notes of orange blossom and white peach. Nicely balanced with a rounded texture, it finishes with lively tangerine and citrus.

Gunderloch Nackenheim Rothenberg Spätlese | 2006 |
RHEINHESSEN

★★★★ $ $ $ From the famed Rothenberg vineyard on the Rhine, this wine is wonderfully concentrated and medium-full on the palate with delicious mango and honeydew fruit and perfectly balanced acidity. The lingering fruit turns to spiced pear offset by minerals.

J.L. Wolf Pechstein Spätlese | 2004 | PFALZ

★★ $ $ The historic J.L. Wolf estate, dating back to 1756, is run by famed Mosel winemaker Ernst Loosen, and this Riesling reflects his deft touch. For a nearly five-year-old white it is quite fresh with lots of floral aromas, grapefruit flavors and a crisp, bright finish.

Joh. Jos. Prüm Wehlener Sonnenuhr Auslese | 2006 |
MOSEL-SAAR-RUWER

★★★★ $ $ $ Even Old World Riesling fans will rally for this extroverted and ripe bottling. The layers of peach, pineapple and apricot are like a canned fruit cocktail; but the rich, almost syrupy fruit allows touches of smoke and mineral to come through, and big acidity keeps it fresh on the palate.

Kruger-Rumpf Münsterer Rheinberg Kabinett | 2006 | NAHE

★★ $ $ Münsterer Rheinberg is a five-acre vineyard rich in quartz and slate, which this Riesling directly channels. A rich, minerally cocktail, this is like white peach nectar balanced by stony acidity.

Maximin Grünhäuser Abtsberg Spätlese | 2006 | MOSEL-SAAR-RUWER

★★★ $ $ $ The 35-acre Abtsberg site is one of the exclusive vineyards of Grünhaus and consistently delivers some of the best wines of each vintage. Case in point: this invigorating and delicious Riesling, with flinty peach, whiffs of petrol and bright acidity.

Mönchhof Mosel Slate Spätlese | 2006 | MOSEL

★★ $ $ While the apple aromas on this tightly knit Riesling are restrained, the palate reveals all the ripeness of the vintage, with a candied-fruit sweetness that evokes summer melon, apricot and even strawberry flavors, balanced with nice acidity.

star producers
german riesling

C.H. Berres

In 2004, after a stint in New Zealand, Markus Berres became this estate's 21st-generation winemaker and immediately replaced the corks with screw-caps.

Dr. Loosen

Not only is Ernst Loosen a champion of spectacular old-vine Rieslings, he's also one of Germany's most valuable ambassadors for the grape.

Gunderloch

Four generations have followed founder Carl Gunderloch, carrying on his pioneering vision for crafting stellar wines from grand cru vineyard sites.

Joh. Jos. Prüm

Since it was established in 1911, Joh. Jos. Prüm has become famous for top-notch Rieslings that are fresh, rich in flavor and yet low in alcohol.

Maximin Grünhäuser

The Maximin Grünhaus estate dates back to the Roman era— vines included. Today it's known for elegant Rieslings with incredible aging potential.

S.A. Prüm

Raimund Prüm is a staunch advocate of eco-friendly farming; his daughter Saskia Andrea (another "S.A. Prüm") shares his vision, and is gearing up to one day take the reins.

135

Reichsgraf von Kesselstatt Scharzhofberger Spätlese
| 2006 | MOSEL-SAAR-RUWER

★★★ $ $ $ Despite a September hailstorm that damaged 85 percent of this vineyard's crop, the winery salvaged enough fruit for this remarkable wine. It's intensely fruity, with rich quince jam, honey and pineapple, all underscored by pleasantly tart lime and minerals.

S.A. Prüm Graacher Himmelreich Spätlese | 2006 |
MOSEL-SAAR-RUWER

★★★ $ $ $ Sourced from a famed vineyard on the right bank of the Mosel, not far from other noted sites such as Bernkasteler Doctor and Badstube, this mouthwatering and electric Spätlese is loaded with apricot fruit and a balancing shiver of acid.

Schloss Reinhartshausen Erbacher Schlossberg Erstes Gewächs | 2006 | RHEINGAU

★★ $ $ $ Crafted at the largest privately owned winery in the Rheingau, this bottling hails from a 37-acre estate vineyard near the village of Erbach. The intensity of its mineral savor is almost briny, while the fruit is all green apple tartness.

Schloss Saarstein Serriger Spätlese | 2006 |
MOSEL-SAAR-RUWER

★★★ $ $ Made with grapes from south-facing vineyards planted in the 1960s and fermented with natural yeasts, this fruit-filled Riesling offers ripe tropical flavors of mango, passion fruit and honeyed citrus with a mineral edge. Full-bodied, it has both power and presence.

Schloss Wallhausen Prinz Salm Estate Kabinett | 2006 |
NAHE

★ $ $ Two estate sites—one featuring red slate soil, the other green—provide the grapes for this Riesling. It's fresh and firm on the palate, with nectarine, pineapple and lime fruit and a nice balance through the finish.

Selbach Kabinett (Fish Label) | 2007 | MOSEL-SAAR-RUWER

★★ $ $ A little spritzy on entry and grippingly tart on the palate, this easy-drinking wine has pleasing hints of quince and red apple. It's a good value, essentially a "second label" from Selbach-Oster's Johannes Selbach.

von Buhl Maria Schneider Medium Dry | 2006 | PFALZ

★★ $ $ This wine is named after jazz composer Maria Schneider, who is a friend of both the von Buhl estate and their U.S. importer, Rudi Wiest. With subtle petrol notes meeting honeydew melon and green apple aromas, it's gently sweet but closes very dry.

von Othegraven Maria V. O. Kabinett | 2006 |
MOSEL-SAAR-RUWER

★★ $$ Named for proprietor Maria von Othegraven, who headed the estate until 1995, this wine offers nice lemon custard aromas with apple and a touch of flint. The up-front peach-nectar sweetness carries nicely on the palate, with plenty of acid offset by tropical fruit.

Wegeler Pure | 2006 | RHEINGAU

★★ $$ Delicate, with floral notes and subtle hints of petrol, this basic QbA Riesling from the Rheingau is quite ripe. A touch of tropical fruit—pineapple and mango—joins its peach flavors, while sprightly acidity gives it a quick, clean finish.

Weingut Johannishof Johannisberger V Kabinett | 2006 |
RHEINGAU

★★ $$ Filled with ripe peach and stone fruit flavors, this Kabinett shows assertive sweetness for this ripeness level, but sweeping acidity brings balance, with a minerally, tart, green apple finish.

Weingut Robert Weil Estate Dry | 2006 | RHEINGAU

★★ $$ Dating back to 1875, the Robert Weil estate is a relative newcomer to the venerable Rheingau region. This Riesling starts out with subtle aromas of green and yellow apple highlighted by notes of flint and gunpowder. Ripe melon flavors explode on the palate, yet they finish dry and crisp.

Weingut St. Urbans-Hof Ockfener Bockstein | 2007 |
MOSEL-SAAR-RUWER

★★★ $$ The steep blue-gray slopes of the Ockfener Bockstein vineyards are captured in this lean and mineral-driven wine, which has distinct blue stone and flint on the nose. Sweet apple and nectarine flavors are quickly subdued by sharp acidity, resulting in a brisk and wonderfully dry pour.

Weingut Zilliken Saarburger Rausch Kabinett | 2006 |
MOSEL-SAAR-RUWER

★★★ $$ Zilliken's slate-filled Rausch vineyard yields Rieslings from Kabinett to Eiswein. This one is a great introduction to the Kabinett style, a pretty wine full of nectarine and stone fruit aromas. Wonderfully juicy up-front and medium-full-bodied, it has great acidity.

Wittmann Trocken | 2006 | RHEINHESSEN

★★ $$ This quaffer is very lean and dry, with bright acidity and restrained stone fruit aromas, like a peach pit with nice mineral and flint character. The palate is compelling, a touch oily in texture, with red apple fruit flavors.

other german whites

Germany's Pfalz and Baden regions benefit from their proximity to France's Alsace and share many of the same white grapes in addition to Riesling. German Grauburgunder (Pinot Gris) and Weissburgunder (Pinot Blanc) compare well to their French counterparts. Scheurebe, from the Rheinhessen region, is intriguing for it black currant and grapefruit flavors, cut by strong acidity. Wines made from Kerner are similar to Riesling, while Huxelrebe and Bacchus resemble Muscat. Muskateller (Muscat) and Gewürztraminer make intensely fragrant wines. Silvaner and Müller-Thurgau are used mainly in lower-quality blends, though both can yield lovely whites, especially in Franken.

news from a wine insider

germany by Philipp Blom, Austria-based wine writer, historian and novelist

Vintage Note

Budding began early in 2007, thanks to a warm spring followed by a relatively moderate summer. The main harvest began in October and lasted well into the following month. Both the quality and quantity of the grapes were excellent. In the Mosel, Saar and Ruwer valleys close to Germany's southwestern border, as well as in the Rheingau, the grapes had particularly dense aromatic concentration and high mineral extract. Farther south, in Pfalz, a sunny autumn resulted in many extremely ripe grapes.

Most Significant Trends

German vintners are making a greater number of high-quality red wines, particularly Pinot Noir (Spätburgunder). Growers are also planting more Cabernet and Merlot. Another notable trend is the increasingly international style of many of the country's Rieslings, with higher alcohol levels and lower residual sugar. But many producers believe that the key to increasing export sales is not in altering the country's unique winemaking style, but in changing the German wine classification system in order to make labels easier to read.

other german white recommendations

Artur Steinmann Pastorius Sommerhäuser Ölspiel Silvaner Kabinett | 2006 | FRANKEN

★ ★ $ $ As it does in almost no other part of the world, the Silvaner grape shines in the Franken region. Steinmann's example is crisp, clean and highly aromatic, a dry but fruity beauty that has great texture and minerality.

Hans Wirsching Dry Silvaner | 2006 | FRANKEN

★ ★ $ $ Another well-made Silvaner from Franken, this bottling from Hans Wirsching is round, floral and peachy. It is not as sharp or acidic as wines made from the more noble Riesling grape, nor as exotically aromatic, yet there's a satisfyingly assertive, granite-hard edge to its minerality.

J.L. Wolf Villa Wolf Pinot Gris | 2006 | PFALZ

★ ★ $ Betraying its red grape origins (Pinot Gris is related to Pinot Noir), this wine offers some subtle red berry fruit in addition to its pear and spiced golden apple flavors. Nicely rounded and full-bodied, it has great acidity and a mineral edge.

P.J. Valckenberg Estate Gewürztraminer | 2006 | PFALZ

★ ★ $ This white shows rose petal and tropical fruit aromas without being overbearing. Flavors of white peach and pear are balanced with mineral in the mid-palate and turn a bit potpourri-like on the finish.

Schloss Castell Silvaner Trocken | 2006 | FRANKEN

★ ★ $ Castell celebrated 350 years of Silvaner cultivation in 2006. While this wine is ambiguous with its fruit, a bit like a hard, unripe peach, its huge acidity and intense minerality, along with an über-dry finish, make it a great aperitif.

Schlossgut Diel Scheurebe Spätlese | 2006 | NAHE

★ ★ ★ $ $ $ Armin Diel is widely considered one of the best Riesling producers in Germany, so it isn't surprising to discover that his Scheurebe is terrific, too. Brimming with ripe, juicy peach and nectarine (with a hint of passion fruit), it's full-bodied and lip-smackingly succulent, serving up wave after wave of tropical fruit.

Weingut Herbert Messmer Burrweiler Altenforst Gewürztraminer Spätlese | 2007 | PFALZ

★ ★ $ $ $ Lovely white flower and citrus aromas announce this Gewürztraminer; in the mouth, however, it's surprisingly concentrated, with lychee and apricot fruit and crisp mineral nuances that render it both medium-bodied as well as subtle and soft in the finish.

austria & switzerland

These two Alpine neighbors share more than just the Alps. Both craft wines that are mostly white and generally excellent. Compared to the white wines of neighboring Germany, Austria's are mainly dry, fuller in body and somewhat racier in character. Switzerland's softer whites are increasingly available in the U.S. as Swiss winemakers have begun to look beyond their borders for customers.

austria

Landlocked Austria is surprisingly uninfluenced by the many great winemaking countries that surround it. Austria's unique identity is largely a product of its rigid wine regulations—the strictest in Europe—which result in exceptionally high-quality wines ranging from dry, minerally whites to stellar reds made from (mostly) indigenous grapes, and concentrated sweet wines. Austria's four major regions are in the eastern third of the country: Lower Austria (the largest region, which includes the stand-out Wachau subregion), Burgenland, Styria (Steiermark) and Vienna. Approximately 70 percent of the country's wines are white. While international varieties are grown here, Austria's native grapes outshine all others.

Austrian Grapes & Styles

Like Germany, Austria is a land of superb white wines. Its most popular grape, covering more than a third of the country's vineyards, is the spicy, citrusy Grüner Veltliner. Many other white grapes are grown, the most prevalent of which is Riesling, though Weissburgunder (Pinot Blanc), Morillon (Chardonnay), Sauvignon Blanc and Welschriesling are scattered throughout the country as well. A few Austrian reds have come to the forefront in recent years, such as peppery Blaufränkisch (Lemberger), juicy Zweigelt, elegant Blauburgunder (Pinot Noir) and smoky St. Laurent.

Austrian Wine Labels

Most Austrian wines list grape and region on the bottle and use a quality system similar to Germany's *Qualitätswein* (see p. 132), though Austria's standards are often higher. Austria's premier area for whites, Wachau, uses its own classification: *Steinfeder* are light wines, *Federspiel* are heavier and *Smaragd* are rich and capable of long aging.

austrian whites

High in minerality and acidity and bursting with expressive fruit flavors, Austrian whites are among the world's most exciting wines. Grüner Veltliner and Riesling are responsible for most of the finest, though some other varieties are worthy of consideration.

AUSTRIAN WHITES

grüner veltliner

Grüner Veltliner, only recently "discovered" by Americans, is a gem of a wine—light-bodied, versatile and perfect for pairing with food. When aged, it develops intense smoky, mineral flavors, whereas young examples are fresh and apple-scented, perfect for everyday drinking.

grüner veltliner recommendations

Domäne Wachau | 2007 | WACHAU

★ ★ $ The historic Domäne Wachau has been taken over by a team of relative youngsters, giving new energy to the cooperative's already well-regarded wines. Here, pear and apple aromas lead to grapefruit and spice flavors balanced with mouthwatering acidity.

Gritsch Mauritiushof Singerriedel Federspiel | 2006 | WACHAU

★ ★ ★ $ $ Aromas of ripe oranges and sweet marshmallows make this wine almost like an orange creamsicle—with a kick. Orange flower water and tangerine on the palate glide beautifully into a long, spicy white-pepper finish.

Johann Donabaum Johann | 2006 | WACHAU

★ ★ ★ $ $ It's a wonder the wines from the tiny nine-acre Donabaum winery ever make it past the Austrian borders. The blend of flavors on this Grüner Veltliner's palate—juicy grapefruit, red apple and pronounced black pepper on peas—is simply gorgeous.

star producers
austrian whites

Domäne Wachau

Domäne Wachau's cooperative of 600 growers contributes grapes to a range of wines, from everyday whites to premium Smaragd bottlings.

Heidi Schröck

Heidi Schröck carries on the traditions of her great aunts, harvesting grapes from the 40-year-old vines they planted.

Hirsch

Josef Hirsch tends the vines while his son Johannes crafts the wines, a partnership that results in distinctive, complex Rieslings and Grüner Veltliners.

Loimer

Quality stickler Fred Loimer's winemaking credo says it all: "My wines are to give people pleasure, not a headache."

Nikolaihof

Nikolaihof's spectacular wines are made following strict biodynamic guidelines, such as scheduling planting and harvesting times around the lunar calendar.

Prager

Prager is easily one of Austria's most famous wineries, thanks to the quality of winemaker Toni Bodenstein's delicious wines.

Loimer Lois | 2007 | **KAMPTAL**
★ ★ ★ $ Fred Loimer doesn't have a standard winemaking formula, preferring to let each harvest guide him. In this case, it resulted in a bright and invigorating lemon-lime flavored white, with crisp green apple, English pea and beeswax aromas and light herbal notes.

Nikolaihof Hefeabzug | 2006 | **WACHAU**
★ ★ ★ ★ $ $ *Hefeabzug* means "on the lees," referring to the aging of the wine on its spent yeasts (lees) after fermentation to increase complexity. One taste and you'll understand: This stunning wine is both crisply acidic and creamy at the same time, with an herbal, peppery edge of fresh watercress in the lovely finish.

Prager Hinter der Burg Federspiel | 2007 | **WACHAU**
★ ★ ★ $ $ $ Brandishing flavors of green pears and unripe stone fruit, this wine is so crisp it almost crunches. Add in a touch of petrol, some birch bark and a long lemon-tangerine finish and Prager has once again earned its reputation as one of Austria's finest vintners.

AUSTRIAN WHITES

riesling

Austrian Rieslings tend to be drier than German versions, though more fruit-driven than those from Alsace. Many have the potential to age for a decade or more.

riesling recommendations

Hirsch Zöbinger Gaisberg | 2006 | **KAMPTAL**
★ ★ ★ $ $ $ This single-vineyard bottling is from the famed Zöbinger Gaisberg vineyard in Kamptal, where 40-year-old vines cling to steep, rocky terraces. Scents of grapefruit, lime and mint mark this concentrated Riesling, with a thick, oily texture uplifted by sharp acidity.

Högl Bruck Smaragd | 2006 | **WACHAU**
★ ★ ★ $ $ $ Grown on precipitous, stone-walled terraces in the highest part of Wachau, this wine is extraordinarily food-friendly. Its fruit-forward style offers baskets full of crisp red apples and sweet peaches, all nicely balanced with mouthwatering acidity.

Rainer Wess Terrassen | 2006 | **WACHAU**
★ ★ $ $ Made by Rainer Wess, a winemaker with both Old and New World training, this medium-bodied white nicely blends candied orange peel and peach aromas with pepper and subtle mineral flavors.

other austrian whites

Austria produces many other wonderfully expressive white wines, most notably Welschriesling and Gelber Muskateller, as well as a small amount of Weissburgunder (Pinot Blanc), Grauburgunder (Pinot Gris), Morillon (Chardonnay) and Muskat-Sylvaner (Sauvignon Blanc). This last comes predominantly from the Styria region, where most of the grapes are handpicked and the wines well crafted.

other austrian white recommendations

Heidi Schröck Grauburgunder | 2006 |
NEUSIEDLERSEE-HÜGELLAND

★ ★ ★ $ $ A seamless Pinot Gris from one of Austria's leading female winemakers, this seductive white melds syrupy banana-apple fruit and acidic zing, a result of six months aging in stainless steel and large neutral barrels.

Nittnaus Sauvignon Blanc | 2006 | BURGENLAND

★ $ $ This Sauvignon Blanc has a flavorful tart-fruit palate. After the initial sulfur character wears off, flavors of sweet, ripe orange and gooseberry lead into a clean finish.

Wenzel Pinot Gris | 2005 | BURGENLAND

★ ★ ★ $ $ Winemaker Michael Wenzel, the latest Wenzel to helm the 400-year-old winery, crafts this delightful Pinot Gris. Its sweet pear and grapefruit aromas are filled out with flinty notes before giving way to tangerine and mandarin orange flavors that linger on the palate.

Wieninger Nussberg Alte Reben | 2006 | VIENNA

★ ★ $ $ $ These *alte Reben* ("old vines") are in an urban center that has been making wine since antiquity. Wieninger's full-bodied, fruity white has a smoky nose filled out with peach flavors and crisp acidity.

austrian reds

Austria's most popular red grape is Zweigelt; it yields light wines with juicy cherry flavors. Blaufränkisch (also called Lemberger) is spicier and more tannic, and responsible for some of the most interesting Austrian reds today. Blauburgunder (Pinot Noir) and St. Laurent (which is similar to Pinot Noir) can also yield some impressive results.

austrian red recommendations

Birgit Braunstein Goldberg St. Laurent | 2004 | **BURGENLAND**

★★ $ $ $ The St. Laurent grape is named for St. Laurentius Day (August 10), the day it reportedly begins ripening. A tough-to-grow variety, it flourishes in the hands of one of Austria's top female vintners, who has created a wine plump with black cherry and plum flavors and nicely balanced by oak and astringent tannins.

Feiler-Artinger Umriss Blaufränkisch | 2005 | **BURGENLAND**

★★ $ $ From a 100-year-old winery in the eastern Austria town of Rust, this muscular wine combines the slightly floral-accented aromas of black fruit and black licorice with the flavor of smoked fruit, firm tannins and loads of acidity.

news from a wine insider

austria by Philipp Blom, Austria-based wine writer, historian and novelist

Vintage Note

The 2007 vintage enjoyed a mild winter and a warm spring followed by rain in late August and a cool, wet fall. At harvest time, vintners had to play a weather guessing game; those who chose the right days to pick experienced a good harvest, producing wines with elegant acidity and good fruit.

Most Significant Trends

Austria's most famous wine producer, Alois Kracher, known above all for his superb sweet wines and his efforts to promote quality and modernization in Austrian winemaking, died at the age of 48 in 2007. Kracher's untimely death has coincided with a challenge to Austrian producers to further define the regional character of their wines. Among the many steps taken in this direction are the planting of old indigenous grape clones, the forming of regional associations and DACs (controlled districts, similar to France's AOCs) and a strong move toward organic and biodynamic winemaking. In fact, the enthusiasm for biodynamic viticulture is so great in Austria that the country now has one of the largest concentrations of biodynamic wine producers in the world.

Moric Neckenmarkt Blaufränkisch Alte Reben | 2005 |
BURGENLAND
★★★ $ $ $ $ This wine could be called the Burgundy of Austria's reds for its elegant expression of place. A complex blend of minty aromas, black fruit and celery seed flavors, bright acidity and formidable tannins make this bottling unique to its Mittelburgenland terroir.

Zantho Zweigelt | 2006 | **BURGENLAND**
★★ $ A medium-bodied Zweigelt, this shows fragrant plums, cinnamon, clove and dried sausage notes. Its fruit-forward flavor bursts with cherries and raspberries, complemented by well-balanced tannins.

switzerland

As in Germany and Austria, the majority of Switzerland's wines are white, but stylistically they are the polar opposite, eschewing acidity in favor of softer flavors. Traditionally, many Swiss wines were made sweet, but Swiss consumers are increasingly favoring drier wines. Most of Switzerland's wine production takes place in the French-speaking western regions and the Italian-speaking southern region, Ticino. Relatively few Swiss wines reach the U.S., but their overall high quality makes them worth hunting for.

Swiss Grapes & Styles

The Chasselas grape accounts for 60 percent of all Swiss wine. Chasselas wines (a.k.a. Fendant in the Valais region) are typically unoaked and minerally. Sylvaner produces fuller-bodied wines. Also planted in Switzerland are Müller-Thurgau (the main white grape in the German-speaking regions), Chardonnay, Sauvignon Blanc, Aligoté, Completer, Kerner and Sémillon. Pinot Noir is the principal red grape, though Gamay is more important in Vaud and Geneva. Merlot yields relatively full-bodied wines in Ticino. Some well-made Syrah is also crafted in the Valais.

Swiss Wine Labels

Wines in Switzerland tend to be labeled by region and grape variety. The country adheres to France's AOC (Appellation d'Origine Contrôlée) classification system as a model.

swiss recommendations

WHITES

Adrian Mathier Coteau de Sierre Fendant | 2006 | VALAIS

★★ $ $ The Mathier family has been making wine in the town of Salgesch for more than a century, and Fendant is the Valais' white wine par excellence. This one is pretty, light and herbal with floral notes, specifically acacia, and a clean, fresh band of soft acidity.

Les Frères Dubois | 2006 | DÉZALEY MARSENS

★★★★ $ $ $ From a family winery that dates its beginnings to AD 800, this is the Chasselas grape at its best, with honeyed chamomile flavor riding over strong minerality. The flavors linger and have a ripe, juicy, pearlike succulence. Exquisite.

René Favre & Fils Petite Arvine | 2006 | CHAMOSON-VALAIS

★★★★ $ $ $ A splendid and powerful white, this Petite Arvine displays seductive dry honey and stone flavors driven by tense acidity. It's impressive now and will be even more amazing with five years of bottle age, served with a slice of Comté cheese.

St. Jodernkellerei Heida | 2005 | VISPERTERMINEN

★★ $ $ $ If you've spent time skiing at Zermatt, you may have run into the Heida grape—it's grown not far away, in the highest vineyards of Europe at 3,770 feet. This wine is surprisingly ripe, with rich, juicy pear flavors deepened by notes of smoke and flint.

REDS

Angelo Delea Carato Merlot | 2003 | TICINO

★★ $ $ $ *Carato* refers to the *barriques* Angelo Delea ages his wines in; this Merlot spent 24 months in French oak and the wood spice is evident but not overpowering. A graceful wine with fleshy plumminess, it has refreshingly high acidity.

Jean-René Germanier Cayas Syrah | 2004 | VALAIS

★★★ $ $ $ $ An elegant Syrah, far leaner than those from the Rhône, this is spicy and gamey, with deliciously dark notes of blackberries and *sous bois* (or "forest floor," as the French speakers of the Valais canton would describe them).

René Favre & Fils Renommée St-Pierre Pinot Noir | 2000 | CHAMOSON-VALAIS

★★★★ $ $ $ A refined yet earthy Pinot Noir from a 40-year-old vineyard, this wine has mellowed with age into a stunning, spicy, warm red, with gingery spice accents and dark, herbal complexities.

greece

Greece has a rich winemaking history dating back to ancient times, but modern Greek vintners have struggled to revive the once-thriving industry left stagnant by centuries of occupation, war, displacement and crop disease. Recently, however, a renewed focus on technology and increased exportation is buoying the country's reputation for quality wine.

Greece: An Overview

Greece encompasses four main viticultural zones: north, central, the Peloponnese and the islands. The northern zone contains the mountainous regions of Macedonia and Thrace, with Naoussa being the area's most famous appellation. Central Greece, stretching from Athens in the south to Mt. Olympus in the north and Albania to the west, features some of Greece's highest-elevation vineyards. The warm valleys and cooler slopes of the Peloponnese peninsula, including the important subregions of Mantinia, Nemea and Patras, boast the greatest number of appellations. Of the islands, Crete is responsible for a significant quantity of wine, while the smaller Aegean islands of Santorini and Samos offer some of the country's finest wines.

Greek Grapes & Styles

Greece is home to more than 300 native grapes—only Italy has more indigenous varieties. International stars such as Chardonnay and Cabernet grow here, too, but are usually blended with local grapes to good effect. Savatiano, used to make Greece's well-known pine resin–flavored wine, Retsina, is the most common grape, but not the most important in terms of quality. Assyrtiko, the best of which comes from Santorini, is used to make crisp, bone-dry wines with pronounced mineral and citrus flavors. Moschofilero is produced as a dry white as well as a dry rosé, both of which are high in acidity, low in alcohol and wonderfully aromatic. Agiorgitiko—also known as St. George, as it is sometimes listed on wine labels—is Greece's most widely planted red grape variety; it often draws comparisons to spicy Cabernet Francs. Xynomavro from the Macedonia region of northern Greece yields red wines that are reminiscent of Piedmont's Nebbiolos, for their high acidity, heavy tannins and impressive aging ability. Honorable mention goes to Roditis, which is responsible for the white wines of Patras, and Mavrodaphne, a red grape that's vinified in both dry and sweet styles.

Greek Wine Labels

As in the European tradition, wine regions take priority over grape names on most Greek wine labels. Reds from Naoussa are required by law to be made from Xynomavro, while those from Nemea are produced with Agiorgitiko. Mantinia wines must be made from at least 85 percent Moschofilero, and wines from Santorini are dominated by Assyrtiko. Grape varieties not traditional to particular areas, however, are usually noted on labels.

greek whites

Greek whites are as distinctive and varied as the appellations that produce them. The volcanic soils on the island of Santorini yield bold, mineral-laden whites. Peloponnesian Moschofilero possesses the spiciness of Gewürztraminer. Floral Roditis from Patras and Assyrtiko from Santorini are universally crisp and dry.

greek white recommendations

Boutari Moschofilero | 2007 | MANTINIA

★ ★ $ $ Hailing from high-altitude vineyards in the Peloponnese appellation of Mantinia, this melony, white peach–flavored wine tingles with the electric acidity typical of the Moschofilero grape. A well-chilled bottle would be a perfect accompaniment to grilled octopus on a warm summer evening.

Costa Lazaridis' Chateau Julia Assyrtiko | 2006 | DRAMA

★ ★ $ This stony, mineral-laden white from Macedonia offers lemon and apple aromas and a slightly viscous texture; its flavors of peach nectar are nicely offset by fresh acidity.

Domaine Hatzimichalis Veriki | 2006 | ATALANTI VALLEY

★ ★ ★ $ $ A new and noteworthy wine from a stalwart producer in central Greece, Veriki combines 50 percent Chardonnay and 50 percent Robola fermented and aged only in stainless steel. The resulting fruit flavors are refreshing and appley, marked by floral notes; the texture is round and substantial.

Gai'a Thalassitis | 2007 | SANTORINI

★ ★ ★ $ $ Intense, mouthwatering acidity characterizes this focused and flavorful island white, which tingles with minerality imparted by Santorini's volcanic soils. Lemony and zesty, it's custom-made for summer drinking, ideally superchilled.

Kouros Patras | 2007 | PATRAS

★ ★ $ From the northwestern Peloponnese region of Patras comes this consistent, value-priced white crafted from the Roditis grape. Not as piercingly acidic as Moschofilero, this has a softer texture, with notes of cantaloupe and tropical fruit.

Sigalas | 2007 | SANTORINI

★ ★ ★ $ $ The Sigalas winery is the premier estate on the island of Santorini. This is their basic white offering, a steely and fragrant beauty made from the delicately fragrant Assyrtiko grape. It possesses a lovely floral perfume followed by hints of bright lemon peel and pear on the palate.

Tselepos Mantinia Moschofilero | 2006 | MANTINIA

★ ★ ★ $ $ This Mantinia white displays a slight coppery color, suggesting some skin contact during fermentation (Moschofilero grapes, like Pinot Grigio, have pink-colored skins). Fresh with pleasant apricot aromas, the wine has an almost tannic quality—and it grips the palate with all its acidic might.

greek reds

Greek reds range in style from simple, everyday wines to complex, often ageworthy bottlings, yet account for less than half of the country's total wine production. The best wines of Naoussa can be compared to quality Barbaresco. Some reds from Nemea possess a Bordeaux-like elegance and others a chewy richness and depth of fruit.

greek red recommendations

Achaia Clauss Chateau Clauss | 2003 | **PATRAS**
★★ **$** This is an eye-opening blend of Cabernet Sauvignon and the local Mavrodaphne grape, grown in the Patras area of northwest Peloponnese. The ripe, sweet cassis fruit of the Cabernet is nicely counterbalanced by a roasted-coffee bass note.

Boutari | 2004 | **NAOUSSA**
★★★ **$ $** The leading name in Greek wine is perhaps best known for this wine from Naoussa, the noted wine zone on the slopes of Mount Vermion in Macedonia. Here, the Xynomavro grape develops complex and perfumed aromas to complement its cedary, licorice-scented fruit flavors.

Domaine Skouras Grande Cuvée | 2005 | **NEMEA**
★★★★ **$ $** Burgundy-trained George Skouras gave this luscious, elegant red a dense core of black cherry fruit flavors offset by an electric charge of acidity. Made from 100 percent Agiorgitiko grown at Skouras's estate in the village of Gymno, it was aged 12 months in Allier (French oak) *barriques.*

Palivou Estate Ammos | 2004 | **NEMEA**
★★★ **$ $** Sourced from high-altitude vineyards in a mountainous area near the Bay of Corinth, the Agiorgitiko grape appears here in a rich, ripe, chocolaty, gamey style. The tannins are sweet and round in this chewy and downright delicious wine.

Pavlou Estate Klima Xynomavro | 2006 | **AMYNDEON**
★★★ **$ $** From the remote Macedonian appellation called Amyndeon (a.k.a. Amynteon), this Xynomavro-based wine is lush with toasty coffee aromas, a result of six months in barrel. Pavlou is a relatively new winery, and one to watch.

other old world wines

In wine terms, "Old World" generally means Western Europe, but in truth, viticulture has far more ancient roots in the "other" Old World—Eastern Europe, North Africa and the Middle East. Although wine production in these regions suffered major setbacks over the last century, in recent years "Other Old World" vintners have been applying new technology and a New World sensibility to their winemaking, with some exciting results.

eastern europe

From the 17th to the early 20th century, Hungary was considered one of the greatest winemaking countries in Europe. Therefore, it's no surprise to see Hungary today reasserting itself and rebuilding its once-great wine industry with confidence. It helps that one of its best wines, Tokaji Aszù, was and continues to be one of the finest dessert wines made anywhere and easily Hungary's most stunning export. But given that Tokaji represents less than 5 percent of Hungary's total production, there is a lot more to be tasted. Other countries in the region, especially Croatia, Slovenia and Bulgaria, also present opportunities for skilled winemakers to produce excellent wines, a growing number of which have the quality to compete in the international market.

Eastern European Wine Labels

While wines in Eastern Europe tend to be labeled according to grape and region, Hungary's famous Tokaji wines (see p. 272)—which do not list varieties—are a major exception.

eastern european whites

If one country in this group stands out for white wines it is Slovenia, whose blends made primarily with Pinot Blanc, Pinot Grigio, Ribolla and Malvasia can hold their own alongside those produced in Italy's Friuli region, just across Slovenia's western border. Look to Hungary for beautiful dry whites from Furmint, and to Croatia for exotic, nutty wines from the Posip grape. Rieslings are made in various parts of Eastern Europe, as is Welschriesling (Laski Rizling in Slovenia or Olasz Rizling in Hungary), which tastes similar but is unrelated. As in most wine regions, Chardonnay and Sauvignon Blanc make cameo appearances.

eastern european white recommendations

Craftsman Zöld Veltelini | 2006 | **NESZMELY, HUNGARY**
★ ★ $ Grown in Aszar-Neszmely—50 miles northwest of Budapest and about halfway to Vienna—this medium-bodied wine is similar to Austrian Grüner Veltliner, with aromas of apples, apricots and flowers that give way to ripe apple, white pepper and citrus flavors.

Katunar Anton Zlahtina Selection | 2006 |
ISLAND OF KRK, CROATIA
★ $ Named for Anton, one of the winemaking brothers of the Katunar family (Ivan is the other), this refreshing white is medium-bodied, with citrus and flower aromas melding with melon and good acidity.

Katunar Zlahtina | 2006 | **ISLAND OF KRK, CROATIA**
★ ★ $ With a relatively low alcohol content (around 12 percent), this Krk Island wine would make a good summertime accompaniment to broiled fish or salad. The scents of herbs, lemons and white pepper lead into a clean, medium-bodied palate of grapefruit and spices.

153

Marko Polo Posip Cara | 2005 | **KORCULA, CROATIA**
★★ $ $ Named for the 13th-century explorer who was born on the Adriatic island where this wine is made, Marko Polo shows notes of citrus and tropical fruit rounded out by white pepper and acidity.

Monarchia Cellars Olivier | 2006 | **BUDA-ETYEK, HUNGARY**
★★★★ $ Light and crisp, this brilliant Hungarian wine teems with citrus fruit. A lemon zest, lemon curd and lemon meringue bouquet opens into delicious lychee, floral and citrus flavors in the mouth.

Pullus Sivi Pinot | 2007 | **MARIBOR, SLOVENIA**
★★★ $ This delectable wine is the medium-bodied Slovenian expression of the grape commonly known as Pinot Gris. Its bright, refreshing aromas of flowers, melon and pink grapefruit meet a citrusy peach flavor that finishes with bracing acidity.

Royal Tokaji Furmint | 2006 | **TOKAJI, HUNGARY**
★★★ $ $ Although Royal Tokaji is legendary for its nectarlike dessert wines, this full-bodied dry Furmint is no less impressive. Oak and herbs mingle with lemon and peach aromas and flavors.

eastern european reds

Bordeaux grapes have long been grown in Eastern Europe, but the most interesting wines here are made from indigenous grapes. Hungary's best-known red, Egri Bikaver ("Bull's Blood from Eger"), is a blend of mainly indigenous grapes. Hungarian vintners also craft wines from Kekfrankos (known elsewhere as Blaufränkisch or Lemberger). Slovenia, Croatia and Bulgaria make fine reds as well. Interestingly, Croatia's Crljenak Kastelanski grape is the parent of California's Zinfandel, and the two share similar taste profiles. Plavac Mali is a more widely grown relative, and it, too, offers Zinfandel-like spicy berry flavors.

eastern european
red recommendations

Bura Estate Dingac Plavak Mali | 2005 | **PELJESAC, CROATIA**
★★ $ $ $ The grapes for this earthy, medium-bodied red were grown on the steep slopes of the Peljesac Peninsula, where they were shielded from the *bura* (Croatian for "north wind"). The wine smells of bramble fruit and forest and tastes of herbs and black fruit.

Craftsman Falconer's Cuvée | 2006 | SZEKSZARD, HUNGARY
★ $ A blend of 80 percent Merlot and 20 percent Kekfrankos (a.k.a. Blaufränkisch), this medium-bodied wine shows black pepper and spice aromas and black and red fruit flavors.

Ivo Skaramuca Dingac Plavac Mali | 2005 |
PELJESAC, CROATIA
★★ $ $ Made entirely of Croatia's native Plavac Mali grape—a cousin of Zinfandel—this medium-bodied wine is bright, sweet and spicy. Peppery red fruit flavors follow a red cherry and raspberry bouquet.

Katunar Anton Riserva | 2004 | ISLAND OF KRK, CROATIA
★★★ $ $ The indigenous Sansigot and Debejan grapes combine with 50 percent Syrah in this ripe and tasty red. Soft red fruit and pepper aromas lead into a blend of blackberry, candy and spice flavors and a clean, bright, fruity finish.

Movia Veliko | 2001 | GORISKA BRDA, SLOVENIA
★★★ $ $ $ Winemaker Ales Kristancic grows his grapes in biodynamic vineyards on the border of Slovenia's Brda region and the Collio region of Italy. His delicious blend of Merlot, Pinot Noir and Cabernet shows raspberry flavors and velvety tannins.

Tibor Gal Pinot Noir | 2004 | EGER, HUNGARY
★★ $ $ Ensconced in the basin of the Western Carpathian Mountains, the vineyards planted by the late Tibor Gal yield a spicy, medium-bodied Pinot Noir with black fruit, cherry, clove and minerals.

Zlatan Plavac Grand Cru | 2004 | HVAR, CROATIA
★★★★ $ $ $ Hvar Island's mild winters, warm summers and abundant sunshine all show in this lovely, food-friendly wine. It smells of rich earth, black fruits and spices with great concentration of fruit on the palate and a long, slightly coarse, tannic finish.

lebanon & north africa

Winemaking in Lebanon has a storied past. (It's not for nothing that the Romans built their temple of Bacchus in the Bekaa Valley, the epicenter of Lebanon's wine production.) In recent years, two producers in particular, Château Musar and Château Kefraya, have helped reinvigorate Lebanon's wine industry and inspire a new generation of vintners. France's colonial involvement in North Africa from the 19th through the mid-20th centuries revived viticulture in the area; for a time, Morocco, Algeria and Tunisia exported vast amounts of wine to France. Since the turbulent post-independence years, creative North African vintners have emphasized quality over quantity, with some good results.

Lebanese & North African Grapes & Styles

While Lebanon is capable of good Chardonnay and Sauvignon Blanc, winemakers here excel with indigenous white varieties: Merweh, thought to be the same as Sémillon, and Obaideh, thought to be identical to Chardonnay. North African white wines are not nearly as compelling, but there are some fresh, crisp examples made from Ugni Blanc, Clairette and Muscat. France's red wine grapes are prolific throughout these regions. Carignane, Cinsault and Grenache vines are widely grown from Morocco to Lebanon; Cabernet, Syrah and Merlot are also popular, especially in Lebanon's Bekaa Valley. The best Lebanese red wines possess a claret-like elegance with slightly fuller body, while most North African reds tend to display earthier flavors.

Lebanese & North African Wine Labels

France's colonial influence over North Africa and Lebanon is still apparent in the labeling of their wines. Regional names are generally emphasized over grape, though labels of wines made exclusively from international grapes like Chardonnay and Cabernet are likely to list them.

lebanese & north african recommendations

WHITES

Château Kefraya La Dame Blanche | 2006 |
BEKAA VALLEY, LEBANON
★ $ Nuances of the rocky soil on Château Kefraya's terraced slopes come through in this well-balanced white. Good acidity upholds the round body, and refreshing notes of stone, mineral and citrus keep it lively and clean.

Ksar | NV | MOROCCO

★ **$** The old-fashioned Rhône variety Clairette performs well in Ksar's soils, a combination of chalk and brick-red clay. The resulting wine is a refreshing white with stone and pear notes on the nose, pear, citrus and green apple on the palate and racy acidity.

Les Trois Domaines Blanc | 2005 | GUERROUANE, MOROCCO

★★ **$** Ugni Blanc, Clairette and Sauvignon Blanc marry nicely in this Moroccan blend from the foothills of the Atlas Mountains. The wine has a round texture and flavors redolent of pear, stone and flowers.

REDS

Château Kefraya Les Bretèches | 2006 | BEKAA VALLEY, LEBANON

★★ **$** This Rhône-style blend from Lebanon's warm, sunny Bekaa Valley is rich in black fruit, spice and complex earthy undertones. The palate strikes a balance between robust body and firm acidity.

Château Musar Hochar Père et Fils | 2002 | BEKAA VALLEY, LEBANON

★★★ **$ $** Despite the constant political upheavals in the Middle East, brothers Serge and Ronald Hochar continue to produce magnificent wines every year. This blend of Cinsault, Carignane and Cabernet gives gorgeous spiced berry flavors with well-integrated tannins.

Château Tellagh | 2004 | MEDEA, ALGERIA

★★★ **$** At heights of more than 4,200 feet, in soils of sand and clay, and through sun-baked summers, the grapes of Medea flourish. In this example, they've produced a beautiful, complex wine, rich in black fruit, spice, floral aromas and vanilla.

Cuvée du Président | NV | ALGERIA

★ **$** The grapes for this easy-drinking red blend come from four appellations in Algeria—Mascara, Dahra, Medea and Tlemcen—creating a wine that integrates black cherry and blackberry flavors with sweet spice and a ribbon of cracked black pepper.

Domaine El Bordj | 2004 | COTEAUX DE MASCARA, ALGERIA

★ **$** Domaine El Bordj has won awards for its wines as far back as the 1858 Paris Expo. This red, made of southern French and local grapes, is floral, sweet-spiced and full of cherry, red currant and cranberry.

Les Trois Domaines Rouge | 2005 | GUERROUANE, MOROCCO

★★ **$** It's easy to imagine pairing this spicy, earthy red with the robust dishes of Morocco. Firmly textured, it has earth, mineral and black fruit notes that mingle with spices and pepper on the palate.

united states

Winemaking in what is now the U.S. dates back to the late 18th century, when Franciscan missionaries planted grapes along the Pacific Coast. The industry began to take off in the early 19th century, and today the U.S. is the world's fourth-largest wine-producing nation. U.S. wine sales have risen steadily for over a decade, as Americans develop a greater interest in wine culture and in the health benefits of moderate consumption.

The United States: An Overview

Today nearly every state can claim at least one winery, a clear sign of the increasing popularity of wine in the U.S. American wine production, however, is still dominated by four states: California, by far the largest U.S. producer, followed by Washington, Oregon and New York. In the U.S., as elsewhere, geography and climate determine where wines of world-class stature are made. The country's finest wines hail from the temperate, often sun-drenched West Coast, where the European *Vitis vinifera* varieties (think Chardonnay, Cabernet, etc.) thrive. In states with harsher climates and severe weather fluctuations, only native American grapes like *Vitis labrusca* or *Vitis rotundifolia* can survive, and unfortunately, they generally don't make great wines. But while the U.S. may rely on European varieties, its wines are a breed unto themselves, typically emphasizing bold fruit flavors over nuances of earth and minerals.

california

The Golden State produces approximately 90 percent of all the wine made in the U.S. One of the challenges for producers is to find areas that are cool enough to keep grapes from ripening too quickly, thus ensuring proper flavor development. Coastal regions tempered by Pacific breezes as well as vineyards at higher elevations are where some of the best wines are made; luckily, California happens to have a bounty of such areas up and down the coast.

Mendocino

Lake   Sierra
        Foothills

Sonoma Napa

San   Contra Costa
Francisco

        Santa Cruz

        Monterey

Pacific Ocean

        San Luis Obispo

        Santa Barbara

            • Los Angeles

                Temecula

        San Diego

**Principal Wine
Region**

California: An Overview

The North Coast is the northernmost of California's important winegrowing regions and includes Napa, Sonoma, Mendocino and Lake counties. Mendocino's Anderson Valley provides the perfect climate for producing Chardonnay and Pinot Noir, as well as high-quality sparkling wines. In Sonoma, the legendary Alexander, Russian River and Dry Creek Valleys are home to elegant Chardonnays, spicy Zinfandels and fruit-forward Sauvignon Blancs. East of Sonoma is the much smaller yet much more renowned Napa Valley, where the country's greatest Cabernets and Bordeaux-style blends are produced. Carneros makes many excellent Chardonnays, Pinot Noirs and sparkling wines. California's vast Central Coast region extends from Santa Cruz to the northern edge of Los Angeles County. Generally speaking, Pinot Noir and Chardonnay grow well throughout this area; Zinfandel and France's Rhône grape varieties—Syrah, Grenache, Mourvèdre and Viognier—also produce some superb wines here. Farther inland, east of San Francisco Bay, Lodi, in California's Central Valley, and the sprawling Sierra Foothills region are famous for old-vine Zinfandels.

California Wine Labels

California labels list the winery name, region (officially known as an AVA, or American Viticultural Area), vintage and grape. U.S. law dictates that a wine labeled with an AVA must contain at least 85 percent of grapes from that specific region. Wines that bear the name of a single grape must contain 75 percent of that variety; a wine labeled "Chardonnay" might contain 25 percent Sauvignon Blanc, for example, though regulations in certain counties are stricter. Blending, however, is an important winemaking technique for many producers, particularly in Napa, where a combination of different grapes often leads to wines of greater complexity. Some of California's finest wines are blends of various Bordeaux grapes (see p. 171), a style that carries the legally recognized moniker "Meritage" (pronounced like "heritage"). While the term "Reserve" appears on some vintners' finer wines, it has no legal meaning.

california whites

California's enormous and varied geography gives its wine-makers the ability to craft white wines in a range of styles, from light, floral and crisp to full-bodied, concentrated and high in alcohol. Many of the best whites, however, are produced in the state's cooler regions, such as Sonoma County's Russian River Valley.

CALIFORNIA WHITES

chardonnay

Chardonnay is California's most planted variety and arguably America's most popular grape; almost every wine-maker in the state makes one. In fact, California's hallmark style of Chardonnay—laden with butterscotch and tropical fruit flavors bolstered by spicy toasted oak—was synonymous with "white wine" in the U.S. for many years. While that opulent style still exists, especially for many mass-produced industrial brands, the trend today among quality vintners is to make leaner, more elegant and food-friendly Chardonnays, balanced with acidity and minerality.

chardonnay recommendations

Buena Vista Ramal Vineyard | 2006 | **CARNEROS**
★★ $ $ $ When Buena Vista purchased 700 acres of land in Carneros in 1969, the area was considered too cold to produce great wine. Forty years later the hits just keep on coming, like this creamy, fig-scented Chardonnay brimming with melon and red apple.

Chalone Vineyard Estate Grown | 2005 | **CHALONE**
★★ $ $ Weighing in at just over 14 percent alcohol, this pear-flavored Chardonnay reflects the extreme heat (balanced by cold nights) experienced by Chalone's high-elevation vineyards. It also possesses a touch of the Burgundian austerity the winery aims for.

Chappellet | 2006 | **NAPA VALLEY**
★★ $ $ Grapes grown in the Napa Valley's southernmost climes benefit from marine influences that enhance their intensity and vibrancy. This lush, rich Chardonnay is a textbook example, layered with ripe pear, spicy oak, roasted pineapple and fresh-grated lemon zest.

Clos du Bois Sonoma Reserve | 2006 | RUSSIAN RIVER VALLEY

★★ $ $ Powerhouse producer Clos du Bois' Russian River Chardonnay, part of its Reserve appellation series, is creamy and viscous, perfumed with Anjou pear and Red Delicious apple, toasted oak and a touch of vanilla.

Concannon Selected Vineyards | 2006 | CENTRAL COAST

★★ $ Tropical fruit dominates this Central Coast Chardonnay from one of California's oldest producers; peach and pear flavors make cameo appearances, too, on the way to a silky smooth finish.

Cuvaison | 2006 | CARNEROS

★★★ $ $ Before bottling, this wine spends nine months in small French oak barrels, which explains its heady, smoky, toasted-oak aromas. Also present are nuances of flower, pear, vanilla and clove, along with a surprising minerality and a creamy, rich finish.

Geyser Peak Winery | 2006 | ALEXANDER VALLEY

★★ $ A blend of Chardonnay lots—most of which were fermented in barrels, the remainder in stainless steel tanks—produced this tasty wine, full of fig, pear and apple notes, and rich butterscotch cut by bright acidity on the palate.

Hayman & Hill Reserve Selection | 2006 |
RUSSIAN RIVER VALLEY

★ $ This crisp, clean Chardonnay comes from a duo of veteran winemakers who struck out on their own in 2004. It's marked by fresh apple, pear and lemon peel flavors.

J. Lohr October Night Vineyard | 2006 | ARROYO SECO

★★ $ $ Winemakers at J. Lohr point to the Chardonnay Musqué clone as the secret behind this wine's floral aromas of acacia and white flowers. Honey and butterscotch follow on the rich palate.

Kendall-Jackson Highland Estates Camelot Highlands
| 2006 | SANTA MARIA VALLEY

★★★ $ $ From the makers of one of California's most recognized Chardonnays—Kendall-Jackson Vintner's Reserve—comes this crème brûlée–flavored wine. Packed with pear, apple and fresh citrus, it has bright acidity and a toasty finish.

Kenwood Vineyards Reserve | 2006 | RUSSIAN RIVER VALLEY

★ $ $ A late bud break and mild summer temperatures allowed Kenwood's Reserve Chardonnay grapes a longer hang time. The resulting concentrated tropical fruit and nut flavors make this a plush, smooth wine.

Landmark Damaris Reserve | 2005 | CARNEROS

★★ $ $ $ John Deere's great-great-granddaughter is the visionary behind the Landmark winery, which crafts sophisticated wines like this tangerine-scented Chardonnay replete with crisp apple and toast overtones and fresh acidity.

MacRostie Wildcat Mountain Vineyard | 2006 | SONOMA COAST

★★ $ $ $ This melon-and-honey-scented Chardonnay comes from the volcanic soils of a sustainably farmed mountainside vineyard; it's ripe with pear and spice and has vivacious acidity.

The Ojai Vineyard Solomon Hills Vineyard | 2006 | SANTA MARIA VALLEY

★★ $ $ $ The winemakers at Ojai "watch the development of the wine carefully, yet prefer to do as little as possible." Rarely do such slacker tactics pay off as handsomely as they do in this Chardonnay, which has fresh citrus and apple notes and a nice heft on the palate.

star producers
california chardonnay

Kendall-Jackson

Although K-J makes wines at every price point, it's probably best known for its iconic, best-selling and much-loved Vintner's Reserve Chardonnay.

Patz & Hall

For more than 20 years, Patz & Hall has been crafting single-vineyard Chardonnays and Pinot Noirs recognized for their evocative character.

PlumpJack

Winemaker Anthony Biagi channels this vineyard's long-established potential (it was the site of the Villa Mt. Eden winery from 1970–1994) into ripe, fruit-driven Chardonnays.

Rochioli

Banker-turned-winemaker Tom Rochioli seems to possess an innate ability to craft world-class wines of mind-blowing flavor dimensions year after year.

Sonoma-Cutrer

This venerable maker of opulent Chardonnays weighs in every year as one of the most popular wineries on American restaurant wine lists.

Talbott

Based in Monterey County, Talbott produces luxurious, full-bodied Chards that stand apart from the fruit-bombs as seriously ageworthy bottlings.

Patz & Hall Zio Tony Ranch | 2006 | **RUSSIAN RIVER VALLEY**
★★★ **$ $ $** Made with grapes sourced from a small crop in the heart of the Russian River Valley, this seductive wine offers pear, apple, melon and vanilla on a plush palate of creamy sweetness.

PlumpJack Reserve | 2006 | **NAPA VALLEY**
★★★★ **$ $ $** As the founder of PlumpJack, Gavin Newsom—also the controversial mayor of San Francisco—styles his wines with characteristic bravado. This heady Chardonnay is like baked apple-pear pie, with a creamy weight balanced by firm acidity.

Rochioli | 2006 | **RUSSIAN RIVER VALLEY**
★★★ **$ $ $** The Rochioli family has long worked the land they now own and are devoted to producing terroir-driven wines like this stunning Chardonnay. It's filled with bright acidity, red apple, Anjou pear and toast aromas and lovely melon flavors.

Roshambo Imago | 2005 | **SONOMA COUNTY**
★★ **$ $** Crafted by the winery of whimsy—their self-proclaimed mantra is "Fighting for Fun in a Winey World"—this unoaked Chardonnay sings with tropical fruit aromas and juicy, pineapple flavors.

Solaire by Robert Mondavi | 2006 | **SANTA LUCIA HIGHLANDS**
★ **$** The Santa Lucia Highlands' cool, foggy climate produces consistently good Chardonnays; this first vintage of Mondavi's Solaire is a worthy example, with aromas of mango and pineapple and crisp, clean fruit flavors spiced with oak.

Sonoma-Cutrer Russian River Ranches | 2006 |
RUSSIAN RIVER VALLEY
★★★ **$ $** No wonder Sonoma-Cutrer Chardonnays are the best-selling Chardonnays in U.S. fine-dining establishments. This one is liquid apple pie. Apple, cinnamon, clove and pecan mingle on the nose; baked apple and pineapple grace the mouthwatering palate.

St. Clement | 2006 | **CARNEROS**
★★ **$ $** A long, even growing season in 2006 contributed to this wine's balance of rich fruit and strong acidity. Lemon peel and cantaloupe dominate the nose, reasserting themselves in creamy, spice- and vanilla-laced flavors.

Stonestreet | 2005 | **ALEXANDER VALLEY**
★★ **$ $** Grown between 700 and 1,800 feet above sea level, the grapes in this blend make up a wine of intriguing complexity: Red apple, citrus, chalk and butter aromas are followed by tropical fruit and peach flavors, great acidity and impressive length.

Talbott Sleepy Hollow Vineyard | 2005 | **MONTEREY COUNTY**
★★★ $ $ Talbott's Sleepy Hollow Chardonnays are always powerful and this big, finessed wine is true to form, full of rich fruit, crisp minerality and a lush palate.

**Woodbridge by Robert Mondavi Select Vineyard Series
Ghost Oak** | 2006 | **LODI**
★ $ This easy-drinking wine comes from grapes grown in the coolest regions of Mondavi's Lodi vineyards. It has crisp apple and citrus notes and refreshing acidity.

CALIFORNIA WHITES

sauvignon blanc

Sauvignon Blanc, the white grape of France's Bordeaux and Loire Valley, has long been second to Chardonnay in California in terms of popularity. Some bottlings are simple, fruity and sweet, but in the hands of a skilled vintner, Sauvignon Blanc displays its inherent citrus, herb and grassy flavors with little interference from oak, which tends to dull the grape's acidity. The term "Fumé Blanc" appears on some labels to evoke a connection to the Loire's Pouilly-Fumé, but few taste anything like their French counterparts.

sauvignon blanc recommendations

Beckmen Vineyards Purisima Mountain Vineyard | 2006 |
SANTA YNEZ VALLEY
★★★ $ $ Thankfully, precipitous slopes never deterred Tom Beckmen from farming this challenging vineyard. Granny Smith apple and lemon-lime flavors wind through his Sauvignon Blanc, and the site's limestone soil is revealed in a lovely minerality on the finish.

Cade | 2007 | **NAPA VALLEY**
★★★ $ $ A superb effort for only a second vintage, this offers intense peach, nectarine, melon and guava aromas, pronounced green apple flavors and a texture that's both rounded and crisp.

Chateau St. Jean La Petite Etoile Vineyard Fumé Blanc
| 2006 | **RUSSIAN RIVER VALLEY**
★★ $ $ Winemaker Margo Van Staaveren's 29 years of experience at St. Jean are evident in this Sauvignon Blanc; white peach, melon and citrus aromas are followed by a rich palate and nice acidity.

Flora Springs Soliloquy | 2006 | NAPA VALLEY

★ ★ $ $ This is a distinctive style of Sauvignon Blanc: Aged *sur lie*, or on the yeasty sediment (the lees) left after fermentation, for seven months, it has a creamy pear quality, soft on the palate, with honey and spice aromas, even a touch of nutmeg.

Fortress Vineyards Musque Clone | 2006 | RED HILLS

★ ★ $ $ By harvesting at two separate times and aging a portion of the second harvest in neutral oak, Fortress delivers a wine with wonderful complexity but no overt oak flavor. Seductive apple pie aromas are followed by flavors of tangerine with juicy acidity.

Grgich Hills Fumé Blanc | 2006 | NAPA VALLEY

★ ★ ★ $ $ Legendary Miljenko "Mike" Grgich has been making wine in Napa Valley for 50 years and continues to be a leader, biodynamically farming his vineyards, running the Grgich Hills Estate on solar power and crafting wines like this one, rich in tropical fruit and citrus, with dried fig flavors and zesty acidity.

Honig | 2007 | NAPA VALLEY

★ $ $ This family winery's history began in 1964 with Louis Honig's visionary purchase of 68 acres in Napa Valley. Now more than 40 years later, their 2007 Sauvignon Blanc explodes with grapefruit and zesty lime, then green pear, eventually turning delightfully figgy.

Markham Vineyards | 2006 | NAPA VALLEY

★ ★ $ Wine has been made on Markham Vineyards' land since 1874, but this Sauvignon Blanc is crafted in a modern style, showing great intensity of citrus and figs, with hints of honeysuckle and grass.

Mason | 2006 | NAPA VALLEY

★ ★ ★ $ $ By strategically picking the grapes at different ripeness levels, winemaker Randy Mason captures a huge range of flavors in this zesty wine, from tropical mango, guava and passion fruit to grapefruit and fresh grass.

Matanzas Creek Winery | 2006 | SONOMA COUNTY

★ ★ $ $ Hailing from Sonoma County's warmer Alexander and Knights Valleys, this white favors the fruity side of the Sauvignon Blanc grape, with intense pear, white peach and fresh-squeezed lime flavors, and just a hint of greenness on the finish.

Patianna Organic Vineyards | 2005 | MENDOCINO

★ ★ $ $ Produced from a biodynamically farmed vineyard, this wine shows superb balance in its delicate citrus flavors, with secondary notes of melon and peach. It's crisp, dry and elegant.

Pomelo | 2006 | CALIFORNIA
★ ★ $ Not content with the success of his eponymous Mason Sauvignon Blanc, Randy Mason offers this great-value wine teeming with guava and papaya fruit, limey freshness and zippy acidity.

Robert Mondavi Winery To Kalon Vineyard Reserve Fumé Blanc | 2005 | NAPA VALLEY
★ ★ ★ $ $ $ Mondavi invented the moniker "Fumé Blanc" back in the sixties, and his version is still defined by lots of winery work—barrel aging and lees stirring. This is a nicely balanced wine with a distinctly herbal edge to its grapefruit and pear aromas.

Robert Pepi | 2006 | CALIFORNIA
★ $ This is a full-bodied, full-flavored rendition of Sauvignon Blanc, heaped with zesty lemon-lime, green apples and grass. Crisp acidity and a pleasing tartness power the flavors through the long finish.

Rodney Strong Estate Vineyards Charlotte's Home | 2006 | SONOMA COUNTY
★ ★ $ The Sauvignon Blanc vineyard started by Rodney Strong in 1971 (and named for his wife) still contributes the core of this wine. With tangy grapefruit and pear, the 2006 vintage is full of acidity.

Shannon Ridge | 2006 | LAKE COUNTY
★ ★ $ $ Utilizing grapes from high-altitude vineyards—at around 2,200 feet above sea level—this wine achieves a terrific balance of ripe tropical fruit and the greener flavors of lime and fresh-cut grass.

Two Angels | 2007 | HIGH VALLEY
★ ★ $ $ As its name implies, the High Valley AVA is a high-altitude region, and its hillside vineyards benefit from the cool breezes that suit Sauvignon Blanc. This shows succulent nectarine and crisp green apple flavors, is tinged with ripe melon and ends in a soft finish.

other california whites

There are more than 100 grape varieties planted in California, but only about 15 are commonly used for the production of white wine. Riesling makes light, floral dry and off-dry wines, as well as some late-harvest dessert wines, sometimes with the addition of Semillon in the style of Sauternes. Floral Gewürztraminers and citrusy Pinot Gris (Pinot Grigio) yield respectable wines in cooler climes, while the Rhône Valley's Marsanne, Roussanne and Viognier thrive in the state's more Mediterranean-like regions.

other california white recommendations

Beaulieu Vineyard Coastal Estates Riesling | 2007 | CALIFORNIA

★ ★ $ Since its start as just four acres in Rutherford in 1900, BV has emerged as a pioneer and leader in California winemaking. BV's Coastal Estates Riesling offers pleasant apple and pear flavors, along with a touch of nicely balanced sweetness.

Blackstone Winery Riesling | 2006 | MONTEREY COUNTY

★ $ This wine handles its subtle sweetness deftly, offsetting nectar-like fruit flavors with crisp acidity. Aromas of spiced baked apples and lime soda meld with a lively citrus quality on the palate.

Ca' del Solo Albariño | 2007 | MONTEREY COUNTY

★ ★ ★ $ $ Bonny Doon's irrepressible Randall Grahm crafts this wine from biodynamic Albariño grapes, a traditionally Spanish variety. Its mineral components are pronounced, making for a stony and bracing refresher, accentuated by crisp lemon-lime verve.

Clos du Bois Pinot Grigio | 2007 | CALIFORNIA

★ ★ ★ $ Alexander Valley stalwart Clos du Bois sources grapes from small-scale growers throughout California to make its basic line of wines, which includes bargains like this floral- and lemon-scented Pinot Grigio packed with generous tropical fruit flavors that finish crisp, thanks to ample acidity.

Estancia Pinot Grigio | 2007 | CALIFORNIA

★ ★ $ Although this is a large-production wine, it receives thoughtful attention—from the use of traditional basket presses to four months of aging in neutral oak—and has the refreshing quality of lemonade and summer peaches, plus a zingy finish.

Fess Parker Viognier | 2006 | SANTA BARBARA COUNTY

★ ★ ★ $ $ Actor Fess Parker's honey-flavored Viognier starts out a bit closed in the glass. Yet in the mouth it reveals explosive flavors of ripe peach, guava and quince paste: a perfect wine for pairing with Manchego cheese.

Hayman & Hill Reserve Selection Interchange | 2007 | SANTA BARBARA COUNTY

★ ★ $ This blend of Chardonnay, Sauvignon Blanc, Muscat, Malvasia Bianca, Semillon and Gewürztraminer may seem "kitchen sink–style" but the result is a complex white with floral nuances, tropical fruit aromas, a rich, lush texture and nice acidity.

Husch Gewürztraminer | 2006 | ANDERSON VALLEY

★ ★ $ The grapes for this fragrant white come from both recent plantings as well as vines dating back to 1968, and they show the essence of Gewürztraminer: exotic aromas of flowers, lychee and pear.

Robert Mondavi Private Selection Pinot Grigio | 2006 | CALIFORNIA

★ ★ $ This expressive Pinot Grigio benefits from the addition of small amounts of Gewürztraminer, Muscat Canelli, Sauvignon Blanc and Malvasia Bianca. The result is a crisp and clean wine whose pear and citrus flavors are tinged with spice notes.

3 Blind Moose Pinot Grigio | 2006 | CALIFORNIA

★ $ Nighttime harvesting maximizes the crispness of this Pinot Grigio, while a touch of Chardonnay adds body and substance. Fresh and fragrant, with pretty floral, pear and nectarine aromas, it's underscored with lively minerality.

Treana Mer Soleil Vineyard | 2006 | CENTRAL COAST

★ $ $ The Monterey Bay–influenced Mer Soleil Vineyard supplies the Viognier and Marsanne grapes for this aromatic Rhône-style blend. Resonating with jasmine and honey, nectarine and fresh lime, it's plush, with a supple finish.

Trinitas Pinot Blanc | 2006 | RUSSIAN RIVER VALLEY

★ $ $ For one of the lesser-planted grapes in California, this full-bodied Pinot Blanc succeeds admirably, serving up soft, lingering melon and white peach aromas, along with nice herb flavors.

Vare Bianco | 2005 | NAPA VALLEY

★ ★ ★ ★ $ $ Vare Vineyards focuses on Italian-style wines like this superb white blend, modeled on those from the Collio region. Richer in style than its Italian siblings, this 500-milliliter bottling exudes delicious ripe apple, flower and exotic spice with fine minerals.

california rosés

Rosé is on the rise. Long the underdog of the wine world—thanks to insipid, sweet White Zinfandels, which gave all pink wines a bad name—rosé is increasingly appreciated as dry and food-friendly. Rosé imports have increased in recent years, and California vintners are responding to the rise in demand, crafting berry-scented wines that are perfect for quaffing during warm weather. The best are made with Sangiovese, Grenache, Pinot Noir or Carignane.

california rosé recommendations

Adi Rosé | 2007 | NAPA VALLEY
★★ $ $ This Syrah-based strawberry-scented wine has wonderful raspberry fruitiness and an appley core. It comes from Abigail Adams Wine Co.—named not for the First Lady but for owner and winemaker Beth Adams's grandmothers, Abigail Phillips and Ruth Adams.

Bonny Doon Vineyard Vin Gris de Cigare | 2006 | CALIFORNIA
★★ $ Grenache Blanc is blended with six other Rhône grapes in this strawberry- and citrus-perfumed blush, which exhibits berry and melon flavors and a touch of vanilla on its mouthwatering finish.

Domaine Chandon Unoaked Pinot Noir Rosé | 2006 | CARNEROS
★★ $ $ From the makers of one of California's most delicious pink sparkling wines—Étoile Rosé—comes this bright cherry-scented wine with whiffs of lime and strawberry-jam flavors balanced by acidity.

Le Printemps Rosé | 2007 | MENDOCINO
★★★ $ The gorgeous rose-petal color of this wine from Copain Wine Cellars is achieved the old-fashioned way: by bleeding color from grape skins (in this case, Pinot Noir and some Grenache) during a pre-fermentation cold soak. The result is an elegant, powerfully berry-flavored wine with perfect acidity.

Philo Rose Day Ranch Pinot Noir | 2006 | ANDERSON VALLEY
★★ $ $ Made with grapes grown on a former apple orchard, this pretty, crimson-colored wine brings to mind aromas of strawberry-rhubarb pie. Cherry and strawberry flavors hover on the nicely weighty palate and good acidity makes it refreshing.

california reds

Cabernet Sauvignon is the wine that put California on the international map back in the 1970s, most famously when a California Cabernet Sauvignon won the top prize at a high-profile tasting in Paris. Although Cabernet remains the state's most iconic wine, fetching the highest praise and prices, there are many other stand-out reds, such as jammy, spicy Zinfandel (especially those crafted from old vines) and the powerful Rhône-style wines championed by the so-called "Rhône Rangers," made from grapes such as Syrah, Grenache, Mourvèdre and Carignane.

CALIFORNIA REDS

cabernet sauvignon & bordeaux blends

Cabernet Sauvignon is the undisputed king of *all* grapes in California, thanks to its ability to create wines of extraordinary complexity, power and longevity. As winemakers have figured out how to manage the development of the grape's formidable tannins, the resulting wines just keep getting more concentrated and better. While plantings of Cabernet on California's valley floors can develop intense berry flavors, the trend of late for expensive Cabernets is toward hillside vineyards, where some growers are cultivating vines that yield wines full of blackberry flavors and earthy, smoky characteristics. Cabernet blends beautifully, too, particularly when paired with other Bordeaux varieties such as Merlot, Cabernet Franc, Petit Verdot and Malbec. These blends may be labeled "Meritage," while others carry their own proprietary names, like Conn Creek's "Anthology." Many Bordeaux varieties, including Merlot (see p. 179) and Cabernet Franc, are also bottled separately.

cabernet sauvignon recommendations

Arrowood | 2004 | **SONOMA COUNTY**
★★ $ $ $ With more than four decades of experience, including a stint as Chateau St. Jean's "winemaster," Richard Arrowood pulls together fruit from numerous sites for this rich, complex and full-bodied wine, nicely balancing its fruit, floral and wood flavors.

Artesa Reserve | 2005 | **NAPA VALLEY**
★★ $ $ $ A relative newcomer to Napa, making wines since 1999, Artesa offers this structured and ageworthy Cabernet, with firm tannins, blackberry fruit and herbal and spice aromas.

Beaulieu Vineyard Georges de Latour Private Reserve
| 2004 | **NAPA VALLEY**
★★★★ $ $ $ $ The crown of the BV collection, this wine beautifully balances its massive black fruit core with cedary oak. On the palate, there's a lively wave of fruit, with peppery spice, supple vanilla and dark licorice accents, plus fine, dry tannins.

Bennett Family The Reserve | 2005 | NAPA VALLEY

★★ **$ $** This bright and fruity Cabernet is ready to drink now. Vibrant red and black fruit and modest tannins are grounded by just a touch of oak and spice, plus nice, fresh acidity.

Cade Napa Cuvée | 2005 | NAPA VALLEY

★★★ **$ $ $** The first vintage of this wine, a project of PlumpJack Group, which includes the nearby PlumpJack Winery, is a superb effort. Good density of fruit turns fleshy and supple on the palate, with flavors of cherries, blueberry preserves and a milk-chocolate finish.

Chappellet Pritchard Hill Estate Vineyard | 2005 | NAPA VALLEY

★★★ **$ $ $ $** This multilayered Napa Cabernet includes small amounts of Petit Verdot and Malbec. Its powerful dark-fruit flavors—cherry, plum, blackberry—are laced with vanilla and smoky oak and balanced with firm tannins.

Chimney Rock | 2005 | STAGS LEAP DISTRICT

★★ **$ $ $** Located on a former golf course (called Chimney Rock), this winery produces a powerful reserve Cabernet, as well as this less expensive bottling: Complex yet approachable, thanks to supple tannins, it has a dense, dark-fruit core that turns chocolaty on the finish.

Cliff Lede | 2005 | STAGS LEAP DISTRICT

★★★★ **$ $ $** Crafted by winemaker Michelle Edwards, formerly of Colgin Cellars, this Cab-heavy Bordeaux blend is intense and exotic, with wild berry aromas augmented by a healthy dose of baking spices and, on the palate, figgy fruit and fine tannins.

Cuvaison | 2005 | MOUNT VEEDER

★★★ **$ $ $** This wine is a great reflection of the Mount Veeder AVA. Dense and chewy, with cherry-preserve flavors and firm, broad tannins, it's rounded out by mocha and vanilla notes.

Dalla Valle Vineyards | 2005 | NAPA VALLEY

★★★ **$ $ $ $** A touch of Cabernet Franc goes into this wine, which is as reliable a winner as you'll find. Lush, supple mixed-berry fruit marries with flavors of mocha, caramel and tobacco. Ample tannins give it a chewy and lingering finish.

Ehlers Estate 1886 | 2005 | ST. HELENA

★★★ **$ $ $ $** Big, bold and tannic, Ehlers' 1886 Cabernet shows layers of wild berries tinged with red pepper and—in a good way—Brussels sprouts. And another good thing: All profits go to the Leducq Foundation, which is devoted to cardiovascular research.

Elyse Morisoli Vineyard | 2004 | **NAPA VALLEY**
★★★ $ $ $ $ Elyse Winery owner Ray Coursen has worked with the Morisoli Vineyard for two decades, and his wines just keep getting better. This stellar bottling showcases the vineyard site's ripe, almost wild fruit with accents of leather, mushroom and Rutherford dust.

Eponymous | 2004 | **NAPA VALLEY**
★★ $ $ $ While it does not literally bear his name, this wine is a project of Bob Pepi, formerly of Robert Pepi Winery. In its fifth vintage, this Cabernet is typically complex and complete, with nice spice and earthy leaves underscoring black plum fruit.

Etude | 2004 | **NAPA VALLEY**
★★★ $ $ $ $ Offering great intensity and power from the onset, this rich and full-bodied Cabernet billows with black fruit, mocha and dried herbs, plus an underlying earthiness. Dried fruit and licorice flavors linger on the long finish.

Faust | 2005 | **NAPA VALLEY**
★★★ $ $ $ A blend of mostly Cabernet Sauvignon, supplemented with Merlot and Cabernet Franc, this wine offers a dense core of smooth and sweet cassis and cherries, with nice peppery aromas.

Geyser Peak Winery | 2005 | **ALEXANDER VALLEY**
★★ $ $ This simple, easy-drinking, fruit-driven wine offers pleasant cherry fruit and hints of raspberry. Touches of sweet spice and vanilla come from 15 months in 100 percent American oak.

Gundlach Bundschu Rhinefarm Vineyard | 2005 |
SONOMA VALLEY
★★★ $ $ $ With a history stretching back 150 years, this winery now makes exclusively estate wines from its Rhinefarm Vineyard. This Cabernet is bold, yet approachable; plush and supple on the palate, it has aromas of plum, blackberry, smoky oak and dark chocolate.

Hanna | 2004 | **ALEXANDER VALLEY**
★★★ $ $ Soft tannins, a silky texture and good acidity make this red ready to drink right now, although it has enough fruit intensity—black cherry and cassis—and structure to develop for a few more years. Aromas of spice and sweet oak round out the long finish.

Honig Bartolucci Vineyard | 2004 | **NAPA VALLEY**
★★★ $ $ $ $ A 100 percent Cabernet Sauvignon wine from a single vineyard, this red has distinctive black cherry and blackberry fruit, with secondary notes of roasted coffee and toasty oak. While big and dense, it shows good balance and a lovely spiciness.

Hundred Acre Kayli Morgan Vineyard | 2005 | NAPA VALLEY

★★★★ $ $ $ $ When Jayson Woodbridge introduced his Hundred Acre wines, he vowed that they'd stand among the best or not at all. He's clearly a man of his word: His 100 percent Cabernet Sauvignon is insanely concentrated and dense, with licorice and cassis up front, followed by plush blackberry, oak and a touch of spice and tobacco.

Judd's Hill | 2004 | NAPA VALLEY

★★ $ $ $ Beginning as a *garagiste* in the 1970s, Judd's Hill founder Art Finkelstein still makes fewer than 3,000 cases of wine annually. His fruit-forward Cab has intense plum fruit, cocoa and just enough oak to add intrigue; it's balanced and soft on the finish.

Kendall-Jackson Vintner's Reserve | 2005 | CALIFORNIA

★★ $ $ This large-production, and very respectable, wine is made by blending fruit from throughout California. Wrapped in modest, ripe tannins, it has a bit of sour-cherry-meets-plum, some bramble and earth, plus notes of vanilla.

La Jota Vineyard Co. | 2003 | HOWELL MOUNTAIN

★★★ $ $ $ Old World fans will love this Cabernet, with its earth, mocha and leather character. Powerful and firm, the wine has plump berry fruit that quickly succumbs to pleasantly dry tannins.

Mandolin | 2006 | CENTRAL COAST

★★ $ Fruit-forward and bold without being onerous, this balanced, small-producer wine has persistent red currant and black cherry flavors that are nicely integrated with oak.

Palmaz Vineyards | 2004 | NAPA VALLEY

★★★ $ $ $ $ The high-tech gravity-flow winery at Palmaz, concealed in tunnels carved within Mount George, offers an elegant Cab with boysenberry, blackberry, milk chocolate and toasty oak finishing with silky tannins.

Peju H.B. Vineyard | 2004 | RUTHERFORD

★★★ $ $ $ This richly layered Cab from a family-owned boutique winery is made from 100 percent estate fruit. The cassis and plum flavors have an underlying pipe tobacco quality, followed by very ripe tannins and hints of clovey spice.

Provenance Vineyards | 2005 | RUTHERFORD

★★ $ $ $ According to winemaker Tom Rinaldi, Provenance Vineyards' 2005 vintage set a new record for hang time, with the grape harvest going into November. The flavor maturity shows in his Cabernet with its rich layers of black cherries, earth, mocha and olives.

Robert Mondavi Winery Reserve | 2004 | NAPA VALLEY

★ ★ ★ $ $ $ $ Made from 86 percent Cabernet Sauvignon, with the remainder Cabernet Franc and Petit Verdot, this wine is opulent, youthful and intense, with firm tannins and fresh fruit flavors of blackberry and plums, lovely licorice and smoke.

Rodney Strong Estate Vineyards | 2004 | ALEXANDER VALLEY

★ ★ $ $ This Cabernet, with a small addition of Merlot, is intense and tightly wound. Powerful and full on the palate, it slowly unleashes black fruit, dusty earth and black olive flavors. The tannins are smooth, but with real presence.

Rubicon Estate Cask | 2004 | RUTHERFORD

★ ★ ★ $ $ $ $ Made from organically grown estate fruit and a proprietary Cabernet clone, this wine is an elegant balance of fruit and floral aromas, underscored by anise and tobacco. Beautifully structured, it has ripe, supple tannins and a chocolaty finish.

star producers
california cabernet sauvignon

Beaulieu Vineyard
BV makes excellent wines for every budget, but earns its first-rate reputation with its amazingly powerful Georges de Latour Private Reserve Cabernet Sauvignon.

Cade
PlumpJack's vaunted sibling Cade continues the tradition of releasing half of its delicious Cabernet juice under screw-cap; no fuss, no muss.

Cliff Lede
Winemaker Michelle Edwards was assistant winemaker at Cabernet icon Colgin Cellars for three years before joining Lede (pronounced: LAY-dee).

Dalla Valle Vineyards
Dalla Valle's Cabernets and proprietary reds are collected—and coveted—for their immense stature and richness.

Hundred Acre
While Philippe Melka consults on the making of Hundred Acre's red-hot wines, owner Jayson Woodbridge is the bigger-than-life force that drives what's becoming a legend.

Robert Mondavi Winery
Mondavi is synonymous with quality and dynamism in Napa winemaking—if not in all of California—and has been for more than 40 years (see "The Year in Wine," page 11).

Sanctuary Usibelli Vineyards | 2004 | NAPA VALLEY

★★★ $ $ $ A vineyard operated by the Usibelli family since the 1950s provides the grapes for this monster Cabernet. Very dark in color, with great extraction, firm tannins, concentrated ripe fruit flavors and accents of toasty oak and cigar box, this wine is well-constructed, powerful stuff.

Shafer One Point Five | 2005 | STAGS LEAP DISTRICT

★★★ $ $ $ $ The Shafer family began their legacy with a Stags Leap Cab back in 1978; this wine is a worthy successor, balanced and supple, but rich in tannins. Heady aromas of dried plum are coupled with figs, tobacco and spice.

Solaire by Robert Mondavi | 2005 | PASO ROBLES

★★★ $ $ This easy-drinking Cabernet is medium-bodied, with bright, juicy blackberry and raspberry flavors. The texture is quite soft, the tannins are gentle and there are some pleasing notes of sweet vanilla on the finish.

Souverain | 2005 | ALEXANDER VALLEY

★★ $ $ Dark, black fruit, espresso and bittersweet chocolate aromas foretell the layers of flavor in this Cabernet. The wine shows good structure and tannic grip, with nice nuances of vanilla and nutmeg from the use of French, American and Hungarian oak.

St. Clement Vineyards Oroppas | 2005 | NAPA VALLEY

★★★ $ $ $ Made of Cabernet Sauvignon from several Napa Valley sources, plus 7 percent Merlot from Star Vineyard in Rutherford, this jammy red balances fruit flavors with generous caramel, chocolate and peppery spice. Cedary oak appears on the finish.

Waterstone Reserve | 2004 | NAPA VALLEY

★★★ $ $ $ $ Despite owning no actual vineyards or winery, the talented *négociants* behind this wine craft a superb Cabernet. With 26 months in new French oak, the wine tastes opulent, and the intense, smoky fruit and cassislike texture handle the oak with ease.

bordeaux blend recommendations

Bennett Lane Maximus | 2005 | NAPA VALLEY

★★★ $ $ $ Named after the wine-loving Roman emperor Magnus Maximus, this blend of Cabernet, Merlot and Syrah has powerful aromas of earth, plum and spice, accented by whiffs of fennel and sage. On the palate, blackberries and blueberries are layered with savory spices and finely integrated tannins.

Charles Creek Vineyard Miradero | 2005 | SONOMA COUNTY
★ ★ $ $ $ Here's a classic Bordeaux-style Cabernet-dominant blend that's been kissed with California sunshine; the dark fruit aromas have been rendered dry and intense—think prune and raisin—resulting in a weighty, tannic wine with shades of cherry, vanilla and spice.

Clos LaChance Special Select Series Meritage | 2004 |
CENTRAL COAST
★ ★ ★ $ $ $ A solid example of California's excellent 2004 vintage at its most balanced, this wine exhibits spice, blackberry and red currant aromas, a lovely jumble of cranberry and cherry flavors and a nicely integrated, tannic finish.

Dominus Estate Napanook | 2004 | NAPA VALLEY
★ ★ $ $ $ This is the second wine from legendary Château Pétrus winemaker Christian Moueix's Napa estate. Earthy-sweet, with spicy eucalyptus aromas, it's powerful in the mouth, displaying loads of black cherries and chewy tannins.

news from a wine insider
california by Laurie Daniel, wine columnist, *San Jose Mercury News*

Vintage Note

California vintners are pleased with the quality of the 2007 vintage, which was marked by moderate weather and a long, leisurely harvest. Yields, however, were down in many areas and the Pinot Noir crop, in particular, was small.

Notable New Wines

The 2005 Freestone Pinot Noir ($75) is an impressive debut from famed Napa producer Joseph Phelps: It's a dense and concentrated yet wonderfully supple wine. Two other notable first bottlings from Napa include the 2004 Tierra Roja ($105), a graceful new Cabernet Sauvignon from the red soils of eastern Oakville; and the first wine from Piero Antinori's Napa Valley venture, Antica (a.k.a. Antinori California), the powerful 2004 Antica Napa Valley Cabernet Sauvignon ($55).

Regions Making News

Paso Robles, one of California's fastest-growing wine areas, is home to two promising new wineries: Booker Vineyard, specializing in big, dense Syrahs; and Terry Hoage Vineyards, which produces several Rhône-style wines.

Girard Artistry | 2005 | NAPA VALLEY

★★ $ $ $ Five Bordeaux grapes are united in this lovely, floral, medium-bodied wine. The bouquet recalls lavender, plum and cherry pie, with nice spicy aromas; the dominant Cabernet endows the wine with bramble fruit, soft tannins and a wonderful nuttiness.

Harlan Estate | 2004 | NAPA VALLEY

★★★★ $ $ $ $ As a much sought after California cult wine, this Bordeaux-style red (mostly Cabernet and often classified as such) doesn't disappoint: Dried cherry, mocha, eucalyptus and blackberry aromas are joined by dark, earthy nuances, a plush texture and layers of black and red fruit, supple tannins, coffee, leather—the works.

Opus One | 2005 | NAPA VALLEY

★★★★ $ $ $ $ Winemaker Michael Silacci has crafted a true Bordeaux blend—in addition to Cabernets Sauvignon and Franc, Merlot and Petit Verdot, there's also 1 percent of Malbec. The wine wafts blueberries, dusty sage and licorice followed by dark, rich flavors of blackberries, cassis, coffee, chocolate and more. Delicious.

Quintessa | 2005 | RUTHERFORD

★★★ $ $ $ $ Quintessa sets the bar high and delivers, producing great wines year after year. This vintage shows heady, earthy aromas of barbecue smoke and tobacco lifted by hyacinth. On the palate there's blackberry, dried cherry, coffee and nicely woven tannins.

Roy Estate Proprietary Red | 2005 | NAPA VALLEY

★★★★ $ $ $ $ Roy Estate's Soda Canyon vineyard was planted under the direction of the legendary Helen Turley, and winemaker Philippe Melka has stepped into her shoes effortlessly. His red Napa blend is packed with bold blackberry and currant flavors, bright acidity and chewy tannins.

Terlato Vineyards Angels' Peak | 2005 | NAPA VALLEY

★★★ $ $ $ This Merlot–Cabernet Sauvignon blend is Anthony Terlato's homage to Bordeaux's Pomerol region, where Merlot is the primary grape and the wines are crafted in a fruit-forward style. Mission accomplished: This boasts raspberry and cherry flavors woven with black fruit and sweet oak nuances.

Vérité La Muse | 2004 | SONOMA COUNTY

★★★★ $ $ $ $ Mostly Merlot, plus splashes of Cabernets Franc and Sauvignon and Malbec, La Muse is concentrated, with plum and blackberry aromas and a hint of chocolate. In the mouth, cherry and blackberry flavors commingle with dusty spices and sweet oak.

CALIFORNIA REDS

merlot

Merlot is back—even though it was never really gone. Despite the rumors of its demise, Americans are still drinking nearly as much Merlot as Cabernet—and consumption is on the rise. The "other half" of the dynamic grape duo that creates the world's great Bordeaux and California Bordeaux-style blends, Merlot is often championed as the softer counterpart to Cabernet's power. In the 1990s, Merlot became immensely popular as people sought out a fruity, accessible red. Unfortunately, with popularity came overproduction. As many lower-quality Merlots flooded the marketplace, the grape earned a reputation for mediocrity. Fortunately, that reputation is increasingly unwarranted. Today, there are countless stellar Merlots worth seeking out for their plush fruit and concentration.

merlot recommendations

Blackstone Winery | 2006 | CALIFORNIA
★ $ Sonoma Valley native Gary Sitton has been producing consistently good, fruit-forward wines at amazingly affordable prices for more than ten years. This Merlot is no exception, with flavors of ripe currant and cherries and pleasingly soft notes of cedar and oak.

Chappellet | 2005 | NAPA VALLEY
★★★ $ $ $ The dark plum, black cherry and mocha in this Merlot are a testament to the flavors that can be coaxed from grapes grown in rocky soil: in this case, the stony soil of Chappellet's 1,200-foot-high Pritchard Hill. Cedary oak and tannins round out this great wine.

Charles Creek Vineyard Sangiacomo Vineyard Pasatiempo
| 2004 | CARNEROS
★ $ $ Husband and wife Bill and Gerry Brinton are known for crafting dependable, fruit-driven wines. Their Merlot brims with black cherries and heady mocha, leading to a toasty oak finish.

Duckhorn Vineyards Estate Grown | 2005 | NAPA VALLEY
★★★ $ $ $ $ Duckhorn's three-decade-long focus on Merlot has undeniably paid off, as this lively, cherry fruit–flavored wine shows; currant, cherry and blackberry flavors are supported by firm tannins.

Ehlers Estate | 2005 | ST. HELENA
★★★ $ $ $ From vineyards planted by Sacramento grocer Bernard Ehlers in 1886 comes this intensely concentrated wine. Rich with red currant, blackberry, mocha and vanilla flavors, it has ripe tannins and a mouthwatering finish.

Gloria Ferrer | 2005 | CARNEROS
★★ $ $ Although Gloria Ferrer is known primarily for California sparklers rooted in the 19th-century Spanish tradition, this medium-bodied still wine is a treat, with blueberry and huckleberry aromas, soft red cherry flavors and sweet tannins.

Hayman & Hill Reserve Selection | 2005 | NAPA VALLEY
★★ $ Aussie David Hayman and Californian Dennis Hill, a duo with more than 40 years of winemaking experience between them, collaborated on this perfumed wine full of dark fruit and sage aromas and raspberry and red cherry flavors balanced by smooth tannins.

Little Black Dress | 2006 | CALIFORNIA
★ $ Like the wardrobe staple this line of wines extols, this fruity, everyday red is basic, straightforward and simple. Notes of cherry dominate at first, then settle with both spice and oak on the finish.

Matanzas Creek Winery | 2004 | BENNETT VALLEY
★★ $ $ Matanzas Creek was once a dairy farm; for more than 30 years, however, vines have occupied the land, producing delicious wines like this one, with plum, red cherry and anise aromas and dried herb and toasty spice flavors.

Miner Stagecoach Vineyard | 2005 | NAPA VALLEY
★★★ $ $ $ Perhaps blessed by the ancient Assyrian sun god (who is commemorated by the winged symbol that graces each Miner bottle), this supple wine possesses wonderfully integrated tannins, ripe plum, black cherry and red currant flavors and a hint of hazelnut.

Newton Unfiltered | 2005 | NAPA VALLEY
★★★ $ $ $ This gorgeous Merlot hails from Newton's steep Spring Mountain vineyards. Black cherry and red currant join fennel and cedar flavors, while firm tannins give the wine power and depth.

PlumpJack | 2005 | NAPA VALLEY
★★★★ $ $ $ Like this wine's portly namesake (Shakespeare's Sir John Falstaff, nicknamed "Plump Jack"), this Merlot is generously proportioned (not to mention outrageously delicious), with aromas of ripe black cherry, toffee and dark chocolate heading into blackberry and soft oak flavors.

Ray's Station Vineyards | 2004 | **NORTH COAST**
★ ★ $ Winemaker Gavin Taylor's Merlot—blended with a bit of Cabernet Sauvignon, Syrah and Cabernet Franc—layers black cherry, ripe plum, licorice and sage flavors and builds to a spicy finish.

Toasted Head | 2005 | **CALIFORNIA**
★ $ This cherry-flavored red combines sweet tannins, anise and licorice aromas and toasty oak flavors. The name refers to the technique of charring the ends of the predominantly American oak barrels in which Toasted Head's wines mature.

CALIFORNIA REDS

pinot noir

Pinot Noir is one of the most persnickety of grapes, hard to grow even in its homeland of Burgundy. California vintners have wrestled with it for decades trying to replicate the spicy, smoky, earthy qualities that characterize French examples. While there are many light, cherry-flavored California Pinots at affordable prices, the better ones are costly, as a result of all the work that goes into making them. The finest come from cool regions like the Russian River Valley, Carneros, Santa Barbara County (especially Santa Maria Valley), the Central Coast and Mendocino.

pinot noir recommendations

Acacia | 2006 | **CARNEROS**
★ ★ $ $ Crafted by one of the pioneering winemaking families of the Carneros region, this is a blend from several fog-blessed vineyards and several Pinot Noir clones. It has notes of sweet blackberry, cherry and cedar and a long, smooth finish.

Buena Vista Ramal Vineyard | 2006 | **CARNEROS**
★ ★ $ $ $ Given Buena Vista's reputation for consistency and the Ramal Vineyard's ideal locale—a south-facing hillside overlooking the San Francisco Bay—it's not surprising how good this wine is, balancing mouthwatering acidity and bright cherry fruit.

Byron Nielson Vineyard | 2005 | **SANTA MARIA VALLEY**
★ ★ ★ $ $ This delicious Pinot began with cool-climate grapes and gentle processing through a gravity-flow winery. The wine shows vivid berry and spice flavors, a whiff of meat and well-integrated tannins.

Cambria Julia's Vineyard | 2006 | SANTA MARIA VALLEY

★★ $ $ The sediment-rich alluvial soil of Julia's Vineyard is partly responsible for this wine's intense flavor: Raspberry and plum aromas are followed by cherry, chocolate and toast flavors.

Carmel Road | 2005 | ARROYO SECO

★★★ $ $ $ Everything about this Pinot says "special": The tiny, hardscrabble site it comes from; the native yeasts used in fermentation; the absence of fining and filtering (processes that remove particulate matter but also, some say, flavor). The final product is sheer delight—a complex and balanced blend of berries, meat and spice.

Carpe Diem Firepeak Vineyard | 2006 | EDNA VALLEY

★★ $ $ This unique, earthy Pinot Noir, made from grapes grown in a mix of clay and volcanic and fossil-laden soils, has black cherry flavors, beefy nuances and a tight, minerally finish.

Chalone Vineyard | 2006 | MONTEREY COUNTY

★★★ $ A difficult growing season that included spring downpours and a summer heat wave somehow ended with ideal harvest conditions and produced this stellar wine, bright with acidity and fragrant with black cherry and raspberry.

Cuvaison | 2006 | CARNEROS

★★ $ $ $ Winemaker Steven Rogstad believes in "doing as little as possible" to grapes, instead allowing them to express the terroir of Cuvaison's Carneros estate. This wine brims with black cherry and leathery aromas, leading to a graceful, nicely balanced finish.

Edna Valley Vineyard Paragon | 2006 | SAN LUIS OBISPO COUNTY

★★ $ $ Edna Valley Vineyard tends to produce Pinots with rich fruit notes. This vintage shows plum, cherry and dusty spice aromas; finely integrated tannins keep the finish soft and supple.

Etude Estate | 2006 | CARNEROS

★★ $ $ $ For Etude founder Tony Soter, Pinot Noir is akin to a technically challenging musical étude; his 2006 performance boasts cherry cola, smoke and oak aromas, a medium-bodied palate and a solid band of minerality.

Goldeneye | 2005 | ANDERSON VALLEY

★★★★ $ $ $ This spectacular wine hits all the high notes. A beautiful, fruit-driven nose redolent of cherry and sweet, ripe raspberries is followed through on the palate with more intense dark fruit flavors, supple, well-integrated tannins and a silky finish.

J. Lohr Fog's Reach Vineyard | 2006 | **ARROYO SECO**
★ ★ **$ $** In this inaugural vintage of J. Lohr's Fog's Reach Pinot, cherry and strawberry mingle with rhubarb pie aromas, while sweet vanilla in the mouth turns a little spicy on the long, oaky finish.

Kendall-Jackson Vintner's Reserve | 2006 | **CALIFORNIA**
★ **$** Made from a blend of Pinot Noir grapes from throughout the state (plus a splash of Syrah), this wine has nicely integrated acidity, balancing cherry and raspberry flavors with a hint of spice.

La Crema | 2006 | **SONOMA COAST**
★ **$ $** A crowd-pleaser, this wine offers zingy cherry aromas and a whiff of spice, followed by juicy, sweet tannins on the palate.

Logan Sleepy Hollow Vineyard | 2005 | **MONTEREY COUNTY**
★ ★ **$ $** Lean, gravelly soils and vigorous pruning keep yields low on the lots of Pinot Noir grapes that go into this sassy wine, whose cherry, plum and spice aromas meld with earth notes on the palate.

star producers
california pinot noir

Byron
Winemaker Jonathan Nagy consistently crafts gorgeous, Burgundian-style wines that, while not inexpensive, cost a fraction of the price of their French counterparts.

Carmel Road
One of the many brands owned by wine mogul Jess Jackson, Carmel Road produces lovely cool-climate Chardonnay and Pinot Noir in Monterey County.

Chalone Vineyard
Chalone has been a Chardonnay trailblazer since the 1960s. Today its Pinots also offer quality and value, thanks to skilled winemaker Robert Cook.

Migration
Migration is the terrific, affordable second label of Goldeneye (which is a sibling of Duckhorn Vineyards), and its Pinot Noirs are outstanding.

Miner
Miner started out making delicious Chardonnays over a decade ago and quickly followed suit with other grapes, Pinot Noir in particular.

The Ojai Vineyard
Ojai may be synonymous with Syrah, but the Pinots it's producing, from the Santa Maria Valley and Santa Rita Hills specifically, expand its portfolio beautifully.

MacRostie Wildcat Mountain Vineyard | 2005 |
SONOMA COAST

★★ $ $ $ MacRostie's fog-shrouded mountaintop vineyard is a classic, cool-climate Sonoma Coast site, endowing this earthy wine with dried cherry and cola aromas at the start and more concentrated dried-berry fruit toward the long finish.

Migration | 2006 | **ANDERSON VALLEY**
★★★ $ $ $ The younger sibling to Goldeneye, Migration is blended from the best lots after those dedicated to the premier label and is therefore a bit less expensive. Intense black cherry and cola aromas are followed by a complex earthiness and fine tannins on the palate.

Miner Garys' Vineyard | 2006 | **SANTA LUCIA HIGHLANDS**
★★★ $ $ $ Miner named this delicious wine after two of the growers whose Pinot Noir grapes contribute to it: Gary Franscioni and Gary Pisoni. It has sweet cherry and dark plum fruit on the nose, leading to a round and supple texture punctuated with sweet oak overtones and firm tannins.

The Ojai Vineyard Clos Pepe Vineyard | 2005 |
SANTA RITA HILLS

★★★ $ $ $ Grapes were picked two weeks apart at different ripeness levels for this wine. The riper batch lends dense blackberry aromas and flavors, while the leaner offers earthiness and tannic structure for a plush, well-balanced vintage.

Orogeny | 2006 | **GREEN VALLEY**
★★ $ $ $ This Pinot is a blend from several vineyards in the Green Valley subappellation of the Russian River Valley. Expressive black cherry flavors dominate the bouquet with a dash of cracked pepper, followed by mouthwatering cherry fruit on the palate and soft, nicely integrated tannins.

Patz & Hall Pisoni Vineyard | 2005 | **SANTA LUCIA HIGHLANDS**
★★★★ $ $ $ $ This concentrated Pinot is packed with aromas of everything from rhubarb and wildflowers to blueberries and black cherries. In the mouth there's rich berry fruit, earthy depth and formidable but well-integrated tannins. Gorgeous.

Sanford | 2006 | **SANTA RITA HILLS**
★★ $ $ $ Two Sanford vineyards, La Rinconada and the historic Sanford and Benedict Vineyard next door, contribute to this blend. Dusty spice and dried berries dominate the nose, and nicely concentrated cherry and berry flavors come through in the mouth, with soft, sweet tannins and bright, balancing acidity.

Sonoma-Cutrer | 2005 | **SONOMA COAST**
★★★ $ $ $ Grapes from more than three dozen individual lots make up this red cherry– and red apple–perfumed Pinot. It's plush in the mouth, well balanced and layered with dark berry fruit flavors, bright acidity and finely focused tannins.

Trinitas | 2006 | **CARNEROS**
★★ $ $ Trinitas Cellars crafts this classic Carneros Pinot, with red cherry and spice flavors offset by soft tannins and acidity, all ending in a delicious finish.

CALIFORNIA REDS

syrah

California's love affair with France's Rhône grape varieties began with Syrah, which grows quite well in various regions throughout the state. In cooler climates it yields wines that are lean and elegant, with spicy, berry flavors and smoky aromas—occasionally comparable to northern Rhône wines such as Crozes-Hermitage. Syrah from warmer parts of California tends to more closely resemble Australian Shiraz (the same grape), displaying brooding, spicy, dark berry flavors and often high levels of alcohol.

syrah recommendations

Beckmen Vineyards Purisima Mountain Vineyard Syrah/ Viognier | 2006 | **SANTA YNEZ VALLEY**
★★★ $ $ $ Purisima Mountain's high elevation and rare limestone subsoil are ideal for Rhône varieties like Syrah and Viognier. Just a touch of the latter goes into this blend, which exhibits beautiful black cherry and blueberry notes, mocha flavors and firm tannins.

Bonny Doon Vineyard Bien Nacido | 2005 |
SANTA MARIA VALLEY
★★★ $ $ $ From Randall Grahm, one of the pioneers of Rhône varieties in California, comes this gorgeous, complex Syrah with a bouquet of sage, herbs and wild berries and a palate thick with tannin, huckleberries and blackberries.

Buena Vista | 2005 | **CARNEROS**
★★ $ $ Selective fruit thinning, nighttime harvesting and 14 months in French oak helped yield this well-rounded, spicy, berry-rich Syrah.

Burgess | 2004 | NAPA VALLEY

★ ★ $ $ Burgess grows its Syrah grapes on the eastern side of How-ell Mountain, where the rough terroir restricts yields and concen-trates flavor; the 2004 vintage is plump with spicy plum, raspberry and mocha notes and an underlining of ripe tannins.

C.G. Di Arie Southern Exposure | 2004 | FAIR PLAY

★ ★ $ $ $ This well-balanced Syrah, layered with blackberry, cassis, tobacco and mocha, comes from the tiny Shenandoah Valley in the eastern foothills of the Sierra Mountains, where days are warm but nights are cool and crisp.

Concannon Selected Vineyards | 2005 | CENTRAL COAST

★ ★ $ In 1883, Irish immigrant James Concannon recognized the Livermore Valley's rocky soils as ideal terrain for creating Bordeaux- and Rhône-style wines. His legacy lives on in bottlings like this Syrah, rich with plum, cassis, cola and spice notes.

Fess Parker | 2004 | SANTA BARBARA COUNTY

★ ★ $ $ Fess Parker crafts his wines with the same adventuresome spirit that defined the TV characters he played (Davy Crockett, Daniel Boone). This intense Syrah is thick with blackberry and smoky vanilla aromas and a licorice- and chocolate-laden palate.

Forth La Rousse Vineyard | 2004 | DRY CREEK VALLEY

★ $ $ Gerry and Jann Forth traded their city lives and careers for a ramshackle ranch in the Dry Creek Valley, where they make tasty wines like this vanilla-spiced, berry- and cherry-scented Syrah.

Kinton | 2005 | SANTA BARBARA COUNTY

★ ★ $ $ "Flying winemaker" Peter Fraser is the man behind this big Santa Barbara Syrah. It boasts fresh-baked blueberry pie aromas and flavors, sleek tannins and a velvety texture.

The Ojai Vineyard Bien Nacido Vineyard | 2004 |
SANTA BARBARA COUNTY

★ ★ ★ ★ $ $ $ This Syrah's grapes come from the cool-climate Santa Maria Valley, resulting in a gorgeously complex wine loaded with fruit, coffee and chocolate notes and well-integrated tannins.

Patianna Organic Vineyards Fairbairn Ranch | 2004 |
MENDOCINO

★ ★ $ $ With grapes from an organic and biodynamic Mendocino vineyard, Patti Fetzer (of the Fetzer wine family) produces this elegant Syrah perfumed with black cherries and blueberries. The fruit flavors repeat on the palate, joined by spicy pepper and soft tannins.

Roshambo Justice | 2005 | **DRY CREEK VALLEY**
★ ★ ★ $ $ This superfruity Syrah shows dense, concentrated layers of blueberries, blackberries and red currants, woven with ribbons of chocolate; the rich flavors are nicely upheld by velvety tannins.

Testarossa Subasio | 2006 | **CENTRAL COAST**
★ ★ ★ $ $ $ The Old World encounters the New World in this beautifully balanced and complex Central Coast Syrah. Made from a blend of Santa Clara and Santa Barbara County grapes, it is bold in structure with dark berry flavors accented by an underlying spicy quality on the nose and palate.

Toasted Head Shiraz | 2005 | **DUNNIGAN HILLS**
★ $ In the 1980s, Karl and John Giguiere converted their family's Dunnigan Hills farm into a vineyard and returned to a winemaking tradition not practiced there since Prohibition. Their 2005 Shiraz is easy-drinking, with blackberry and cassis notes.

star producers
california syrah

Beckmen Vineyards
Predominantly self-taught, the talented Steve Beckmen crafts amazing Syrahs at his family's decade-old Santa Barbara County vineyard.

Bonny Doon Vineyard
Maverick winemaker Randall Grahm's superb Rhône-inspired Syrahs express California's regional terroir—and are biodynamically produced.

Burgess
Since 1972, Tom Burgess has patiently figured out which sites on his estate grow which grapes best; his Syrahs from the eastern slope of Howell Mountain are exquisite.

The Ojai Vineyard
When disease destroyed Ojai's vines in the 1990s, the owners began buying Syrah from other vineyards, including Roll Ranch, whose grapes have turned out to be among California's best.

Roshambo
Roshambo's mastermind Naomi Brilliant takes a fresh, un-serious approach to making seriously good wine.

Testarossa
Though Rob and Diana Jensen established Testarossa to create terroir-driven, vineyard-designated Chardonnays and Pinot Noirs, they also make fantastic Syrahs.

CALIFORNIA REDS

zinfandel

DNA testing in the early 1990s shattered the myth that Zinfandel was a native American grape variety, as many had long believed. Alas, Zinfandel turns out to be identical to an obscure Croatian grape called Crljenak Kastelanski, though how exactly it became Zinfandel, an important variety in California capable of producing world-class wines, remains a mystery. Regardless, Zinfandel's long-established relationship with California (dating as far back as the 1850s) gives it a uniquely American identity. Though numerous styles exist, many of the finest offer exuberant berry fruit aromas and flavors. The most prized Zinfandel bottlings come from vineyards planted with gnarled old vines—some a century old—whose low yield results in grapes of extraordinary richness and concentrated flavors.

zinfandel recommendations

Alexander Valley Vineyards Alexander School Top of the Crop Old Vine | 2005 | ALEXANDER VALLEY

★★ $ $ $ Dark and daring, this wine is a mixed berry jam of boysenberry, blackberry and black raspberry, with nice allspice and pepper aromas. A touch of smoke makes it ideal for barbecue.

Blackstone Winery | 2006 | CALIFORNIA

★ $ Exploiting Zinfandel's affinity for blending, winemaker Gary Sitton typically includes various grapes from various regions in this wine for added structure and sophistication. His 2006 vintage brings to mind raspberries, plum preserves, raisins and baking spices.

Clos du Bois Sonoma Reserve | 2005 | DRY CREEK VALLEY

★★ $ $ This perfect pizza wine shows fruity intensity, with dark bramble berries, peppery spice aromas and firm tannins, probably from the addition of a tiny amount of Petite Sirah.

Dashe | 2006 | DRY CREEK VALLEY

★★★ $ $ Husband-and-wife winemaking team Michael and Anne Dashe craft this velvety Zin. It's got dark flavors of licorice, spice, supple black cherry and blueberry plus ripe tannins and a lingering vanilla-accented finish.

Di Arie | 2006 | **AMADOR COUNTY**

★ ★ **$ $** This wine is rich and ripe without straying into cooked-fruit territory. Pure black cherry and blackberry flavors meet mocha and sweet vanilla on the palate with nuances of herbal, loamy soil.

Edmeades | 2006 | **MENDOCINO COUNTY**

★ ★ ★ **$ $** Small amounts of Petite Sirah, Merlot, Syrah and Grenache add an extra layer of complexity to this full-bodied wine, which offers berry, spiced cherry compote, espresso and even some minerally earth aromas.

Francis Ford Coppola Director's Cut | 2005 |
DRY CREEK VALLEY

★ ★ ★ **$ $** From Francis Ford Coppola's appellation wine series, this Zin comes with a dose of Petite Sirah for added structure. It's supple in texture and nicely balances toasty oak, sweet vanilla and raspberry with fine but firm tannins.

star producers
california zinfandel

Alexander Valley Vineyards
The Wetzel family's long list of wines includes a terrific old-vine Zinfandel and three spicy ones: Sin Zin, Temptation Zin and Redemption Zin.

Clos du Bois
Megawinery Clos du Bois has been making delicious wines endowed with excellent quality-for-price goodness since 1974; their first Zinfandels hit the markets in the early 1990s.

Dashe
The winemaking Dashes, Michael and Anne, craft amazing single-vineyard wines—most famously, their mind-blowing Zins.

Grgich Hills Estate
Miljenko "Mike" Grgich put California Chardonnay on the world map in the mid-1970s; today, all of his eponymous wines are landmarks.

Lolonis
Winemaker Lori Knapp is dedicated to organic viticulture, and her Mendocino vines yield wines comparable in quality to those from Napa Valley for about a third less cost.

Roshambo
Don't be fooled by Roshambo's whimsical wine names ("The Reverend" Zinfandel, "Justice" Syrah): This Dry Creek Valley vintner makes profound wines.

Grgich Hills Estate | 2005 | NAPA VALLEY

★ ★ ★ **$ $ $** Decades before DNA testing came along, it was Mike Grgich who first suspected Zinfandel might be a grape originally from his native Croatia. He was right, and so is this delicious rendering of the grape; it's lean and spicy, with berry flavors and great acidity.

Hayman & Hill Reserve Selection | 2004 | DRY CREEK VALLEY

★ ★ **$** Dennis Hill and David Hayman, both of Blackstone Winery, lend their names to this fruit-driven Zinfandel redolent of raspberries and cherry pie. The palate offers more berry flavors and just a touch of supple, dusty tannins.

Lolonis | 2005 | REDWOOD VALLEY

★ ★ **$ $** The organic viticulture pioneers at Lolonis have been using ladybugs as pest control since the 1950s and started making wine in 1982. Their experience shows in this tasty yet reserved Zinfandel, with plummy aromas, nice cassis and forest flavors and a spicy finish.

Murphy-Goode Liar's Dice | 2005 | SONOMA COUNTY

★ ★ **$ $** Sweet wild raspberry flavors are matched with plenty of spice and white pepper in this Zinfandel; 14 months in French and American oak give it nice tannins and structure.

Noceto OGP The Original Grandpère Vineyard | 2005 | AMADOR COUNTY

★ **$ $** From the Sangiovese specialists at Noceto comes this food-friendly Zin, boasting fruity and floral flavors and peppery spice and showcasing the grape's potential for acidity and modest tannins.

Ottimino Little 8 Rancho Bello Vineyard | 2004 | RUSSIAN RIVER VALLEY

★ ★ **$ $ $** This toothsome wine is downright chewy in its blackberry and blueberry flavors, with nice peppery nuances, touches of sweet vanilla and a tannic finish.

Pezzi King Old Vines | 2005 | DRY CREEK VALLEY

★ **$ $** Dry Creek Valley's warm climate comes through in this Zinfandel's caramel and chocolate flavors. Dense and full-bodied, the wine also reveals blackberries, a hint of stewed spiced prunes and plums and ripe tannins.

Robert Mondavi Private Selection | 2005 | CENTRAL COAST

★ **$** A good sipper on its own, this value-priced, widely available Zinfandel is a solid example of what the grape can do: It's medium-bodied, with subtle pepper aromas, enjoyable blueberry flavors and softened, minimal tannins.

Roshambo The Reverend | 2005 | DRY CREEK VALLEY
★ ★ ★ $ $ Roshambo may not take itself very seriously, but it certainly makes serious wine. The Reverend's jammy, dark berry flavors come with nicely detailed notes of cigar box, cedary spice and dark chocolate and just the right amount of tannin.

Trinitas Old Vine | 2005 | CONTRA COSTA COUNTY
★ ★ $ $ This black fruit–driven wine is marked by rich notes of chocolate syrup and cassis on the palate, offset by earth and dusty tannins. There are even hints of peppery spice and cocoa on the finish.

Z-52 Agnes' Vineyard Old Vine | 2005 | LODI
★ ★ $ $ This is a small-production Zinfandel crafted with grapes from warm-climate Lodi. Its ripe cherry flavors are accented by notes of licorice and herbs and upheld by tart acidity. It is medium-bodied and finishes with a spicy earthiness.

other california reds

European immigrants brought many different Mediterranean grape cuttings with them long before U.S. Customs prohibited such souvenirs, though most were used to produce simple jug wines. In the 1980s, a group of winemakers calling themselves the "Rhône Rangers" looked beyond the popular Cabernet Sauvignon and began experimenting with varieties such as Grenache, Mourvèdre, Carignane and Petite Sirah, which they claimed were ideally suited to California's Mediterranean climate. The gamble paid off, as these grapes are producing some of the state's most interesting and delicious wines. A similar movement to establish Italian grapes such as Sangiovese, Dolcetto and Barbera as "Cal-Italia" varieties has had mixed results, though some of these wines are quite good.

other california red recommendations

Beckmen Vineyards Purisima Mountain Vineyard Grenache
| 2005 | SANTA YNEZ VALLEY
★ ★ ★ $ $ $ Purisima Mountain's high elevation and unusual limestone subsoils seem to agree with Rhône grape varieties like Grenache. In this wine, gorgeous raspberry notes fuse with a hint of black pepper and the palate is juicy with berries and cassis.

Ca' del Solo Sangiovese | 2005 | SAN BENITO COUNTY

★ ★ $ Bonny Doon proprietor Randall Grahm sources grapes from the Gimelli Vineyard in the sunny, cool breeze–blessed Cienega Valley for this Italian varietal wine. It's redolent of cassis, black cherry, chocolate and tobacco with a touch of minerality on the finish.

Concannon Limited Release Petite Sirah | 2005 | CENTRAL COAST

★ $ From a 125-year-old winery comes this great value with bright berry fruit and cherry flavors grounded by soft, sweet tannins.

Di Arie Estate Grown Block #4 Primitivo | 2006 | SHENANDOAH VALLEY

★ $ $ If Di Arie's Block #4 is any indication, Zinfandel's cousin Primitivo is getting comfortable in the Sierra Foothills' Shenandoah Valley; this wine's cherry flavors sing with notes of earth, pepper and spice.

Earthquake Petite Sirah | 2005 | LODI

★ ★ $ $ Although 7 Deadly Zins may be their most popular label, brothers Michael and David Phillips (at their Michael-David Winery) produce other Lodi wines worth noting, like this Petite Sirah with blackberry and plum notes, toasty oak and well-integrated tannins.

Ehlers Estate Cabernet Franc | 2005 | ST. HELENA

★ ★ ★ $ $ $ In 1987, Parisians Jean and Sylviane Leducq replanted this vineyard with Bordeaux varieties. One of the results is this marvelous, complex Cabernet Franc, rich in firm tannins, black cherry, currant and spicy sage notes.

Elyse Hudson Vineyard Le Corbeau | 2005 | LOS CARNEROS

★ ★ ★ $ $ $ Dusty spice and dried berry aromas dominate this gorgeous Grenache-centric wine, rounded out with blueberry, black pepper and violet flavors, supple weight and nicely integrated tannins.

Epiphany Rodney's Vineyard Petite Sirah | 2005 | SANTA BARBARA COUNTY

★ ★ $ $ $ Winemaker Eli Parker, son of actor-turned-wine-mogul Fess Parker, founded the Epiphany label to showcase amazing grapes, primarily from Santa Barbara County. His inky Petite Sirah has fruit-forward notes of blackberry balanced by coffee and leather.

Foppiano Vineyards Petite Sirah | 2004 | RUSSIAN RIVER VALLEY

★ $ $ Like many Italians who turned to winemaking when gold mining didn't pan out, Giovanni Foppiano purchased a winery in 1896. It remains in the family and produces this bold, cherry-flavored red.

Kokomo Windsor Oaks Vineyards Malbec | 2006 | CHALK HILL
★★ $ $ $ With only a few vintages under their belt, Indiana transplants Erik Miller and Josh Bartels are producing impressive wines, like this soft, spicy Malbec with notes of berries, vanilla and toast.

Kuleto Estate Sangiovese | 2005 | NAPA VALLEY
★★ $ $ $ This juicy Sangiovese from Pat Kuleto's mountain estate is packed with plum, date, fig and spicy dust aromas and blackberry and a hint of tobacco on the palate.

Lolonis Orpheus Heritage Vineyards Petite Sirah | 2005 | REDWOOD VALLEY
★★ $ $ $ From one of California's northernmost appellations comes this big, well-balanced wine. Thirty-five-year-old vines instill it with a range of notes, from luscious blackberry to earth and coffee.

Noceto Sangiovese | 2005 | SHENANDOAH VALLEY
★ $ $ Yearning to plant something different in Zinfandel-saturated Amador County, Jim and Suzy Gullett turned to an old Italian favorite: Sangiovese. Of their multitude of bottlings, this one has bright cranberry and cherry flavors.

Peju Province Cabernet Franc | 2005 | NAPA VALLEY
★★★ $ $ $ Cabernet Franc, long a favorite of Bordeaux and the Loire, flourishes in California too, as this well-balanced Peju example proves. Spicy oak and blackberry aromas lead to cassis, coffee and beautifully integrated tannins on the palate.

Pietra Santa Sangiovese | 2005 | CIENEGA VALLEY
★★ $ $ In the foothills of the Gabilan Mountains lies Pietra Santa's granite- and limestone-rich vineyard, cooled by Monterey Bay breezes. The winery's Sangiovese is a spicy wine with intriguing black cherry, dried sausage and earth notes.

Ridge Lytton Springs | 2005 | DRY CREEK VALLEY
★★★ $ $ $ Wet, cold conditions started the 2005 season in Lytton Springs, in Dry Creek Valley, but production was still healthy and flavorful. This blend of Zinfandel, Petite Sirah and Carignane shows gorgeous aromas of black cherry, licorice and violet and a full palate of dark berries and generous tannins.

Stags' Leap Winery Petite Sirah | 2005 | NAPA VALLEY
★★★ $ $ $ Former cinematographer Kevin Morrisey did stints at Bordeaux's Château Pétrus and California's Domaine Chandon and Etude before becoming head winemaker at Stags' Leap. His muscular Petite Sirah blend displays pepper, blackberry, coffee and leather.

Thomas Fogarty Gist Ranch Cabernet Franc | 2004 |
SANTA CRUZ MOUNTAINS
★★ $ $ $ A warm September in the Santa Cruz Mountains may have contributed to the roundness of this Cabernet Franc, ripe in plum and black cherry notes with hints of chocolate and violet.

Two Angels Petite Sirah | 2006 | HIGH VALLEY
★★ $ $ One of the lesser-known AVAs of California, High Valley produces this Petite Sirah, a wine with solid tannic structure, raspberry and plum mingling on the nose and black cherry, marmalade and licorice on the dense palate.

Valley of the Moon Sangiovese | 2005 | SONOMA COUNTY
★★ $ $ From a warm Sonoma County microclimate and red volcanic soils, this raspberry- and cranberry-nuanced wine has pepper and berry jam–like flavors and a kiss of vanilla on the finish.

star producers
other california reds

Beckmen Vineyards
The Beckmens see the "convergence of soil, microclimate, wind and sun" on their hillside Purisima Mountain Vineyard as the perfect setting for growing Rhône varieties.

Ehlers Estate
Ehlers is a not-for-profit winery whose proceeds benefit the Leducq Foundation, one of the world's largest supporters of cardiovascular research.

Elyse
When Ray Coursen left the restaurant business, his goal was to make rich, juicy, voluptuous Zins. It appears he has a way with Grenache, too.

Peju Province
Not only is Peju dedicated to organic and sustainable viticultural practices, the family-owned winery is solar powered, too—and the wines are spectacular.

Ridge
Paul Draper was a pioneer in the blending of grape varieties such as Carignane, Petite Sirah and Grenache with Zinfandel—long before it was in fashion.

Stags' Leap Winery
Stags' Leap cemented its reputation by making superb Cabernets, but its Petite Sirah and its Rhône field blend are equally deserving of praise.

oregon

Oregon vintners have wisely focused on what their climate allows them to do best: Pinot Noir. Which isn't to say that the state's cool, often uncommonly wet weather doesn't pose its share of problems. But vintners who understand the region have tailored their viticulture accordingly, and are today responsible for some of the best Pinot Noirs in the U.S., and a few stellar whites as well.

Oregon: An Overview

The hub of Oregon wine production is the Willamette Valley. Located in the state's northwest corner and protected against strong winds from the Pacific by the Oregon Coast Range mountains, the region experiences cool temperatures and abundant moisture. Fortunately for vintners, Pinot Noir has taken to the area particularly well. To the south, in the warmer regions of Umpqua, Rogue and Applegate Valleys, some Pinot Noir is grown, though Bordeaux and Rhône varieties tend to perform better. East of the Willamette Valley on the Washington State border are the Columbia Gorge and Valley and the Walla Walla Valley, where warm-climate-loving Syrah has made a good home for itself.

Oregon Wine Labels

Oregon's traditionally tight labeling restrictions have loosened recently; where the state once required that most wines labeled by variety contain 90 percent of that grape, the minimum has been reduced to 75 percent for some varieties. This will not apply to Pinot Noir, Pinot Gris or Chardonnay, however, which are still held to the 90 percent standard. In addition, wines bearing specific region names may now contain 95 percent of grapes from that region, rather than the previously required 100 percent. In regions such as Columbia Valley or Walla Walla Valley that straddle the Washington–Oregon border, winemakers must follow Oregon state appellation rules, although they may default to the federal standard of 85 percent with respect to regional labeling.

oregon whites

While most of Oregon's vintners focus on reds, their whites can still be impressive. Two of the most notable types are Pinot Gris and Pinot Blanc, with the former showing a bit more substantial body than the latter. The success of Chardonnay in Oregon has been spotty, though several winemakers have managed to use the cooler climate to their advantage, crafting elegant, mineral-laden examples. Lighter, drier Rieslings also achieve some success in certain areas, particularly the Willamette Valley.

oregon white recommendations

Abacela Albariño | 2007 | UMPQUA VALLEY
★ ★ $ $ Beginning with a quest to make Tempranillo, Abacela winery now specializes in growing Iberian grapes in Oregon's Umpqua Valley. Here, the Galician grape Albariño makes a stony, minerally wine with lemon and green apple flavors and good acidity.

Adelsheim Pinot Gris | 2006 | WILLAMETTE VALLEY
★ ★ $ $ Made from grape clones imported from Alsace, this wine typifies the adventurous spirit of Adelsheim. The nose shows chalky-flinty character, with peach and pretty floral notes. On the palate, white stone fruit and grapefruit emerge.

Anna Maria Chardonnay | 2006 | ROGUE VALLEY
★ ★ $ $ This premium label from Valley View Winery marks its 30th vintage of Chardonnay with this wonderfully flinty, smoky bottling, almost Chablis-like in its lean stature, crisp minerality and bright acidity woven with a hint of butterscotch and pear.

Anne Amie Vineyards Cuvee A Amrita | 2007 |
WILLAMETTE VALLEY
★ ★ $ Fresh and floral, with aromas of white peach, apricot and fresh-cut grass, this blend of Pinot Blanc, Müller-Thurgau, Chardonnay and Riesling features a zesty palate of grapefruit, more stone fruit and a crisp finish.

A to Z Pinot Gris | 2007 | OREGON
★ ★ $ A to Z's masterful blending of wines offers great value, as in this floral and stone fruit–laden Pinot Gris, whose mineral streak underscores its crisp, off-dry style. Watch for the producer's latest from the recently acquired Rex Hill Winery.

Benton Lane Pinot Gris | 2007 | WILLAMETTE VALLEY

★ $ $ This balanced, bright easy-to-drink white showcases a vibrant nose of grass and grapefruit. More citrus shows up on the palate, along with yellow apple and crisp pear.

Chateau Lorane Viognier | 2006 | OREGON

★ ★ $ $ This Viognier is almost mainstream compared to Chateau Lorane's more eccentric efforts (Melon de Bourgogne, Huxelrebe), but it's also a delight for its intense tangerine and petrol nose, lush, full body and interesting citrus and orange blossom flavors.

King Estate Signature Collection Pinot Gris | 2007 | OREGON

★ ★ $ $ Produced from a mix of organic and sustainably grown grapes, this Pinot Gris shows concentrated pear and apple fruit, a fresh flavorful palate of citrus and spice and wonderfully refreshing acidity with mineral nuances.

Methven Family Vineyards Chardonnay | 2006 | WILLAMETTE VALLEY

★ ★ $ $ The newest single-variety wine from this small family estate, this Chardonnay has aromas of tropical and sweet candied fruit, with an intriguing Riesling-like petrol quality. On the palate, it's medium-bodied with loads of red and green apples, finishing crisp.

RoxyAnn Pinot Gris | 2006 | ROGUE VALLEY

★ $ $ Founded in 2002, this family-run winery has hit its groove with this fresh, easy and pleasing wine. Creamy flavors of peach and mango are bright and mineral-laden on the finish.

Sienna Ridge Estate Gewürztraminer | 2006 | RED HILL DOUGLAS COUNTY

★ ★ $ This white is almost ostentatious in its aromatics, with heaps of flowers, sweet lychee and succulent peach. On the palate, it's juicy and refreshing, with stone fruit, bright acidity and a mineral edge.

Sokol Blosser Winery Evolution 12th Edition | NV | AMERICA

★ ★ $ $ Food-friendly and easy-drinking, Sokol Blosser's blend of nine white grapes has achieved an almost cultlike following. The latest version is typically aromatic, with pretty floral, spice and lychee nuances and loads of apple and nectarine fruit.

Willamette Valley Vineyards Riesling | 2007 | WILLAMETTE VALLEY

★ ★ ★ $ Wafts of citrus, apple, pear and jasmine mark this aromatic Riesling. Seductive flavors of juicy peach and apricot are slightly sweet, yet perfectly balanced by bright, refreshing acidity.

oregon reds

Oregon's Pinot Noirs are highly susceptible to vintage variation, especially in the Willamette Valley's challenging climate. The drier, hotter years of 2003 and 2006 produced a crop of bold, high-alcohol versions, while the cooler years of 2005 and 2007 tempered the grape's intensity and yielded subtler, more elegant and refined wines. Both Cabernet and Syrah seem to be finding a niche in the state's warmer southern regions, although the majority of Oregon's vintners continue to focus on Pinot Noir.

pinot noir recommendations

Adelsheim Calkins Lane Vineyard | 2006 |
CHEHALEM MOUNTAINS
★★★ $ $ $ This single-vineyard wine is made from multiple Pinot Noir clones, including new Burgundy clones and Oregon standbys. They manifest themselves in complex black cherry and berry aromas that evolve into spiced berry flavors underscored by smooth tannins.

Andrew Rich Vintner Reserve | 2006 | **WILLAMETTE VALLEY**
★★★★ $ $ $ Andrew Rich is one of several vintners working out of the Carlton Winemakers Studio, a "green" cooperative wine production facility. His Reserve Pinot explodes with gorgeous raspberry, blackberry and cherry from start to finish. Touches of cigar box and licorice make it even more interesting.

Atticus | 2006 | **WILLAMETTE VALLEY**
★★ $ $ Winemaker Scott Shull—of Raptor Ridge fame—had a hand in creating this elegant, earthy Pinot Noir. It's medium-bodied, with a bouquet of cherry, vanilla and cola, soft tannins and a lengthy finish.

Bethel Heights Flat Block | 2006 | **WILLAMETTE VALLEY**
★★ $ $ $ Located in the Eola-Amity Hills subappellation of Willamette Valley, Pinot Noir specialist Bethel Heights produces several delicious bottlings; this one has nicely layered cherry, huckleberry and blueberry fruit and pungent spice and forest floor aromas.

Boedecker Cellars Stewart | 2005 | **WILLAMETTE VALLEY**
★★ $ $ $ The small-production Boedecker Cellars sources fruit from throughout the valley to make this rich yet balanced Pinot. Filled with flavors of cherry, wild strawberries and a little tobacco, it offers delicious drinking and is food-friendly, too.

Carlton Hill | 2006 | YAMHILL-CARLTON DISTRICT
★★★ $ $ $ Just six acres in size, Carlton Hill's Dijon clone vineyard has yielded a wonderfully floral wine, gorgeous in its violet-berry aromas, with bright cherries and wild berries on the palate. Earth and tobacco linger on the finish.

Chehalem 3 Vineyard | 2006 | WILLAMETTE VALLEY
★★★ $ $ $ Combining grapes from three vineyards, this wine achieves the glorious trinity of great availability, reasonable price and delectable taste. Cherry, raspberry and vanilla dominate the nose, followed by black cherry, earth and pepper flavors and sweet tannins.

Domaine Serene Evenstad Reserve | 2005 |
WILLAMETTE VALLEY
★★★ $ $ $ The seven vineyards of Evenstad Estate range in elevation from 520 to 800 feet, giving this lush, delicious wine a diversity of flavors, from black fruit and plum to pomegranate.

star producers
oregon pinot noir

Adelsheim
David and Ginny Adelsheim established their Chehalem Mountains vineyard in 1972; today, Pinot expert Dave Paige continues to craft their richly textured, fruit-driven wines.

Andrew Rich
Andrew Rich spent six years at California's Bonny Doon Vineyard before moving to Oregon, where he makes beautiful Pinot Noirs and Rhône-style reds.

Domaine Serene
Ken and Grace Evenstad have been making some of Oregon's finest Pinots since they moved to the Willamette Valley in 1989.

Penner-Ash
Lynn Penner-Ash earned her winemaking reputation at Stag's Leap Wine Cellars and Rex Hill before launching her own label with impressive Pinot Noirs and Syrahs.

Retour
The winery may be new but the vines are among the Willamette Valley's oldest; winemaker Eric Hamacher is a seasoned crafter of supple, balanced Pinot Noirs.

Stoller
On land that was once a turkey farm, the Stollers planted Pinot Noir and Chardonnay in 1995; as it happens, their wines pair perfectly with turkey.

Firesteed | 2006 | OREGON
★ $ Fermented in stainless steel with Burgundian yeasts and then blended with a smidgen of barrel-aged wine, this youthful, bright and lively value wine offers a pleasant, juicy mouthful of black currants, raspberries and flinty minerals.

Lachini Ana Vineyard | 2006 | DUNDEE HILLS
★★★ $ $ $ With grapes coming from 28-year-old Pommard clones, this wine is richly layered and immensely drinkable, with smoked pork, red cherry, blackberry, earthy mushroom and forest floor aromas. It's heady and wonderful stuff with soft tannins.

Lachini S | 2006 | WILLAMETTE VALLEY
★★★ $ $ $ Peter Rosback of Sineann winery crafts this wine from the young estate vineyard at Lachini. It offers a dense, chewy core of black currant and plum, mingled with black pepper and gamey animal notes on the long finish.

Merriman Estate | 2006 | YAMHILL-CARLTON DISTRICT
★★★ $ $ $ With just over 100 cases produced, you'll have to act quickly for a taste of this supple Pinot, marked by flavors of huckleberry and blueberry, baking spice and toasty oak. The fine tannins and nice balance offer real elegance.

Penner-Ash | 2006 | WILLAMETTE VALLEY
★★★ $ $ $ This wine's cherry and berry fruit benefits from a dash of exotic spice and black pepper, a result of the exclusive use of French oak barrels. Its generous, dense fruit flavors carry through the lengthy finish, accented by notes of sweet vanilla.

Raptor Ridge Reserve | 2006 | WILLAMETTE VALLEY
★★ $ $ $ Thoughtful blending of grapes from throughout the valley results in an enjoyable wine with good texture and balance. Red and black fruit drive the palate, with hints of earth and leather, and the rather high alcohol level (15.2 percent) never reveals itself.

Retour | 2006 | WILLAMETTE VALLEY
★★★★ $ $ $ $ Eric Hamacher's meticulous winemaking shows in every aspect of this brilliant Pinot Noir, from the bright fruit aromas mixed with sweet spice, earth and rose petals to the muscular yet refreshing flavors of black raspberries, milk chocolate and smoky oak.

Rex Hill Reserve | 2006 | WILLAMETTE VALLEY
★★ $ $ $ This Willamette Valley wine has an abundance of dark fruit aromas—black cherry and blackberry—with an underlying earthiness. It's fresh and easy on the palate, with a lightly toasty oak finish.

Stoller Estate Grown Cathy's Reserve | 2004 | DUNDEE HILLS
★★★★ $ $ $ $ This small-production wine is worth its price tag. On the nose, it weaves together red fruit, charcoal smoke and violet aromas, while on the palate it achieves good balance given its considerable power, with hints of kirsch ending in a soft finish.

William Hatcher | 2006 | WILLAMETTE VALLEY
★★ $ $ $ The lone wine crafted personally by A to Z Wineworks and Rex Hill partner Bill Hatcher, this is very Burgundian in style, with spicy dried cherries and delicate fruit, alongside a touch of fresh soil. The palate is soft and supple with generous acidity.

washington state

Washington continues to search for a signature grape, though many now believe it will be Syrah. Yet as the country's second-largest wine producer, Washington is home to a wide range of varieties, which vintners use to make wines of excellent quality and often exceptional value. Syrah, Cabernet and Bordeaux-style blends dominate the state's red wine production. While Chardonnay is the most important white, Sauvignon Blanc, Riesling and Semillon also perform exceptionally well here.

Washington State: An Overview

Most winemaking in Washington takes place inland, where vineyards are sheltered from the coastal weather by the Cascade Range and enjoy sunny, relatively dry summers. The state's largest region is the Columbia Valley, which encompasses many prominent subregions, including Yakima Valley, Red Mountain and Walla Walla Valley (the last of which straddles the border with Oregon).

Washington State Wine Labels

Washington wine labels include basic information such as grape variety, winery, vintage and region where the grapes were grown. Some Washington wines are blends of Bordeaux grape varieties and are labeled "Meritage" (see p. 160), which is rare in the U.S. outside of California; other wineries give proprietary names to their signature blends.

washington state whites

Washington was a white-wine-centric state before its reds gained success. The often chilly summer nights allow vintners to produce crisp, citrusy Chardonnays, which display a lighter, more refreshing texture compared to the full-bodied California style. Riesling also grows well under these conditions, producing wines with vivid fruit flavors, complemented by floral aromas and either a dry or off-dry taste profile. Crisp, refreshing and often possessing a hint of sweetness, Washington Chenin Blanc is a nice surprise, as is Sauvignon Blanc, with its trademark herbal and grassy flavors that don't overwhelm the palate.

washington state white recommendations

Abeja Chardonnay | 2006 | **WASHINGTON STATE**
★ ★ $ $ $ Located just a few miles outside the town of Walla Walla, Abeja makes this creamy, balanced Chardonnay with butter, macadamia and caramel flavors, highlighted by apple and bright acidity.

Andrew Rich Vintner Roussanne | 2006 | **COLUMBIA VALLEY**
★ ★ ★ $ $ Relatively unknown in Washington, Roussanne shows real potential in this delicious pear- and floral-scented white. It's plump and lush on the palate with apricot flavors and good acidity.

Buty Sémillon/Sauvignon Blanc | 2006 | **COLUMBIA VALLEY**
★ ★ $ $ This traditional blend of Bordeaux grapes has all the juicy, thirst-quenching character you'd expect from a New World wine. Bright tangerine and melon aromas give way to a palate of grapefruit and a zesty, spicy finish.

Forgeron Cellars Chardonnay | 2006 | **COLUMBIA VALLEY**
★ $ $ A sure crowd-pleaser, this crisp Chardonnay with lively acidity leads off with smoky oak and minerals, then offers green apple and citrus flavors, courtesy of a small addition of Orange Muscat.

Hogue Riesling | 2006 | **COLUMBIA VALLEY**
★ $ One of Washington State's largest wineries makes this delicious everyday Riesling. Green apple, white flower and a whiff of petrol join off-dry apple juice and apricot nectar flavors, with plenty of zingy acidity to balance the sweetness.

Milbrandt Vineyards Legacy Evergreen Chardonnay | 2006 |
WASHINGTON STATE
★ ★ $ $ Part of longtime grape-growers Butch and Jerry Milbrandt's
new line of eponymous wines, this Chardonnay is tropical, with mango
and banana turning to green apple on the palate and vanilla and oak
on the finish.

Pacific Rim Dry Riesling | NV | **WASHINGTON STATE**
★ ★ $ Riesling devotee Pacific Rim produces both sweet and dry ver-
sions of the variety; their dry Riesling—made with 80 percent Washington State grapes and 20 percent from Germany's Mosel region—
combines classic apple and bright citrus flavors with a crisp finish.

Poet's Leap Riesling | 2007 | **COLUMBIA VALLEY**
★ ★ $ $ Quite rare for Riesling, this wine is partially (just 3 percent
of the blend) fermented in oak. The result is gorgeous: Spiced-pear,
melon and flinty aromas are followed by a slightly off-dry palate, with
sweet apricot flavors and zesty acidity.

Stonecap Monson Family Estates Riesling | 2006 |
COLUMBIA VALLEY
★ $ This pretty wine, bottled under the Stonecap label, comes from
grapes grown on the Monson family's esteemed Goose Ridge Vineyard. It has basketfuls of stone fruit aromas and flavors—apricot and
peach—along with crisp apple and flinty notes and a touch of petrol.

Waterbrook Mélange Blanc | 2006 | **COLUMBIA VALLEY**
★ ★ $ Waterbrook's aromatic blend gets its perfumey quality from
Viognier and lychee-scented Gewürztraminer. Pink grapefruit on the
palate makes for a captivating and beautifully balanced wine.

washington state reds

Merlot continues to be one of Washington's primary red
grapes but is increasingly used in blends. Cabernet and
especially Syrah have risen to the top ranks of fine red wines
coming out of Washington. The best Cabernet Sauvignons,
Cabernet Francs and Bordeaux-style blends exhibit smooth
textures and bold fruit flavors. Syrah, Washington's bright-
est up-and-comer, can be more subtle here than elsewhere,
though it still displays exuberant spiciness. While vintners
have experimented with varieties like Sangiovese and Nebbiolo, the only other red really worth mentioning is Lemberger, a fruity, low-acid wine meant to be enjoyed young.

washington state red recommendations

Amavi Cellars Syrah | 2005 | WALLA WALLA VALLEY

★ $ $ Slow to reveal itself, this Syrah shows real Rhône character once it opens, with smoked meat and bacon-fat aromas drizzled with cassis, a ripe core of blackberry and earth, and refined tannins.

Cayuse Vineyards Cailloux Vineyard Syrah | 2004 | WALLA WALLA VALLEY

★★★★ $ $ $ $ This is an absolute blockbuster, with incredibly dense fruit flavors—like the filling of a blueberry pie—along with chocolate and allspice. The texture is silky, syrupy and viscous, with nicely integrated oak and a touch of gamey meat.

Columbia Winery Red Willow Vineyard Cabernet Sauvignon | 2004 | YAKIMA VALLEY

★ $ $ Founded in 1962, Columbia Winery offers both experience and value. Their juicy Cabernet is well structured, with black and red fruit, a sour cherry quality, hints of spice and pepper and sweet tannins.

Dunham Cellars Lewis Vineyard Merlot | 2005 | COLUMBIA VALLEY

★★★ $ $ $ $ This excellent single-vineyard wine shows dense, chewy fruit with blueberry, blackberry and sweet, brandied flavors that are nicely balanced by fine tannins and a cedary finish.

Goose Ridge Vineyards Cabernet Sauvignon | 2005 | COLUMBIA VALLEY

★★★ $ $ Made with 9 percent Malbec, this full-bodied Cab could almost be from Rutherford (California), with its fine, dusty tannins and ripe berry fruit. Mocha and mint aromas and some olive and leafy notes round out the beautifully long finish.

Hogue Reserve Cabernet Sauvignon | 2004 | COLUMBIA VALLEY

★★ $ $ At the top of Hogue's range of wines is its Reserve line, which includes this Cab, layered with cherry and raspberry aromas and whiffs of wet leaves, sweet tobacco and spice. On the palate, fresh berry and dried cherry meet earth and sage.

Kiona Reserve Syrah | 2003 | RED MOUNTAIN

★★★ $ $ Located within the Yakima Valley (which is within the Columbia Valley), Washington's smallest AVA, Red Mountain, serves up this fruity and floral Syrah, fragrant with violet, hyacinth, baking spice and black peppercorns. Gorgeous blueberry fruit drives the flavor.

L'Ecole Nº 41 Seven Hills Vineyard Syrah | 2006 |
WALLA WALLA VALLEY
★★★ $ $ $ The 220-acre Seven Hills Vineyard provides fruit for several wines, which all show dense black fruit like this one; pine needle, licorice, mineral and cocoa flavors add complexity.

The Magnificent Wine Co. House Wine Red | 2006 |
COLUMBIA VALLEY
★★ $ With spice-rack aromas reminiscent of Christmas cake and plum pudding, this refreshing red blend is an excellent bargain. Nicely integrated fruit develops into vanilla and oak on the finish.

Nicholas Cole Cellars Michele | 2005 | **COLUMBIA VALLEY**
★★★ $ $ $ Cabernets Sauvignon and Franc, Merlot and Petit Verdot make up this dark and decadent red. Its bright fruit and lean tannins are wrapped in black cherry, caramel and molten chocolate aromas accented with some pipe tobacco and earth.

star producers
washington state reds

Cayuse Vineyards
Having grown up in a Champagne house in France (Baron Albert), Christophe Baron brings years of experience to his stony-soiled Walla Walla vineyards, where he makes earthy, complex reds.

Dunham Cellars
Hand-harvesting grapes from some of Washington's finest vineyards, Dunham crafts elegant, ageworthy wines.

Goose Ridge Vineyards
Winemaker Charlie Hoppes renders multilayered and much-praised wines from relatively young vines at this Columbia Valley estate.

L'Ecole Nº 41
Produced just outside of Walla Walla in what was once a schoolhouse in historic Frenchtown, L'Ecole Nº 41's rich, full-bodied reds earn A's under managing winemaker Marty Clubb's tutelage.

The Magnificent Wine Co.
Deceptively simple labels and under-$15 price tags belie the quality of these handsome Columbia Valley wines.

Sol Duc
Precept Wine Brands went to one of the best—Goose Ridge—to source grapes and skill for Sol Duc's well-balanced Bordeaux-style blends.

Novelty Hill Merlot | 2005 | COLUMBIA VALLEY
★★ $ $ Red and black fruit, licorice and burnt matches along with some slightly savory bell pepper and sage make this an intriguing Merlot. The red fruit lingers on the palate, while youthful tannins provide good structure and grip.

Otis Kenyon Syrah | 2005 | WALLA WALLA VALLEY
★★ $ $ This delicious Syrah is ripe with black cherry and prunes, flavors of hickory smoke and bacon fat and touches of violet. It's incredibly lush on the palate with nicely integrated vanilla and oak.

Reininger Merlot | 2003 | WALLA WALLA VALLEY
★★ $ $ With black fruit, mocha, an herbal, minty quality and wisps of smoke, this big Merlot shows complexity and intensity, turning to cassis on the palate. Time in both French and American oak contributes good tannic grip and a bit of dill on the finish.

Sequel Syrah | 2005 | COLUMBIA VALLEY
★★ $ $ $ Crafted by winemaker John Duval, who for 15 years brought us Australia's iconic Penfolds Grange, this wine has a dense blueberry core wrapped in earth, cedar and mocha. With bright acidity, it's all-around lovely.

Sol Duc Goose Ridge Estate Meritage | 2004 | COLUMBIA VALLEY
★★★ $ $ $ This classic Bordeaux-style blend of Cabernet and Merlot is tarlike, with black fruit, licorice and hints of pine. The chewy fruit and sweet, firm tannins are nicely integrated.

Tamarack Cellars Merlot | 2006 | COLUMBIA VALLEY
★★★ $ $ Careful blending of grapes from the best vineyards makes this a complex Merlot, with a spicy cinnamon-chocolate, cassis and black cherry nose. Big tannins arrive on the palate and power through the long finish. It's also refreshingly moderate in alcohol.

Trio Vintners Sangiovese | 2006 | WALLA WALLA COUNTY
★★★ $ $ This wine's sour cherry pie fruit, hints of spice and intriguing leather and deli-meat character are a testament to the potential of Sangiovese in Washington. Grippy tannins and zippy acidity make it ideal for food.

Waterbrook Reserve Syrah | 2006 | COLUMBIA VALLEY
★★★ $ $ Rich, dark and supple, this Syrah is a blueberry-and-milk-chocolate smoothie with a shot of espresso for good measure. The wine includes a small amount of Mourvèdre, adding to its Rhône impression, fine tannins and lingering dark fruit.

other united states

While California is in no danger of losing its place as the country's largest wine producer (second-place Washington State accounts for less than 5 percent of the national wine total), new wineries are appearing across America. Although they try to emulate the success of California and the Pacific Northwest, winemakers in the rest of the country struggle with issues of climate, soil, restrictive trade laws and a highly competitive wine market. A handful, however, are achieving great success.

Other United States: An Overview

Of all the problems facing vintners in the majority of American states, climate is probably the most troublesome. While there may be plenty of inexpensive land to be had, much of it is affected by the country's notoriously cold winters and/or hot, humid summers, conditions that can sustain certain native grape varieties, but spell trouble for traditional European *Vitis vinifera* (Chardonnay, Cabernet, etc.).

Winemakers outside of the country's principal wine-producing states are often forced to choose between growing the generally lower-quality native American or hybrid grapes that may perform well in their region's climate, or trying to work with European grapes that may not thrive in less than ideal soil and weather conditions. One state where winemakers don't have to make this choice is New York. Its two main wine regions, the east end of Long Island and areas in the northern part of the state surrounding the Finger Lakes, experience temperatures that are moderated by nearby bodies of water, conditions in which European *Vitis vinifera* grapes fare well. Long Island produces some exceptional Merlot, Cabernet Franc, Chardonnay and Sauvignon Blanc, while areas surrounding the Finger Lakes produce noteworthy Chardonnay, Riesling, Gewürztraminer and Pinot Noir.

Outside of New York, wine regions are developing in northeastern states such as New Jersey, Connecticut and Rhode Island. Parts of Pennsylvania are capable of producing good wines from European varieties. The same is true of Virginia, where a surprisingly large number of successful wineries are moving away from local hybrid grapes toward *vinifera* varieties such as Chardonnay and the red Bordeaux varieties. In the hot southwest, Arizona, perhaps the most unexpected wine producer, is currently focusing on Rhône Valley varieties. Texas, too, is making considerable quantities of *vinifera*-based white and red wines. New Mexico's high-elevation vineyards are the source of fine sparkling wines as well as some nice reds crafted from Cabernet, Merlot and Pinot Noir.

Still, many wineries in Virginia, North Carolina, Missouri, Ohio and other states continue to rely on hybrid or native grape varieties such as Baco Noir, Concord, Seyval Blanc, Vignoles and Vidal Blanc to make wines that are sold mostly to visitors as part of local tourist industries. With the increasing popularity of wine in America and the dedication of many local governments to bringing modern viticulture to their states, the future is looking bright for many of these small U.S. winemakers.

other u.s. whites & rosés

Parts of the northeast—especially New York's Finger Lakes region—enjoy ideal conditions for growing Riesling and Gewürztraminer. Chardonnay and Sauvignon Blanc benefit from the slightly longer growing season on Long Island, where some lovely sparkling wines and dry, crisp rosés are also crafted. Hybrid grapes such as Vidal Blanc are used to make delicious dessert wines in New York, Virginia and Texas. Despite a relatively warm, humid growing season, Virginia's winemakers are producing a number of high-quality, dry white wines from Chardonnay, Viognier and other *vinifera* grapes. With a growing season marked by cool nights and warm, dry days, Idaho is also a source of many good *vinifera*-based whites.

other u.s. white & rosé recommendations

Bedell Cellars Taste White | 2006 |
NORTH FORK OF LONG ISLAND, NEW YORK

★ ★ ★ $ $ This wonderfully layered blend of Chardonnay, Sauvignon Blanc, Viognier, Gewürztraminer and Riesling brims with aromatic white flowers, red apples and ripe peaches.

Benmarl Winery Seyval Blanc | 2007 |
HUDSON RIVER REGION, NEW YORK

★ $ Seyval Blanc is considered one of the most dependable and hard-working grapes among the French-American hybrids that survive the cold Northeast winters. In this crisp, clean wine, it boasts citrus and pear aromas and creamy red apple flavors.

Callaghan Vineyards Lisa's Proprietary White | 2006 |
SONOITA, ARIZONA

★ ★ $ $ Though the Callaghan family originally focused on Bordeaux grapes in the 1990s, they've since explored other European varieties with greater success. Here, Viognier, Riesling, Marsanne, Roussanne and Malvasia Bianca create a floral, juicy peach-flavored wine that's full-bodied and complex.

Chaddsford Philip Roth Vineyard Chardonnay | 2005 |
PENNSYLVANIA

★ ★ $ $ $ This is a powerful, aromatic New World Chardonnay from an unlikely place. Toasted hazelnut, smoky vanilla and red delicious apple in the nose lead to a well-balanced mouthful of wine with bright citrus acidity and creamy oak.

Corey Creek Chardonnay | 2006 |
NORTH FORK OF LONG ISLAND, NEW YORK

★ ★ $ $ The lovely citrus and honeysuckle aromas might lead you to guess this is Viognier, but the crisp Granny Smith and apple pie spices confirm it's Chardonnay, and a good one at that.

Gruet Barrel Select Unfiltered Chardonnay | 2006 |
NEW MEXICO

★ ★ $ $ Citrus zest and fresh pear dominate the nose of this crisp, minerally, unfiltered Chardonnay from one of the best sparkling wine producers in the West—outside of California. Moderate contact with oak lends the slightest hint of vanilla to the wine, but it's otherwise clean and refreshing.

Hermann J. Wiemer Reserve Chardonnay | 2003 |
FINGER LAKES, NEW YORK

★★ $ $ While the Wiemer estate, under its German founder, is best known for excellent Rieslings, it also capably handles Chardonnay, conjuring soft vanilla and acacia aromas with flavors of apricot and good acidity on the light, crisp palate.

Horton Vineyards Rkatsiteli | 2007 |
ORANGE COUNTY, VIRGINIA

★★★ $ The most widely planted grape in the country of Georgia, Rkatsiteli seems more than at home in Virginia, if this honeysuckle-scented white is any indication. Horton's luscious bottling is full of apple, pear and orange fruit, all balanced with fresh citrusy acidity.

Hunt Country Vineyards Dry Riesling | 2006 |
FINGER LAKES, NEW YORK

★★ $ Over the course of six generations, the Hunt family made its name crafting ice wines, and now they make quality dry wines, too. The petrol and chalk on the nose of this dry Riesling are straight out of Alsace; the ripe green apple flavors, however, are all American.

Konstantin D. Frank & Sons Salmon Run Riesling | 2007 |
NEW YORK

★ $ Dr. Konstantin Frank had a vision for growing great European wine grapes in New York and this Riesling is part of the fruition of his dream, with its solid stone fruit and white flower nose and lovely ripe peach palate, finishing soft and clean.

Lieb Reserve Pinot Blanc | 2006 |
NORTH FORK OF LONG ISLAND, NEW YORK

★★ $ $ Made from the oldest Lieb vines, dating to 1983, this is crisp, clean, easy-drinking stuff, perfect for a balmy afternoon in the back-yard. Its flavors of honeydew melon meet zesty lemon on the palate.

Macari Reserve Chardonnay | 2005 |
NORTH FORK OF LONG ISLAND, NEW YORK

★★★ $ $ Located on a 500-acre waterfront estate, Macari crafts this creamy yet balanced Chard. It is medium-bodied, with sweet-toasty vanilla, tangerine and creamsicle on the nose and summery, citrus-kissed white peaches in the mouth.

Millbrook Chardonnay | 2006 | NEW YORK STATE

★★ $ $ This Chardonnay marks the 21st vintage for owners John and Kathe Dyson and Millbrook Vineyards & Winery. Made from grapes from three New York regions, it shows aromas of herbs and fragrant spices and crisp citrusy flavors.

Stone Hill Winery Reserve Chardonel | 2006 | **MISSOURI**
★ ★ $ $ A 12-month sojourn in small French oak barrels is the calling card of this heady, buttery, pear-kissed white made with Chardonel (a hybrid grape developed in the 1950s by crossing Chardonnay and Seyval). The result is a rich, creamy, delicious wine.

Zhoo Zhoo Reserve Chardonnay | 2006 |
SNAKE RIVER VALLEY, IDAHO
★ ★ $ $ Part of a playful series of wines created by three sisters and featuring labels by artist Babette Beatty, this barrel-fermented beauty offers generous aromas of quince and Granny Smith apples.

ROSÉS

Channing Daughters Croteau Farm Vineyard Rosato di Cabernet Franc | 2007 | **NORTH FORK OF LONG ISLAND, NEW YORK**
★ $ $ This crisp, dry pink wine boasts tropical-floral aromas spritzed with citrus. Medium-bodied, with bright acidity and lean minerality, it screams for summer sipping around a raw bar full of chilled shellfish.

Wölffer Rosé Table Wine | 2007 | **THE HAMPTONS, NEW YORK**
★ ★ $ Given winemaker Roman Roth's talent with Merlot, it's not surprising that he included some in this lovely, dry rosé (rounded out with Chardonnay and Cabernets Sauvignon and Franc). Strawberry and raspberry aromas are followed by citrus notes and dry minerals.

other u.s. reds

A growing number of quality red wines are coming out of states other than California, Washington and Oregon. In New York's Long Island, vintners rely mainly on Cabernet Sauvignon, Merlot and Cabernet Franc, with the latter two showing particular promise. Delicate Pinot Noir fares better in the Finger Lakes region farther north. In Virginia, local grapes such as Norton are grown alongside increasing amounts of *vinifera,* especially Cabernet and Merlot, but also Tannat, the powerful red grape from France's Madiran region, which has found a home in the state's gravelly soils. In the relatively hot regions of Texas and Arizona, sturdy Merlot and Cabernet vines thrive, and Grenache, Mourvèdre, Tempranillo and Sangiovese are capable of some truly interesting wines. Pinot Noir does surprisingly well in New Mexico's high-elevation vineyards.

other u.s. red recommendations

Barboursville Vineyards Reserve Nebbiolo | 2004 | **VIRGINIA**
★★★ $ $ $ Italy's famed Zonin family set up shop in Virginia in 1976 and have proven again and again that there's good wine to be had from the Old Dominion. Here, winemaker Luca Paschina has crafted a Piedmont-inspired red with black cherry and violet aromas and berry and tobacco flavors that go on and on.

Bedell Musée | 2005 | **NORTH FORK OF LONG ISLAND, NEW YORK**
★★★★ $ $ $ $ Bedell's newest wine is an impressive blend of Merlot, Cabernet Sauvignon and Petit Verdot. Aromas of sweet spice and black fruit arrive first, building intensity on the palate with layers of black and red fruit and silky, generous tannins.

Benmarl Estate Red Baco Noir | 2007 |
HUDSON RIVER REGION, NEW YORK
★★ $ $ Benmarl is the current name of a vineyard established in the mid-1800s, making it one of our nation's oldest. The viticulture practiced there, however, is thoroughly modern, as evidenced by this toothsome red with black cherries and soft, well-integrated tannins.

Brotherhood Pinot Noir | 2005 | **NEW YORK**
★★ $ Brotherhood claims to be America's oldest winery—John Jaques produced the first commercial vintage there in 1839—but some beg to differ. What is without doubt is that this lovely violet- and black cherry–scented Pinot possesses mouthwatering fruit, nice minerality and a fine, balanced finish.

Callaghan Vineyards Padres | 2005 | **SONOITA, ARIZONA**
★★ $ $ Spain's Tempranillo grape headlines in what would otherwise be a typical Bordeaux blend of Cabernet Sauvignon, Petit Verdot and Cabernet Franc. Fresh-cut herbs, red currants and black cherry aromas and flavors balance the fine tannins in the finish.

Chaddsford Merlot | 2005 | **PENNSYLVANIA**
★ $ $ The Keystone State's most famous winery has been demonstrating for more than a quarter century that Pennsylvania wines deserve attention. This Merlot is no exception, with its smoky, red berry fruit aromas and black pepper and red cherry jam flavors.

Gruet Cuvée Gilbert Gruet Pinot Noir | 2006 | **NEW MEXICO**
★★ $ $ A fitting tribute to the Gruet family patriarch, this Pinot is a gathering of cherry, black pepper and earthy-sweet spice aromas that grow more complex over time. Spicy, with raspberry and cherry nuances, it finishes dry, with a touch of chocolate on the palate.

Horton Vineyards Pinotage | 2006 |
ORANGE COUNTY, VIRGINIA

★★ $ $ Pinotage—a cross between Pinot Noir and Cinsault—is South Africa's signature red wine grape. In this Virginian example, it yields a dark, spicy red wine with savory nuances and a touch of bitter herbs in the otherwise fruity finish.

Kluge Estate New World Red Wine | 2004 |
ALBEMARLE COUNTY, VIRGINIA

★★ $ $ $ Consulting winemaker Michel Rolland had a hand in this blend from Thomas Jefferson's home state, and it's imbued with Rolland's signature New World characteristics: ripe black fruit aromas with highlights of cassis, sweet spice, vanilla and eucalyptus.

Macari Cabernet Franc | 2004 |
NORTH FORK OF LONG ISLAND, NEW YORK

★★★ $ $ Blackberries and dusty, earthy aromas compete for attention on the nose of this delicious North Fork Cabernet Franc. Sweet, ripe berry fruit in the mouth takes on spice and a touch of vanilla as it heads toward a balanced, succulent finish.

Pellegrini Vineyards Vintner's Pride Encore | 2005 |
NORTH FORK OF LONG ISLAND, NEW YORK

★★★ $ $ $ The name of this peppery red is completely appropriate: After the first sip you'll keep going back for more red currant and dusty sage aromas, more red berry fruit balanced by tealike tannins, more hints of sweet tobacco.

Shinn Estate Vineyards Nine Barrels Reserve Merlot
| 2005 | **NORTH FORK OF LONG ISLAND, NEW YORK**

★★★ $ $ $ Ex-Manhattan restaurateurs Barbara Shinn and David Page have found their calling as winemakers, as this delicious Merlot attests. Figs, sweet spices, violets and vanilla aromas lead to cherry pie and blackberry confiture flavors that come in powerful waves.

Stone Hill Winery Norton | 2005 | HERMANN, MISSOURI

★★ $ $ This sweet, spicy red is made with a native North American grape called Norton; thanks to its success in Missouri, it also happens to be the official state grape. Stone Hill's rendering is medium-bodied and well balanced, with blackberry fruit and lively acidity.

Wölffer Cabernet Franc | 2004 | THE HAMPTONS, NEW YORK

★★★ $ $ $ The principal grape of France's Chinon seems to fare well in the Hamptons. Here it takes on bell pepper and black cherry aromas spiked with cracked black pepper, then bursts with blueberry and blackberry flavors, followed by chocolate on the finish.

australia

The surge of growth in Australian wine production over the past ten years or so has been nothing short of phenomenal. Today, Australia is home to the sixth-largest wine industry in the world. By embracing technological innovation and savvy marketing strategies and displaying an untiring dedication to their craft, Australian vintners not only dominate the bargain-priced wine landscape, they are also producing wines that are among the world's finest.

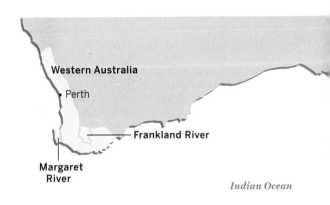

Western Australia

Perth

Frankland River

Margaret River

Indian Ocean

Principal Wine Region

Australia: An Overview

With more than 2,000 wineries spread across its six wine-producing states, Australia takes advantage of its varied climate and geography. South Australia is the undisputed hub of the industry. The Barossa Valley is responsible for much of the country's acclaimed Shiraz, while Coonawarra is ideal for Cabernet. Tasmania and Victoria produce excellent, cool-climate wines including many elegant Pinot Noirs. Yarra Valley, near Melbourne, continues to perfect delicate Pinot Noirs and Chardonnays, as well as some interesting Sauvignon Blancs. The Hunter Valley region in New South Wales is known for its Shiraz, Semillon, Cabernet and Chardonnay. Chardonnay also shines in the New South Wales district of Tumbarumba, whose high-altitude vineyards yield some of Australia's greatest whites. For other quality whites, look to the Clare and Eden Valleys and the Margaret River.

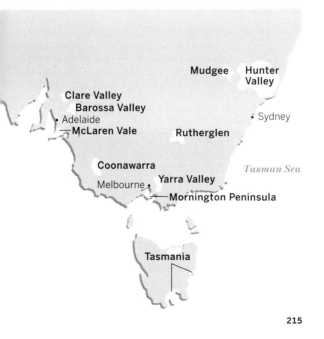

Australian Wine Labels

Australian labels specify producer, region, vintage and variety. Blends are named with the dominant grape listed first.

australian whites

White wines account for around 40 percent of Australia's production. The most popular white is Chardonnay, which winemakers craft in a wide variety of styles. Also grown are Riesling, Semillon and Sauvignon Blanc, as well as lesser-known varieties such as Verdelho and Colombard.

AUSTRALIAN WHITES

chardonnay

Australia was slow to embrace Chardonnay. Little of it was planted there until the early 1980s, yet today it is the country's primary white grape. Chardonnay is made into simple fruity wines as well as lush, complex masterpieces. Lighter-bodied versions hail from cooler regions, like South Australia's Adelaide Hills, Mornington Peninsula in Victoria and Tasmania. Chardonnays from the Margaret River region express exquisite elegance, while voluptuous examples are made in South Australia's Riverland, as well as the Hunter Valley, Mudgee and Riverina regions of New South Wales.

chardonnay recommendations

Giaconda Estate Vineyard | 2005 | **VICTORIA**
★★★ $ $ $ $ From vineyards located in the foothills of the Victorian Alps comes this plush, full-bodied Chardonnay brimming with powerful fruit flavors and balanced with minerals and acidity.

Giant Steps Sexton Vineyard | 2005 | **YARRA VALLEY**
★★ $ $ The crisp, cool conditions and gravelly soils of the Yarra Valley's slopes yield this tasty wine with flavors of nectarine, citrus, melon and peach offset by white pepper and lemon undertones.

Grant Burge Barossa Vines Unoaked | 2006 | **BAROSSA**
★★ $ The southern Barossa's premium terroir imparts creamy, buttery flavors to this full-bodied though balanced wine.

Hope Estate | 2006 | HUNTER VALLEY
★ $ Buttery, rich and round, Hope Estate's Hunter Valley Chardonnay oozes simple pleasure in the form of toasty oak and citrus flavors with a creamy, vanilla-accented finish.

Innocent Bystander | 2006 | YARRA VALLEY
★★ $ $ Former Devil's Lair owner-winemaker Phil Sexton set up shop in the Yarra Valley to build a sprawling, state-of-the-art, gravity-fed winery where he makes this elegant, mineral-laden Chardonnay noted for its appealing stone fruit flavors.

Jacob's Creek Reserve | 2006 | SOUTH AUSTRALIA
★ $ Jacob's Creek has been Australia's leading export brand for more than a decade, thanks to crowd-pleasing wines like this one; crisp and light, it shows lime and pear flavors with a balanced finish.

Slipstream | 2006 | ADELAIDE HILLS
★★ $ $ Winemaker Stephen Pannell ages this round, juicy peach- and pear-scented Chardonnay in neutral French oak barrels to produce a pure wine that expresses the grapes' inherent fruit flavors.

Stonier Reserve | 2005 | MORNINGTON PENINSULA
★★ $ $ $ Stonier's Chardonnay vines are planted on protected north- and northeast-facing slopes on the chilly, sea wind–blasted Mornington Peninsula. The stony, volcanic soils give the grapes fresh, mineral-flecked flavors, as in this apple- and lemon-scented wine.

Yalumba Y Series Unwooded | 2007 | SOUTH AUSTRALIA
★ $ Now in their sixth generation of winemaking, Yalumba's Smith family focuses on the sustainability of natural resources. Their techniques are reflected in this rich, tropical fruit– and peach-scented wine; its melon and peach flavors are followed by a soft finish.

other australian whites

Riesling is Australia's second most important white wine. The Clare Valley produces mainly dry versions with mineral flavors and an ability to age nicely. Good Sauvignon Blanc can also be found in Australia, though the Semillon grape fares better, often yielding dry wines with intriguing honey flavors. Rhône grape varieties Marsanne, Roussanne and Viognier are sometimes bottled on their own but generally used in blends. The Portuguese grape Verdelho is widely grown, but produces only a few noteworthy examples.

other australian white recommendations

Betts & Scholl Riesling | 2007 | EDEN VALLEY
★ ★ ★ **$ $** Colorado sommelier Richard Betts and venture capitalist and art collector Dennis Scholl collaborated with Australian wine-maker Trevor Jones on this gorgeous Riesling full of pear and citrus aromas, elegant minerality and crisp acidity.

d'Arenberg The Hermit Crab Viognier/Marsanne | 2006 | MCLAREN VALE
★ ★ ★ **$ $** d'Arenberg named this Rhône grape blend "The Hermit Crab" as a nod to the calcareous deposits of prehistoric sea creatures that enhance the soil of many McLaren Vale vineyards. In this expression, Viognier and Marsanne take on rich, luscious flavors of tropical fruit balanced by fresh grapefruit notes.

Glen Eldon Wines Riesling | 2005 | EDEN VALLEY
★ ★ **$ $** The Eden Valley has a long history of producing high-quality Rieslings, and Glen Eldon makes one of the area's finest; spicy citrus aromas are grounded by mineral flavors and mouthwatering acidity.

Hanenhof Viognier | 2005 | BAROSSA VALLEY
★ ★ **$ $** Viognier is still relatively rare in Australia, but this beautifully made wine suggests there should be more. Produced from some of the first-planted Viognier vines in Barossa, it offers quince, melon and pear flavors with tropical highlights.

Kaesler Viognier | 2006 | BAROSSA VALLEY
★ ★ ★ **$ $** Although the Kaeslers planted vines in the Barossa Valley as long ago as 1893, this full-bodied Viognier, bursting with succulent peach and apricot flavors, is made from a tiny plot of grapes planted just eight years ago.

Petaluma Hanlin Hill Riesling | 2007 | CLARE VALLEY
★ ★ ★ **$ $** This exceptional Riesling gives credence to the claim that Clare Valley produces the best Rieslings on the continent. Delicious ripe white peach flavors predominate, filled out with notes of lime zest and balancing acidity.

Peter Lehmann Riesling | 2007 | EDEN VALLEY
★ ★ ★ **$ $** Peter Lehmann's Riesling is crafted from grapes grown on the cooler slopes of the Eden Valley. The superb terroir results in this stunning wine, rich with honey and zesty citrus flavors underscored by a firm minerality.

Pewsey Vale Individual Vineyard Selection Riesling | 2007 |
EDEN VALLEY

★ $ $ The 2007 vintage in Australia's Eden Valley was warmer and drier than normal, causing these Riesling grapes to ripen almost a full month earlier than usual. Remarkably, this wine retains good acidity, which supports lush, ripe fruit flavors.

Poonawatta Estate The Eden Riesling | 2006 | EDEN VALLEY

★ ★ ★ $ $ Although Poonawatta is known for their cool-climate Shiraz, they produce some magnificent Riesling, too. This powerful wine is made with grapes from vines that are more than 30 years old, and it delivers wonderfully vibrant flavors of lime, pronounced acidity and a lengthy finish.

St Hallett Poacher's Blend Semillon/Sauvignon Blanc/ Riesling | 2007 | BAROSSA

★ $ This delicious medium-dry white blend is made from a combination of Semillon, Sauvignon Blanc and Riesling grapes picked at night, while the air is cool, which yields a crisp, tropical fruit–flavored wine that's immensely drinkable.

Stonehaven Winemaker's Selection Riesling | 2006 |
SOUTH AUSTRALIA

★ $ Abundant and refreshing mineral notes run throughout the bold, ripe stone fruit and fresh white peach flavors in this lovely, citrus-scented Riesling.

Wakefield Riesling | 2005 | CLARE VALLEY

★ ★ $ $ Subtle aromas of petrol give way to generous, full-bodied flavors of zesty lemon, lime and grapefruit followed by an impressively long finish.

australian reds

Robust, ripe, berry-flavored Shiraz is Australia's claim to wine fame, though Cabernet Sauvignon is widely produced and performs well in many regions. Merlot plantings have increased significantly, though the grape has yet to yield results on a par with the country's Shiraz and Cabernet Sauvignon. There is a niche-following for some high-quality Pinot Noirs from a handful of the country's cooler wine regions, and the more obscure varieties of Grenache and Mourvèdre are gaining ground, especially in McLaren Vale and the Barossa Valley.

AUSTRALIAN REDS

cabernet sauvignon

Cabernet Sauvignon may be second to Shiraz in popularity among Australians when it comes to red wine, but it is still held in high esteem and is responsible for producing many of the country's most exceptional reds. Australian Cabernets run the gamut from simple, often over-acidified wines to wonderfully ripe, full-bodied and fruit-driven examples; the finest are capable of extensive aging. The country's warmer regions tend to highlight berry and chocolate flavors, while cooler climes enhance the grape's mineral qualities. Western Australian regions, like Margaret River, produce refined Cabernets. Some of the very best Cabernets hail from the relatively tiny region of Coonawarra in South Australia.

cabernet sauvignon recommendations

Faldo Nick Faldo Selection | 2005 | COONAWARRA
★★ $ Named for golfer Nick Faldo, this Cabernet shows classic Coonawarra character, with big, black fruit (plums and berries), hints of peppery spice and a distinctive minty quality topped off with nice balance and obvious craftsmanship.

Henschke Cyril Henschke | 2003 | EDEN VALLEY
★★★★ $ $ $ $ The typically cool Eden Valley is home to fifth-generation winemaker Stephen Henschke, who, with his wife, Prue, acting as viticulturist, crafts legendary red wines, including this plush Cab filled with dense plum and prune and notes of sage and thyme.

John's Blend No. 31 Individual Selection | 2004 |
LANGHORNE CREEK
★★ $ $ $ This New World Cabernet is a product of winemaker John Glaetzer, who lists more than 30 years with Wolf Blass on his résumé. Initially soft and plush on the palate, the wine finishes with firm but pleasant tannins.

Penley Estate Phoenix | 2005 | COONAWARRA
★★ $ $ Showcasing the estate's trademark balance, Penley's Cabernet offers ripe cherry fruit, with pretty black pepper spice and anise aromas. The finish is long and satisfying, with good complexity from the use of both new and used French and American oak.

Peter Lehmann | 2005 | BAROSSA

★ ★ $ $ With values like this one it's easy to understand Barossa Valley's fame. Ripe Cabernet fruit comes wrapped in flavors of cocoa, toast and sweet vanilla. The oak is a bit dominant on the finish, but all in all it's a solid effort for the price.

Tatachilla | 2005 | MCLAREN VALE

★ $ $ At Tatachilla, young French winemaker Fanchon Ferrandi exploits the coastal climate and cooling sea breezes to craft this supple, silky red. Black currant and blackberry are married with black pepper and dusty sage, while the finish offers juicy, soft tannins.

Vasse Felix | 2004 | MARGARET RIVER

★ ★ $ $ The peregrine falcon on Vasse Felix's labels is a nod to the trained creatures that once deterred foraging birds from the vineyards. The falcons flew away long ago but the winery still manages great wines like this example, with its subtle herb notes, red currant fruit flavors and hints of mint and spice.

Woop Woop | 2006 | SOUTH EASTERN AUSTRALIA

★ $ This multiregion wine represents what Australia does so well—maximizing flavor and value through broad-based blending. In classic Woop Woop style, this wine offers big, easy-drinking flavor with black-cherry fruit, a full-bodied palate and a subtly spicy finish.

AUSTRALIAN REDS

shiraz

Shiraz is Australia's iconic red wine grape, beloved and revered for producing the country's greatest wines. It is also Australia's most widely planted red grape. The Shiraz of Australia is remarkably different from its counterpart, the Syrah of France. With a spicier, more explosive array of concentrated red and black berry flavors as well as spice, Shiraz is without a doubt Australia's defining wine. Grown in a variety of regions throughout the country, Shiraz is at its best in the Barossa Valley and McLaren Vale in South Australia, Hunter Valley in New South Wales and several Victoria regions. Most examples are drinkable when young, though some well-made versions have the ability to benefit from long aging, sometimes even more so than comparable Cabernet Sauvignons.

shiraz recommendations

Angove's Vineyard Select | 2005 | MCLAREN VALE

★ ★ ★ **$ $** Natural yeasts kick off the fermentation in this wine, yielding a peppery, jammy Shiraz with a lovely touch of cassis sweetness on the finish.

Charles Cimicky The Autograph | 2005 | BAROSSA VALLEY

★ ★ ★ ★ **$ $** Charles Cimicky learned to make wine from his dad, Karl, and now under his own label creates world-class wines like this Shiraz; powerful flavors of plums, dates and figs are woven with highlights of cigar.

Corrina Rayment Revolution | 2006 | MCLAREN VALE

★ ★ **$ $** Rayment is considered a terroirist, crafting wines that express their sense of place above all else. In this Shiraz, soil from the McLaren Vale subregion called Seaview imparts pronounced cherry, chocolate and espresso flavors and a distinctive meaty quality.

star producers
australian shiraz

Charles Cimicky
When Charles Cimicky took over his father's winery (then called Karlsburg), he raised the quality and soon became known as one of South Australia's most meticulous winemakers.

Domaine Terlato & Chapoutier
French winemaker Michel Chapoutier and importer/ marketer Anthony Terlato are the team behind this highly praised venture.

Jacob's Creek
Australia's leading export brand for more than a decade, this Barossa producer makes robust and well-priced wines.

Layer Cake
Winemaker Jayson Woodbridge's grandfather described vineyard soil as a layer cake with potential for yielding richly layered wines. Woodbridge has brought the idea to life.

Penley Estate
A descendant of two great winemaking families (the Penfolds and the Tolleys), Penley's Kym Tolley makes stunning wines in Australia's Coonawarra region.

Two Hands
The famed *négociant* team of Michael Twelftree and Richard Mintz creates some of the best Shiraz on the continent.

d'Arenberg The Footbolt | 2004 | MCLAREN VALE
★★ $ $ "Footbolt" was the name of a chestnut colt whose racing successes helped fund the purchase of d'Arenberg's first vineyards in 1912. Today, vines more than a century old yield this blackberry-flavored Shiraz, offset by notes of anise, cherry and pepper.

Domaine Terlato & Chapoutier lieu dit Malakoff | 2006 | PYRENEES
★★★ $ $ The partnership between biodynamic northern Rhône guru Michel Chapoutier and importer Anthony Terlato of Terlato Wines International results in this luscious Shiraz full of smoke, licorice and hints of dusty spices and chalky minerals.

Heartland Directors' Cut | 2006 | SOUTH AUSTRALIA
★★ $ $ $ Heartland wines are made with fruit from mature vine-yards in the Limestone Coast and Langhorne Creek regions of South Australia. Their Directors' Cut Shiraz exhibits bountiful waves of berry flavors underlined by an earthy meatiness.

Henry's Drive | 2006 | PADTHAWAY
★★ $ $ $ Lively aromas of mint and eucalyptus mark this wine as a classic Padthaway Shiraz. In the mouth it's silky, with blackberry and blueberry flavors leading to touches of spice and cedar.

Jacob's Creek Centenary Hill | 2003 | BAROSSA VALLEY
★★★★ $ $ $ This full-bodied Barossa Shiraz from an excellent vintage oozes heady eucalyptus and sweet spice aromas, a mouthful of black fruit flavors and soft vanilla notes on the finish.

John Duval Wines Entity | 2006 | BAROSSA VALLEY
★★★ $ $ $ This is only the third vintage for this terrific Shiraz, yet it possesses the character of a more established wine, full of berry, plum and cassis flavors balanced by substantial but sweet tannins.

Layer Cake | 2006 | BAROSSA VALLEY
★★★★ $ $ From Jayson Woodbridge, vintner and proprietor of California cult-Cab winery Hundred Acre, comes this incredibly well-priced Shiraz overflowing with mocha and dark berry flavors. It hails from Barossa's Golden Mile, a coveted area where some of the grapes are grown for Penfolds' venerable Grange.

Mr. Riggs | 2006 | MCLAREN VALE
★★ $ $ $ Three of McLaren Vale's best-known growers—Ian Leask (Breakneck Creek), David Paxton (Quandong Farm) and Tony Parkinson (Penny's Hill)—contributed grapes for this smoky, spicy, blackberry-flavored Shiraz.

Penley Estate Hyland | 2005 | COONAWARRA
★★★ $ $ The sunny summer of 2005 is credited with imparting concentration and weight to this full-bodied yet elegant Shiraz, which offers aromas of red and black berries and flavors ranging from raspberry to savory spices.

Petaluma | 2005 | ADELAIDE HILLS
★★ $ $ The terroir of Petaluma's B&V Vineyard resembles that of France's northern Rhône Valley, where Shiraz (Syrah) and Viognier are the primary grapes. A bit of Viognier is added to this cherry- and cedar-scented Shiraz, which shows hints of chocolate and licorice.

Peter Lehmann Stonewell | 2002 | BAROSSA
★★★ $ $ $ $ Lehmann believes that the Stonewell district of Barossa possesses the region's finest terroir, and this dense, rich Shiraz might prove him right; red and black fruit flavors are layered with anise, licorice and soft oak nuances on a long finish.

Tintara | 2005 | MCLAREN VALE
★★ $ $ Flavors of cocoa predominate in this complex wine packed with dried plum, blueberry, sweet vanilla and touches of spice and cigar, bolstered by soft oak.

Two Hands Bella's Garden | 2006 | BAROSSA VALLEY
★★★★ $ $ $ This beautiful, intensely concentrated Shiraz possesses a rare density and purity of fruit, ranging from black cherry compote to blueberry flavors studded with notes of cedar and vanilla, and ending with a remarkably long finish.

Wyndham Estate Black Cluster | 2003 | HUNTER VALLEY
★★ $ $ $ This light, fruity and refreshing Shiraz offers ripe blueberry flavors accented by notes of spice, licorice and pepper.

other australian reds

Australia's unheralded gems are Grenache and Mourvèdre, both originally from France's Rhône Valley. Grenache displays many of the same fruity characteristics as Shiraz but with a lighter body, while Mourvèdre shows a smokier, spicier composition. Vintners often combine the two with Shiraz in blends labeled "GSM." Pinot Noir has tried to take hold in several regions, though success is mainly restricted to Tasmania and the Yarra Valley. Merlot has increased its presence in South Australia over the last decade.

other australian red recommendations

Anaperenna by Ben Glaetzer | 2006 | BAROSSA VALLEY
★★★ $ $ $ Intense blackberry and black currant fruit dominate this excellent dry-farmed blend, whose grapes were watered only with natural rainfall. The Shiraz and Cabernet Sauvignon vines used for the wine are 85 and 60 years old, respectively, which accounts for its concentration of flavors and complexity.

Chateau Reynella Basket Pressed Grenache | 2004 | MCLAREN VALE
★★★ $ $ From South Australia's oldest operating winery comes this jammy, rhubarb pie–scented Grenache. The wine rests for more than a year in old French oak *barriques,* which impart a smooth richness on its long finish.

Cimicky Trumps Grenache/Shiraz | 2005 | BAROSSA VALLEY
★★ $ $ This spicy Barossa blend is dominated by Grenache, which imparts its telltale characteristics of pepper, black cherry and blueberry flavors.

Cullen Diana Madeline | 2004 | MARGARET RIVER
★★★ $ $ $ $ Cabernet Sauvignon takes the lead in this impressive Bordeaux-style blend from the Margaret River, rounded out with small amounts of Merlot and Cabernet Franc. Generous, luscious currant and cherry flavors are accented by intriguing meaty notes and supported by formidable tannins on a plush, lingering finish.

d'Arenberg The Galvo Garage | 2004 | ADELAIDE HILLS
★★ $ $ A blend of Cabernets Sauvignon and Franc, Merlot and Petit Verdot, this d'Arenberg is replete with earthy coffee aromas, red currant and tobacco flavors and big, brawny tannins that seem to go on forever on the finish.

De Lisio Grenache | 2006 | MCLAREN VALE
★★★ $ $ $ Winemaker Tony De Lisio has been making wine in McLaren Vale for some 30 years, and it just keeps getting better. His dry-grown bush vine Grenache, made in part with grapes from an 80-year-old vineyard in Blewitt Springs, bursts with black cherry, raspberry, currants and spice.

Henschke Henry's Seven | 2005 | BAROSSA
★★ $ $ This ripe, spicy blend of Shiraz, Grenache, Mourvèdre and Viognier brims with plum and currant fruit. Its name commemorates Henry Evans, who planted the first vineyard in the district of Keyneton, where the Henschke winery is located, in 1853.

John Duval Wines Plexus | 2006 | BAROSSA VALLEY

★★★ $ $ $ Lavender dominates the fragrant floral bouquet in this elegant, fruity yet powerful GSM (Grenache, Shiraz, Mourvèdre). It's crafted by John Duval, one of Australia's most highly regarded wine-makers, who made Penfolds Grange from 1986 to 2002.

Kaesler Avignon Grenache/Shiraz/Mourvedre | 2005 | BAROSSA VALLEY

★★ $ $ Working with vines that are up to 105 years old, winemaker Reid Bosward has been perfecting this GSM since 1997, aiming for a seamless, voluptuous texture. He achieves it in the 2005 vintage, with its earthy aromas and blueberry and black-cherry fruit flavors.

Parson's Flat Shiraz/Cabernet | 2004 | PADTHAWAY

★★★ $ $ $ This inky, richly concentrated 70/30 blend of Shiraz and Cabernet Sauvignon was aged in American and French oak, the result of which is an earthy, powerful wine redolent of vanilla and packed with dark plum flavor.

Penley Estate Condor Shiraz/Cabernet | 2005 | COONAWARRA

★★ $ $ Penley's Condor is rich and complex, with ripe fig, cherry and plum aromas and juicy berry flavors. Though soft initially, it opens up beautifully, revealing layers of complex berry and cassis flavors.

Petaluma | 2004 | COONAWARRA

★★★ $ $ $ The Petaluma team considers the 2004 vintage to be one of Australia's greatest. Founder Brian Croser's Cabernet-Merlot blend is no exception, possessing a lovely floral nose spiked with cherry and vanilla notes followed by cassis and berry flavors.

Peter Lehmann Clancy's Shiraz/Cabernet Sauvignon/Merlot | 2004 | BAROSSA

★★ $ $ Blending Shiraz and Cabernet (nearly equal parts of each in this case) is common in Australia. The addition of 15 percent Merlot makes Clancy's red something of a standout—and a delicious one, too—exuding berries of every variety and tealike tannins.

Pillar Box Red | 2006 | PADTHAWAY

★ $ This well-priced red, another Shiraz-Cabernet blend with a bit of added Merlot, shows crowd-pleasing flavors of plum and raisin with a hint of cocoa and a refreshing, satisfying juiciness.

Razor's Edge Shiraz/Grenache | 2006 | MCLAREN VALE

★ $ Following the wildly successful Razor's Edge McLaren Vale Shiraz, the debut vintage of this well-crafted blend gets its lush fruit opulence from Shiraz, while Grenache adds spice and structure.

S.C. Pannell Shiraz/Grenache | 2006 | MCLAREN VALE

★★★ $ $ $ The powerful depth of this inky purple blend can be attributed to the age of the vines that contributed the grapes—45 years for the Shiraz and 70 years for the Grenache—endowing the wine with layers of plush berry flavors.

Tintara Grenache | 2005 | MCLAREN VALE

★★ $ $ Soft, violet and dusty spice aromas abound in this juicy, raspberry-flavored Grenache. It's made in Tintara's 1878 facility, where they still use the wooden basket presses that the winery has employed for more than a century.

Wakefield Promised Land Shiraz/Cabernet | 2005 | SOUTH AUSTRALIA

★ $ Raspberry fruit and soft, chalky tannins define this delightful everyday Shiraz–Cabernet Sauvignon blend; it finishes as juicy as it starts, thanks to mouthwatering tannins and a hint of spice.

news from a wine insider

australia by Sophie Otton, Australia-based wine buyer, judge and journalist

Vintage Note

Unlike the 2007 vintage, which suffered through drought and frost resulting in a more than 25 percent decline in production, the 2008 vintage was relatively easy and seems to have yielded promising wines, especially in key regions such as Victoria and Western Australia. Two exceptions are South Australia, where a heat wave significantly condensed the harvest, and the Hunter Valley region; though some terrific white wines were produced here, winemakers have struggled with reds due to late-ripening grapes.

Winemakers to Watch

Larry Cherubino, a consultant vintner in Western Australia, has begun making his own range of beautifully crafted wines under three labels: Cherubino, The Yard and Ad Hoc. Also look for Andrew Thomas's Hunter Valley Shiraz and unusually delicate, flavorful Semillon. In Victoria, Michael Glover is making superb wines at Bannockburn Vineyards, an established brand known for Chardonnay and Pinot Noir. Glover's first release—the 2006 vintage—has taken the producer to even greater heights.

new zealand

Sauvignon Blanc is the wine that first earned New Zealand international acclaim. Winemakers have since broadened their horizons with other whites like Chardonnay and Riesling, as well as many excellent reds. Their success with Pinot Noir, Syrah, Cabernet and Merlot has further established New Zealand's vintners as some of the world's most talented.

Principal Wine Region

Kumeu
Auckland — Waiheke Island

Tasman Sea

Gisborne

Hawkes Bay

Wairarapa
Martinborough
Nelson
Blenheim — ☆ Wellington
Marlborough

Waipara

Canterbury • Christchurch

Central Otago
Queenstown

South Pacific Ocean

New Zealand: An Overview

New Zealand is home to the southernmost vineyards in the world. Winemaking takes place on the country's two long main islands, pragmatically called North Island and South Island. Though the latitudes of some of New Zealand's winemaking regions aren't far apart, their respective climates can vary substantially. The South Island is home to the Marlborough region, famous for its Sauvignon Blanc and Chardonnay, and Central Otago, known for fine Pinot Noir. North Island producers focus on Pinot Noir and Syrah in Martinborough; the warmer Hawkes Bay region produces many elegant Bordeaux-style wines.

New Zealand Wine Labels

Labels generally list region, grape and vintage and in some cases, vineyard name. The term "Reserve" may be used to designate higher-quality wines, but has no legal meaning.

new zealand whites

Historically, New Zealand has been known as a white wine country. Although many excellent Chardonnays and Rieslings are crafted here, it is Sauvignon Blanc that has emerged as the defining white grape of New Zealand.

NEW ZEALAND WHITES

sauvignon blanc

Sauvignon Blanc is the keystone of New Zealand's wine identity. The grape here yields wines with a freshness that recalls examples from Sancerre in France's Loire Valley. Yet New Zealand Sauvignons are in a category of their own, possessing flavors of grass, limes and exotic tropical fruit. This distinctive flavor profile, in combination with a comparatively low mineral content and high acidity, results in fresh, citrusy wines unburdened by overtly herbal flavors.

sauvignon blanc recommendations

Brancott B | 2007 | **MARLBOROUGH**
★ ★ ★ **$ $** There's a faint whiff of grassiness in the nose of this otherwise tropical fruit–dominated wine, with crisp mineral overtones and refreshing lime-grapefruit citrus flavors.

Dashwood | 2007 | **MARLBOROUGH**
★ ★ ★ **$ $** Grapes sourced from Marlborough's Wairau Valley contribute pronounced flavors of lime and guava, while those from the region's Awatere Valley add a firm backbone of minerals to this well-built, multilayered wine.

Drylands | 2007 | **MARLBOROUGH**
★ ★ ★ **$** The 2007 harvest featured the ideal combination of dry weather, warm days and cool nights, which brought out ripe grapefruit flavors in this smooth wine, balanced by crisp acidity and pronounced minerality.

star producers
new zealand sauvignon blanc

Brancott
Brancott helped establish Marlborough Sauvignon Blanc as New Zealand's signature wine by planting the region's first modern vineyards.

Dashwood
Dashwood's excellent, fruit-forward whites are made by Vavasour Wines, the producer that pioneered viticulture in Marlborough's Awatere Valley.

Drylands
The terroir at Drylands—where the vineyards' soil is layered with gravel and silt deposited over time by the shifting Wairau River—is reflected in the wines' intense flavors and fresh acidity.

Kim Crawford
Crawford's path to success—from sourcing grapes and facilities to owning his own winery and vineyards—has been steeped in quality all the way.

Nobilo
Nikola Nobilo was considered a maverick when he first planted *Vitis vinifera* grapes on New Zealand's North Island, but his efforts paid off handsomely.

Spy Valley
Bryan and Jan Johnson located a great growing region in Marlborough's Waihopai Valley (called Spy Valley for a nearby "spy base") and launched their label in 2000 to great acclaim.

Kim Crawford | 2007 | MARLBOROUGH
★ ★ $ $ From this consistently high-quality producer comes another succulent medium-bodied Sauvignon, layered with flavors of passion fruit, grass and herbs offset by refreshing acidity.

Nobilo Regional Collection | 2007 | MARLBOROUGH
★ ★ $ A late-arriving summer full of long, warm, sunny days has accentuated the bold fruit notes in this Sauvignon Blanc, yet it remains crisp and light-bodied with accents of spice and minerals.

Redcliffe | 2006 | MARLBOROUGH
★ $ Thanks to the clay-rich and stony soils in which its grapes are grown, Redcliffe's Sauvignon Blanc possesses classic aromas of herbs, grass and citrus as well as a refreshing crispness.

Spy Valley | 2007 | MARLBOROUGH
★ ★ ★ ★ $ $ This stand-out wine shows intriguing notes of chalky minerals and lime juice (thanks to grapes grown in stony riverbed soils) woven with captivating grapefruit and gooseberry flavors.

other new zealand whites

Chardonnay is New Zealand's second most planted white grape, and it thrives in many regions. Skilled vintners have worked hard to produce high-quality Rieslings, though it still ranks fourth in total acreage behind Pinot Gris.

other new zealand white recommendations

Drylands Dry Riesling | 2007 | MARLBOROUGH
★ $ A touch of natural sweetness highlights this Riesling's luscious stone fruit and fragrant honeysuckle flavors, which are nicely balanced by zesty notes of lime and grapefruit and crisp acidity.

Gunn Estate Unoaked Chardonnay | 2007 | EAST COAST
★ ★ $ $ A long, warm and dry summer in 2007 allowed these Chardonnay grapes to achieve a mouthwatering ripeness and intensity. The result is a layered, complex wine full of zesty grapefruit, white peach and tropical fruit flavors.

Staete Landt Chardonnay | 2005 | MARLBOROUGH
★ ★ ★ $ $ Handpicked grapes yield a gorgeous, Burgundy-style Chardonnay with generous aromas of vanilla and toast and a lush, medium body. Though fermented in French oak, it's not overly oaky.

new zealand reds

New Zealand's efforts in red wine have been focused mainly on Pinot Noir, a grape that has succeeded admirably in parts of both the North and South Islands. Many refined Cabernets and Merlots are produced as well, and some Syrahs are worth noting.

NEW ZEALAND REDS

pinot noir

Pinot Noir is New Zealand's most planted red grape. This notoriously finicky variety thrives on both islands, thanks to cool temperatures moderated by the ocean's influence; no vineyard on either island is located more than 80 miles from the coast. On the North Island, Pinot Noir performs especially well in Martinborough. On the South Island, it excels in Marlborough and particularly in Central Otago, near the southern end of the island, where the country's finest Pinot Noirs are made from low-yielding vines that produce intensely concentrated yet elegant wines.

pinot noir recommendations

Amisfield | 2006 | **CENTRAL OTAGO**
★★★ $ $ $ Amisfield winemaker Jeff Sinnott employs a minimalist winemaking approach in order to allow the inherent character of the grapes and the terroir to shine. His brooding, black cherry–scented Pinot is truly delicious, with earthy richness and sweet tannins.

Bird Old Schoolhouse Vineyard Big Barrel | 2006 |
MARLBOROUGH
★★ $ $ Named for the 900-liter barrels in which the wine is fermented and aged, Steve Bird's Pinot is a complex, rich wine brimming with cherry, chocolate and dried fruit flavors bolstered by tannins.

Craggy Range Te Muna Road Vineyard | 2006 |
MARTINBOROUGH
★★★ $ $ $ Craggy Range's managing director Steve Smith focuses on single-vineyard wines such as this Pinot Noir, the jewel in the crown of his North Island wines. Bold black cherry fruit flavors show impressive intensity.

Mt. Difficulty | 2006 | CENTRAL OTAGO
★ ★ ★ $ $ A warm, near-perfect growing season in 2006 yielded a bounty of delicious Pinot Noirs like this beautifully crafted example; bright cherry and wild strawberry flavors are underscored by stone and mineral nuances.

Spy Valley | 2006 | MARLBOROUGH
★ ★ ★ $ $ Pinot Noir grapes were specially handpicked for this ripe, robust wine that's bursting with red plum and blackberry fruit flavors; a year of aging in oak barrels has endowed it with a fuller body and smooth finish.

Te Kairanga | 2006 | MARTINBOROUGH
★ ★ $ $ This crisp, tart Martinborough Pinot shows sweet cherry, raspberry and currant flavors layered with waves of freshly ground pepper, all balanced with moderate tannins on a soft finish.

other new zealand reds

The warmer pockets of both the North and South Island produce New Zealand's finest Cabernet Sauvignon, Merlot and Cabernet Franc, most of which are used in blends. An increasing number of winemakers work with Syrah, and the grape is starting to show real promise here.

other new zealand red recommendations

Craggy Range Gimblett Gravels Sophia | 2004 | HAWKES BAY
★ ★ ★ ★ $ $ $ From a producer known for dependable and delicious Pinot Noirs comes this hefty Bordeaux-blend of Merlot, Cabernet Franc and Cabernet Sauvignon, with generous black fruit flavors and muscular tannins on a powerful finish.

Gunn Estate Syrah | 2007 | HAWKES BAY
★ ★ $ $ The Ohiti Valley, located in the heart of Hawkes Bay, yields this dense and concentrated Syrah boasting black plum and black cherry flavors with highlights of spice and a velvety texture.

Trinity Hill Syrah | 2006 | HAWKES BAY
★ ★ $ $ A fruity, spicy Syrah full of lovely berry aromas followed by soft fruit flavors with notes of cracked pepper, herbs and cola and sweet tannins on the finish.

argentina

South America's second-largest country has long been one of the world's largest wine producers (it currently ranks fifth), yet only in the last few decades have Argentine wines become widely available in the U.S. Argentine reds are globally acclaimed, and quality is continually on the rise.

Principal Wine Region

CHILE

South Pacific Ocean

Salta
• Cafayate

ARGENTINA

La Rioja

Aconcagua
Valparaíso
Casablanca
Maipo — ☆ Santiago
Colchagua
Curicó
Maule
Concepión

Mendoza
•Maipú
•Luján
•Tupungato
Mendoza

Buenos Aires ☆

South Atlantic Ocean

Argentina: An Overview

Argentina's most famous wine region, as well as its largest and most productive, is Mendoza. The continental climate here provides moderate temperatures and cooling breezes, while runoff from the nearby Andes mountains offers ample natural irrigation. Mendoza's important subregions of Maipú and Luján de Cuyo produce some of the country's finest red wines, specifically from Malbec and Cabernet Sauvignon grapes. High-altitude regions, such as Tupungato in the Uco Valley, support Argentina's relatively small white wine production. This consists primarily of fruit-forward yet balanced and often noteworthy Chardonnay and Sauvignon Blanc.

Argentine Wine Labels

Most Argentine wine labels identify grape variety, the region where the grapes were grown, the producer's name and the vintage. Proprietary names are sometimes listed as well. The terms "Reserva" and "Reserve" are commonly used on higher-quality wines, though these terms have no legal meaning.

argentine whites

Argentina's distinctive white grape is Torrontés, which typically manifests itself in a light-bodied, floral and refreshing wine. Chardonnay, however, is a far more important grape in terms of export and is increasingly grown throughout the country; winemakers use it to craft wines that range from lightly oaked and crisp to full-bodied, rich and creamy. Argentina's Mendoza Chardonnay clone flourishes in higher-altitude regions such as Tupungato. Simple though satisfying Sauvignon Blanc is also widely planted throughout Argentina, as are small amounts of other international grape varieties such as Pinot Gris (Pinot Grigio), Riesling, Semillon and Viognier.

argentine white recommendations

Colomé Torrontés | 2007 | CALCHAQUÍ VALLEY
★ $ Restored by Donald Hess, who owns the Hess Collection on Mt. Veeder in Napa, this winery has become known for its stand-out Torrontés, such as this tropical fruit–scented example with a crisp, refreshing palate.

Elsa Bianchi Torrontés | 2007 | SAN RAFAEL
★ $ This Torrontés makes for a pleasant honey- and spice-scented pour. Freshly cut citrus and mineral flavors dominate the nicely balanced palate, followed by a crisp, mouthwatering finish.

Felipe Rutini Chardonnay | 2005 | MENDOZA
★ $ $ The Rutini family was the first to recognize the potential of Mendoza's Tupungato Valley. They've been perfecting viticulture here since 1925, and continue to produce well-built wines like this honeyed Chardonnay, full of vanilla, toast and creamy richness.

Graffigna Centenario Pinot Grigio | 2007 | SAN JUAN
★ $ Made by one of Argentina's oldest wineries—and the very first to export Argentine wine—this mineral-laden, fruity Pinot Grigio is an enjoyable quaffer, perfect for pairing with seafood.

Inacayal Vineyards Pinot Grigio | 2007 | MENDOZA
★ ★ ★ $ Named for the last leader of Argentina's native Tehuelche people, Inacayal crafts an exquisite Pinot Grigio from hand-harvested grapes that are fermented—as with traditional Italian versions—in stainless steel tanks. Generous flavors of stone fruit are balanced by refreshing acidity and delicate traces of licorice.

Las Moras Chardonnay | 2007 | SAN JUAN
★ ★ $ From San Juan's relatively warm Tulum Valley comes this creamy, delicious Chardonnay with expressive ripe fruit flavors and a substantial body.

Tamarí Reserva Torrontés | 2006 | MENDOZA
★ ★ $ A wonderfully expressive and well-made Torrontés with bold tropical fruit and nut flavors underscored by an intense minerality, all for a very fair price.

Villa Viña Torrontés | 2006 | SALTA
★ ★ $ This wine illustrates why Torrontés is the white wine to watch in Argentina right now; with bright acidity, herbal aromatics, lush mango and fresh melon flavors, it offers a lovely alternative to many traditional, oaky whites.

argentine reds

Malbec has never been as important in France, its homeland, as it is in Argentina. Vintners here have realized the grape's potential, producing robust wines full of intense fruit flavors concentrated by oak aging. Over the years, Malbec has become Argentina's most widely planted and important variety, and it is largely responsible for the country's distinctive profile in the international market. Bonarda, a variety thought by some experts to be the Italian Charbono grape, also thrives in Argentina. Cabernet Sauvignon's presence continues to spread and the quality of its wines is improving. Merlot, Pinot Noir and the Spanish Tempranillo grape also have a presence, and the more recent success of Syrah in the hot San Juan valley has made Argentina worthy of its distinction as a top producer of a diversity of red wines.

argentine red recommendations

Antucura Calvulcura | 2003 | UCO VALLEY
★ ★ ★ ★ $ $ The grapes used in this Merlot–Cabernet Sauvignon blend were grown at 3,300 feet above sea level in the heart of the Uco Valley, producing a wonderfully rich, dark wine with generous ripe fruit aromas followed by a captivating array of cassis and berry flavors.

Antucura Valle de Uco Vineyards Antucura | 2004 | MENDOZA
★ ★ ★ ★ $ $ $ With help from friend and Uco Valley neighbor Michel Rolland, Antucura has produced a beautifully constructed Cabernet-Merlot blend with a Bordeaux-like finesse that perfectly complements its luscious, ripe black fruit flavors.

Bodega Norton Privada | 2005 | LUJÁN DE CUYO
★ ★ ★ ★ $ $ Once made exclusively for the Norton family's private *(privada)* cellar, this stunningly complex blend of Malbec, Merlot and Cabernet Sauvignon is aged in new French oak barrels. Revealing layer upon layer of dark fruit flavors and a profound earthiness, this is a wine that should be able to age for some time.

Bodega Norton Reserva Malbec | 2005 | LUJÁN DE CUYO
★ $ Made with grapes from 30-plus-year-old vines, this medium-bodied, fruit-forward Malbec makes for an enjoyable everyday pour.

Colomé Estate Malbec | 2006 | CALCHAQUÍ VALLEY
★★★ $ $ Malbec alone appears on the front label, though Cabernet and Tannat contribute to this blend, adding darker fruit flavors, spice notes and a fuller body to Argentina's signature grape; a perfect red for exotic game, lamb or beef.

Crios de Susana Balbo Malbec | 2007 | MENDOZA
★ $ Crios (Spanish for "offspring") wines—made by the legendary Susana Balbo (see facing page)—deliver delicious, everyday enjoyment for a low price. This Malbec is brimming with blackberry fruit and chalky, earthy nuances.

Domaines Barons de Rothschild (Lafite) and Nicolas Catena Amancaya Malbec/Cabernet Sauvignon | 2006 | MENDOZA
★★ $ $ This joint venture between a French and an Argentinean producer yields a delicious full-bodied Cabernet-Malbec blend that shows concentrated berry flavors with accents of cedar and a round, supple mouthfeel.

Famiglia Bianchi Cabernet Sauvignon | 2006 | SAN RAFAEL
★★★ $ $ This muscular Cabernet from one of Mendoza's oldest winemaking families is dominated by black pepper, cedar and blackberry notes, offset by vanilla nuances that lead to a soft, silky finish.

Furque 3 Cepas | 2005 | MENDOZA
★★★ $ Founder Alberto Furque's daughter Carolina is the winemaker at this high-elevation winery. Offering great value for the price, this full-bodied Malbec-Syrah-Tempranillo blend is made with hand-harvested grapes that deliver juicy black cherry and plum flavors.

Inacayal Select Malbec | 2005 | MENDOZA
★★★ $ $ Though Inacayal built its reputation on luscious Pinot Grigios, the Mendoza vintner has great talent with red wines, too, as this outstanding, black cherry–flavored Malbec illustrates.

Kaiken Ultra Malbec | 2006 | MENDOZA
★★★ $ $ From Aurelio Montes, one of Chile's most renowned winemakers, comes this beautifully layered, powerful Malbec, weaving plum, roasted coffee and currant flavors with substantial tannins.

Las Moras Reserve Tannat | 2004 | SAN JUAN
★ $ Black cherries and mocha are on display in this relatively rare Argentine Tannat that is decidedly softer than its counterparts from France's Madiran region; notes of sweet vanilla and toast round out the smooth finish.

Luca Malbec | 2006 | ALTOS DE MENDOZA
★ ★ ★ $ $ $ Laura Catena (of the esteemed winemaking family) crafts this small-quantity, terroir-driven line of wines, and her dark, inky Malbec, perfumed with cola, black cherry and spice, achieves uncommon depth and flavor.

Susana Balbo Signature Malbec | 2006 | MENDOZA
★ ★ ★ $ $ Susana Balbo has more than two decades of winemaking experience, and her name on the label is a guarantee of quality; this delicious Malbec is bolstered by the addition of 10 percent Cabernet and shows violet and cherry aromas with velvety tannins on the finish.

Tikal Patriota | 2006 | MENDOZA
★ ★ $ $ Named Patriota ("patriot") in honor of the two grapes that have shaped Argentina's winemaking identity, this Bonarda-Malbec blend from famed producer Ernesto Catena offers beautiful fruit flavors nicely balanced with notes of earth and spice.

news from a wine insider
argentina by Nick Ramkowsky, partner,
Vine Connections, specializing in Argentine wine

Most Significant Trends
Patagonia and Salta are two emerging wine regions in Argentina definitely worth paying attention to. In the Calchaquí Valley in Salta, Bodega Colomé, one of Argentina's oldest wineries with some of the highest vineyards in the world, underwent a significant makeover and is currently producing intense red blends and some very good Torrontés. The winery is also home to a beautiful nine-room hotel. Another winery with plans for a boutique hotel is Bodegas y Viñedos O. Fournier, in the Uco Valley of Mendoza. Already operating a noteworthy restaurant, O. Fournier specializes in a wide range of wines, from Tempranillo to Sauvignon Blanc to Malbec.

Notable Hotels
A great addition to the Buenos Aires hotel scene is the Legado Mitico, recently restored and converted into a gorgeous boutique hotel in the city's chicly bohemian Palermo Soho district. In the city of Mendoza, at the heart of Argentina's main wine region, the 26-room Villagio Hotel is just a block from Plaza Independencia.

chile

Chile's wine industry is like an undiscovered stock. It has strong fundamentals: a warm, dry climate tempered by cool Pacific winds; fertile soils and ample irrigation; and geographic isolation, which has helped Chile's vines remain disease-free. It has also attracted international attention in recent years, as Chilean vintners have modernized their techniques and explored new regions. In the process, they've succeeded in producing some of the world's best-value wines, as well as truly world-class Bordeaux-style wines.

Chile: An Overview

Chile's wine regions stretch north to south along 600 miles of this narrow country (see map, p. 234). Most wine production takes place in the interior Central Valley, although coastal regions such as Casablanca are being developed. Emerging regions include San Antonio; Aconcagua, a hotbed of organic farming; Colchagua, for top-notch reds; and Elqui. Near Santiago is Chile's best-known region, Maipo, most notable for its Cabernet. Other regions owe their reputations to a few star producers, such as Casa Lapostolle and Los Vascos in Rapel and Miguel Torres in Curicó.

Chilean Wine Labels

Chilean labels list grape and often a proprietary name for blends. Single-vineyard designations are increasingly used, and the term "Reserva" is found on some quality wines.

chilean whites

Cooler regions like Casablanca and San Antonio are broadening the scope of Chile's white wine production, primarily with a growing number of crisp, clean Sauvignon Blancs. Some wineries in the country's southern regions have had success with Chardonnay, and occasionally Riesling.

chilean white recommendations

Amaral Unoaked Chardonnay | 2006 | SAN ANTONIO VALLEY
★ ★ $ $ This mineral-laden Chardonnay shows aromatic floral notes and flavors of green apple; it hails from San Antonio's Leyda Valley, a region on the rise for its beautifully balanced cool-climate wines.

Casa Silva Sauvignon Gris | 2006 | COLCHAGUA VALLEY
★ $ $ Casa Silva's Sauvignon Gris balances herbs and flinty mineral flavors with grapefruit, white peach and subtle banana notes.

De Martino Sauvignon Blanc | 2007 | MAIPO VALLEY
★ ★ ★ $ An excellent value from De Martino's Isla de Maipo estate, this organic Sauvignon is made from handpicked grapes that are fermented in their own yeasts, a technique that results in an expressive, crisp wine with vibrant acidity.

Montes Leyda Vineyard Sauvignon Blanc | 2007 |
LEYDA VALLEY
★ ★ ★ $ $ An amazingly fresh Sauvignon Blanc bursting with fresh-squeezed lime, sweet grassy notes, lush grapefruit flavors and a pronounced, mouthwatering acidity from start to finish.

Valdivieso Reserva Sauvignon Blanc | 2007 | CENTRAL VALLEY
★ $ Century-old Valdivieso made a name for itself as Chile's first Champagne-style house. Today, winemaker Brett Jackson makes still wines, too, like this vibrant tropical-flavored Sauvignon.

Veramonte Reserva Chardonnay | 2006 |
CASABLANCA VALLEY
★ ★ $ Veramonte, a producer known for the quantity and the quality of its wines, has crafted this elegant, tropical fruit–scented Chardonnay brimming with pineapple and nectarine flavors.

chilean reds

Chile, sometimes called "the Bordeaux of South America," stakes its reputation on fruit-driven reds such as Cabernet Sauvignon and Merlot. Chile's distinctive grape is Carmenère, an old Bordeaux variety first officially identified here in 1994; it has been replacing the humble País as Chile's national grape ever since. Emerging reds such as Pinot Noir and Syrah are experiencing a rise in production, especially in coastal regions like Casablanca and San Antonio.

chilean red recommendations

Baron Philippe de Rothschild Escudo Rojo | 2006 | MAIPO
★★ $ The name of this delicious currant- and cedar-scented red blend from the famed Bordeaux-based Rothschilds is a nod to their family crest, which was originally a red shield, or *"escudo rojo."*

Concha y Toro Casillero del Diablo Reserve Carmenère | 2006 | RAPEL VALLEY
★ $ This appealingly plum-scented Carmenère is from a line of wines named in honor of Concha y Toro founder Don Melchor, who, in an effort to discourage theft at his winery, renamed his most treasured aging cave Casillero del Diablo, or "Cellar of the Devil."

Emiliana Los Robles Estate Gê | 2003 | COLCHAGUA VALLEY
★★★★ $ $ $ $ Crafted by Chilean winemaker Álvaro Espinoza, this powerful—and organic—red blend from Concha y Toro is dominated by Syrah (rounded out with Cabernet Sauvignon, Merlot and Carmenère) and delivers black currant, fig and chocolate flavors.

Intriga Cabernet Sauvignon | 2005 | MAIPO VALLEY
★★★★ $ $ Viña MontGras owners Hernán and Eduardo Gras teamed up with winemaker and co-owner Cristián Hartwig to make this extraordinarily earthy Cabernet from the Maipo Valley; dense flavors of coffee, leather and pepper show hints of eucalyptus.

Kingston Family Vineyards Bayo Oscuro Syrah | 2004 | CASABLANCA VALLEY
★★★ $ $ Winemaker Byron Kosuge spent 14 years at California's Saintsbury before branching out on his own to consult at smaller California wineries and in Chile, where he crafts big, bold wines like this Syrah; ripe black cherry and blackberry flavors are woven with notes of dust, spice, black pepper and toasty oak.

Montes Purple Angel | 2005 | COLCHAGUA VALLEY

★★★★ $ $ $ Montes's efforts to enhance the image of the Carmenère grape have yielded impressive results, as this velvet-textured and inky, dark purple–hued wine demonstrates. Its layers of ripe dark berry flavors take some time to emerge from the glass.

MontGras Reserva Cabernet Sauvignon | 2006 | COLCHAGUA VALLEY

★ $ Esteemed California winemaker Paul Hobbs had a hand in this juicy, youthful and affordably priced Cabernet, which displays exuberant cherry fruit and sweet vanilla flavors, bolstered by soft tannins.

Viu Manent Secreto Carmenère | 2006 | COLCHAGUA VALLEY

★ $ Meant for everyday pleasure, this well-constructed 85 percent Carmenère brims with dark berry fruit; what makes up the remaining 15 percent is the winemaker's secret.

news from a wine insider

chile by Peter Richards, UK-based wine writer and broadcaster

Vintage Note

Chilean wine producers are excited about the 2007 vintage; the cool, dry end of the harvest benefited both red and white wines, which show good balance and integration.

Most Significant Trends

New Chilean wine regions continue to emerge and plantings in places like Bío Bío, Elqui, Choapa and Limarí have begun to bear fruit. Producers along the Colchagua coastline are crafting lovely, fresh reds, and Errazuriz's Aconcagua vineyard, Chilhué, is making beautiful wines. In the south, Miguel Torres's new Empedrado vineyard in Maule's coastal hills is poised for stardom, while new plantings of Pinot Noir and Riesling in Bío Bío are already yielding fresh, promising wines.

New Wines to Look For

Two of Chile's biggest producers, Concha y Toro and Cono Sur, have released new sparkling wines from opposite ends of the country: the Concha y Toro sparkler is from Limarí, while Cono Sur's is made in the southerly Bío Bío district. New sweet wines worth noting include De Martino's botrytised Semillon from Maipo and Caliboro's late-harvest Torontel from Maule.

south africa

Vines have been planted in South Africa for centuries, but its modern wine industry is still young. Over the past two decades, great strides have been made toward fully realizing the potential of South Africa's stellar terroir, with the Paarl, Stellenbosch, Swartland, Constantia and Walker Bay regions leading the way. Today, the best producers are streamlining their portfolios by focusing on grapes that excel in their respective regions.

Atlantic Ocean

Coastal Region

Paarl

Robertson

Cape Town
Constantia

Stellenbosch

Elgin

Walker Bay

Indian Ocean

Principal Wine
Region

South Africa: An Overview

For many years, most forward-looking South African wine-makers produced a Chardonnay, a Sauvignon Blanc, a Riesling, a Cabernet, a Merlot and perhaps a Syrah (usually called Shiraz in South Africa). This scenario is changing, however, as producers realistically assess which grapes perform best in their regions and vineyards. As a result of such careful study, several South African wine regions are taking the lead with certain varieties—Stellenbosch, for instance, is known for Cabernet Sauvignon–based Bordeaux-style blends; Swartland and Paarl for Syrah and other Rhône varieties; and the cooler growing areas of Walker Bay, Constantia, Overberg and Cape Agulhas for Sauvignon Blanc, Chardonnay and Pinot Noir.

South African Wine Labels

The straightforward labels used by South African wine-makers list the winery name, grape, region and vintage. Blends may be given proprietary names, but the varieties that went into them will usually appear on the back label.

south african whites

Whites of practically all styles are made in South Africa from the Chenin Blanc grape. Sometimes referred to as "Steen," the variety shows a lighter, more citrusy flavor profile than the traditional Chenin Blanc wines of France's Loire Valley. The other main varieties, Sauvignon Blanc and Chardonnay, generally yield medium-bodied wines with mineral flavors; Sauvignon Blancs sometimes stray into herbal and exotic fruit flavors as well. The remaining white wine production is less significant, consisting mostly of examples made from Colombard (sometimes referred to as Colombar in South Africa), Cape Riesling (also known as Crouchen, an obscure French grape with no relation at all to Riesling), Semillon, Gewürztraminer and various Muscats.

south african white recommendations

Black Rock White Blend | 2006 | SWARTLAND
★★ $ $ Chenin Blanc dominates in this superb blend, rounded out with Chardonnay and a dash of Viognier, yet it displays the toasty oak, apple flavors and creamy texture of a rich New World Chardonnay.

Buitenverwachting Sauvignon Blanc | 2007 | CONSTANTIA
★★ $ Brad Paton recently joined longtime winemaker Hermann Kirschbaum at Buitenverwachting, where the pair trade off overseeing the reds and whites each year. This, Brad's first turn at the Sauvignon Blanc, is packed with herbs, limes, stone fruit and minerals.

The Foundry Viognier | 2006 | COASTAL REGION
★★★ $ $ Meerlust Estate's lauded young winemaker Chris Williams somehow found time to make this delicious Viognier under his own label; full-bodied and ripe, it's packed with apricot, melon and apple flavors with a refreshing kick of lime.

Glen Carlou Chardonnay | 2006 | PAARL
★★ $ $ This fruit-driven, full-bodied, mouthwatering Chardonnay was crafted by third-generation wine professional David Finlayson.

Jardin Nine Yards Chardonnay | 2006 | STELLENBOSCH
★★★ $ $ $ Old World meets New in this powerful yet elegant expression of Chardonnay bursting with toasty, buttery flavors layered with hazelnut, green apple and citrus, balanced by wonderful acidity.

Le Bonheur Sauvignon Blanc | 2007 |
SIMONSBERG-STELLENBOSCH
★★ $ This winery's Gallic name means "happiness" and is a nod to the original owners of the property, French Huguenots who settled in the Cape in 1689. Classic Sauvignon Blanc flavors of grass, herbs and pink grapefruit mark this bright, lively wine.

Mulderbosch Sauvignon Blanc | 2007 | WESTERN CAPE
★★★ $ $ The vineyards over which winemaker Mike Dobrovic presides in the Koelenhof area of Stellenbosch benefit from cooling winds that temper the long, hot summers, giving this stone fruit–scented wine wonderful balance.

Raats Family Wines Original Unwooded Chenin Blanc
| 2007 | COASTAL REGION
★★ $ This zippy Chenin Blanc from winemaker Bruwer Raats is made without oak, which allows the grape's fresh flavors of juicy pear and pineapple to shine, alongside refreshing mineral notes.

Sauvignon Republic Sauvignon Blanc | 2007 |
STELLENBOSCH

★★★ $ $ Winemaker John Buechsenstein's assertive Sauvignon Blanc is a perfect match for spicy foods. Its mineral-laced tropical flavors are balanced by a crisp acidity imparted by grapes grown in the highest vineyard site in Stellenbosch.

Sequillo White | 2006 | **SWARTLAND**

★★★ $ $ $ Acclaimed South African terroir-ist Eben Sadie crafts this white blend from Chenin Blanc, Grenache Blanc, Roussanne and Viognier fermented in French oak barrels, which results in a gorgeous wine brimming with stone fruit flavors.

Simonsig Chenin Blanc | 2007 | **STELLENBOSCH**

★★ $ The legendary Malan family named their winery after its view of the nearby Simonsberg mountain (Simonsig means "Simon's view"). This deliciously drinkable, medium-bodied Chenin Blanc has lovely honeysuckle and apricot aromas and silky honey flavors expertly balanced by acidity.

Thelema Chardonnay | 2006 | **STELLENBOSCH**

★★★ $ $ Thelema was once a run-down fruit farm at the top of the Helshoogte Pass before Gyles and Barbara Webb converted it into one of Stellenbosch's best winemaking operations. Their crisp, clean Chardonnay offers apple and marmalade flavors woven with intriguing yeasty nuances.

south african reds

For better or for worse, the signature grape variety of South Africa is Pinotage, a cross between French natives Cinsault and Pinot Noir. With its pungent aromas and decidedly eccentric, earthy taste profile, Pinotage is far from a crowd-pleaser, though carefully made, full-bodied, smooth versions attract some admirers. Vintners have more commercial success with international grape varieties like Cabernet Sauvignon, Merlot and Cabernet Franc, which are often blended together to yield complex, enjoyable reds. South Africa's Merlots and Pinot Noirs are comparable to some examples from America's Pacific Northwest, and Shiraz plantings—which yield assertive, jammy Australian-style wines as well as versions with an earthier, more French-like refinement—are on the rise.

south african red recommendations

Black Rock Red Blend | 2006 | SWARTLAND

★★ $ $ The old bush vines used to compose this berry-flavored blend of Shiraz, Carignane, Grenache, Mourvèdre and Viognier grow on the rugged slopes of Swartland's Perdeberg mountain, where they are deeply rooted in granite.

Cirrus Syrah | 2005 | COASTAL REGION

★★★★ $ $ $ A trio of partners—Ray Duncan of California's Silver Oak Cellars, Jean Engelbrecht of Rust en Vrede and golf pro Ernie Els—came together to create this plush Syrah full of extremely ripe fruit flavors offset by silky tannins.

De Toren Fusion V | 2005 | STELLENBOSCH

★★★★ $ $ $ Named for the five red Bordeaux varietals combined to produce it—Cabernet Sauvignon, Merlot, Cabernet Franc, Malbec and Petit Verdot—De Toren's flagship wine is a powerful, earthy gem.

Engelbrecht Els Vineyards Proprietor's Blend | 2004 | WESTERN CAPE

★★★★ $ $ $ This explosive, fruit-driven Bordeaux-inspired blend—a collaboration between South African wine producer Jean Engelbrecht and golf pro Ernie Els—shows impressive depth and complexity with robust cocoa- and pepper-dusted blackberry flavors rounded out by lush tannins and notes of leather.

The Foundry Syrah | 2004 | COASTAL REGION

★★★ $ $ $ Chris Williams—who is the winemaker at Meerlust—also makes a gorgeous Syrah under his own Foundry label. His 2004 bottling delivers ample rich, ripe red and black fruit, underscored by nuances of earth and spice with plush tannins.

Glen Carlou Gravel Quarry Cabernet Sauvignon | 2004 | PAARL

★★★ $ $ $ From the base of the Simonsberg mountain in the Paarl region comes this smoky, licorice- and plum-scented Cabernet that shows rich flavors of ripe fruit and tobacco followed by notes of coffee and leather in the huge finish.

Guardian Peak Lapa Cabernet Sauvignon | 2005 | STELLENBOSCH

★★★★ $ $ $ A top-notch Cabernet from a winery named after the highest peak on the Stellenbosch mountain range, this wine is brimming with layers of black cherries, berries, dates and figs filled out with plush tannins and a long finish.

Kanonkop Kadette | 2005 | STELLENBOSCH

★★★ $ The Kanonkop estate, situated on the lower slopes of the Simonsberg mountain, has been run by four generations of the Sauer family. Their well-priced 2005 Kadette, a blend of Pinotage and Bordeaux varieties, displays a powerful spectrum of spice-infused fruit flavors with a touch of mint.

Paul Cluver Pinot Noir | 2006 | ELGIN

★★★ $ $ The Elgin region's relatively cool climate is sometimes compared to France's Burgundy, and this smoky, cherry-scented Pinot Noir is indeed Burgundian in style, with a gorgeous, velvety mouthfeel and bright black cherry and chocolate flavors.

Sequillo Red | 2004 | SWARTLAND

★★★ $ $ $ Winemaker Eben Sadie makes this southern Rhône Valley–style blend of Syrah, Mourvèdre and Grenache that's both fruity and elegant, balancing ripe red and black berry flavors with notes of dates and vanilla enlivened by vibrant acidity.

Stormhoek Pinotage | 2006 | WESTERN CAPE

★★★ $ This ripe, jammy, fruit-forward Pinotage hails from vineyards in a hidden valley halfway up the Bains Kloof Pass in Wellington in the Western Cape. It's overflowing with flavors of berries, honey, coffee and chocolate, yet is nicely balanced.

Thelema Cabernet Sauvignon | 2005 | STELLENBOSCH

★★★ $ $ $ Thelema's winemaker, Gyles Webb, crafts this standout, complex Cabernet; dark black fruit flavors are layered with notes of earth, coffee and chocolate and a hint of leather on the finish.

Thelema Shiraz | 2005 | STELLENBOSCH

★★ $ $ $ From the slopes of the Simonsberg mountain in the Stellenbosch region comes this rich, robust Shiraz with flavors of blackberries and spice that lead to a balanced, toasty finish.

other new world wines

Led by Ontario and British Columbia, Canada's wine industry has grown tremendously in recent years. On North America's warmer end, Mexico is crafting some excellent wines, mainly in Baja California. In South America, the wine industries of Brazil and Uruguay are on an upswing, producing higher-quality wines that are beginning to reach U.S. wine shops with greater frequency.

Canada, Mexico, Brazil, Uruguay: An Overview

Nothing about making wine in Canada is easy. Still, the country's vintners manage to produce quality red and white wines despite extreme winters and early frosts. The Canadian winemaking industry is centered in Ontario and British Columbia. Ontario's Niagara Peninsula and Pelee Island regions benefit from the moderating influences of the Great Lakes (Ontario and Erie), which allow winemakers here to succeed with Riesling, both as a dry wine and in the regions' famous ice wines. The Okanagan Valley, British Columbia's preeminent subregion, produces elegant wines primarily with Chardonnay, Pinot Noir and Bordeaux varieties.

Vintners in Mexico, Brazil and Uruguay make the most of their warmer climates. The Mediterranean-like conditions in Mexico's Baja California region result in full-bodied reds from Petite Sirah, Zinfandel, Nebbiolo and Tempranillo.

About 90 percent of Brazil's wine comes from Serra Gaú-cha, the main appellation in the state of Rio Grande do Sul, whose temperate climate and hillside vineyards are ideal for growing Tannat and other French transplants like Cabernet and Merlot. Tannat is even more important in Uruguay, where it thrives near the capital city of Montevideo.

other new world whites

Riesling is successfully grown in Ontario and British Columbia along with Gewürztraminer, Chardonnay and Pinot Gris. Canada is also the world's largest producer of sweet ice wine, made from Riesling or Vidal Blanc grapes that are left to freeze on the vine before they are harvested. Mexico produces Sauvignon Blanc, Chenin Blanc and Semillon, while Brazil's cooler regions support Chardonnay, Muscat, Semillon and Sauvignon Blanc. Uruguay makes a few nice whites from Chardonnay, Sauvignon Blanc and Torrontés.

other new world white recommendations

Aurora Cellars Chardonnay | 2006 | SERRA GAÚCHA, BRAZIL
★ **$** One of Brazil's largest cooperatives produces this fresh, fruit-driven Chardonnay. It hints at oak but isn't the least bit heavy-handed, instead boasting ripe pear fruit and crisp acidity.

Cave Spring Estate Bottled Riesling | 2006 |
BEAMSVILLE BENCH, CANADA
★★★ **$** From Lake Ontario's long, narrow Niagara Escarpment, this terrific dry Riesling is intensely perfumed with acacia flower, stone and ripe, juicy pear; in the mouth, overripe peach flavors and more minerality are well balanced by a touch of grapefruit in the finish.

Henry of Pelham Reserve Riesling | 2006 |
SHORT HILLS BENCH, CANADA
★★ **$** Henry of Pelham Rieslings are made in the Mosel style; this one shows apple and lemon flavors underlined by a lovely minerality and accented by a waxy hint of petrol.

L.A. Cetto Chenin Blanc | 2006 | **GUADALUPE VALLEY, MEXICO**
★ $ Family-owned L.A. Cetto has been making wine in Baja California for more than three-quarters of a century. This affordable and fairly rich Chenin Blanc has a hint of sweetness; overall, it's delicious.

Mioranza Chardonnay | 2007 | **SERRA GAÚCHA, BRAZIL**
★ $ Fermented in stainless steel, this fruit-driven Chardonnay is perfumed with heady tropical fruit accented by white floral notes; in the mouth, it's crisp and clean with bright minerality.

Peninsula Ridge Estates Inox Chardonnay | 2006 |
NIAGARA PENINSULA, CANADA
★★ $ $ Inox means "stainless steel" in French (it's short for *inoxydable*). In this acacia flower–scented Chardonnay's name, it alludes to the fact that the wine was vinified without any oak contact. The result is bright Granny Smith apple fruit and mouthwatering acidity.

other new world reds

In Ontario, the hybrid grape Baco Noir produces rustic, smoky reds. British Columbia's Bordeaux blends resemble Washington State reds and are some of the region's most successful wines. Most of Mexico's robust reds are made from Tempranillo, Cabernet, Petite Sirah and Nebbiolo. In Brazil, France's Tannat grape makes quality reds, as do Cabernets Sauvignon and Franc, Merlot and Pinot Noir. But it's in Uruguay that Tannat reigns supreme, yielding dark, tannic wines that are a bit softer than most French examples without losing the luscious, full body the grape is known for.

other new world red recommendations

Aurora Cellars Cabernet Sauvignon | 2004 |
SERRA GAÚCHA, BRAZIL
★ $ The palate of this violet-scented wine brims with Christmas spices and blackberry fruit. Having spent eight months in oak barrels, it's got nice structure for a wine so affordable.

Bodega Carlos Pizzorno Don Próspero Tannat | 2004 |
CANELONES, URUGUAY
★ $ Given the racy, robust and astringent features typical of the Tannat grape, this pleasing wine is decidedly tame—mouth-filling yet soft, with black currant fruit, black pepper and other spicy notes.

Domaine Monte de Luz Carquera Cabernet Franc | 2007 |
SAN JOSÉ, URUGUAY

★ $ Cool climate–loving Cabernet Franc shines in this delicious bargain bottling from Uruguay. Intense and fruity, it has raspberry and violet aromas, soft tannins and a touch of spice on the palate.

Henry of Pelham Reserve Baco Noir | 2005 |
ONTARIO, CANADA

★ ★ $ $ Although there was a movement in Canada in the 1980s to pull up the hybrid grape Baco Noir, Henry of Pelham continued to grow the variety and refine its bottlings. This aromatic example displays vanilla and clovey spice and loads of black fruit, with a good grind of pepper in the finish.

L.A. Cetto Petite Sirah | 2005 | GUADALUPE VALLEY, MEXICO

★ ★ $ This intensely fruity wine is made by one of Baja California's oldest wineries. Heightened by a touch of black pepper, its aromas and flavors of blackberry, violet, blueberry and sweet spice extend straight through the mouthwatering finish.

Marson Gran Reserva Cabernet Sauvignon | 2002 |
SERRA GAÚCHA, BRAZIL

★ ★ $ $ Marson's top-of-the-line wine, this Reserve Cabernet is made only in the best vintages and then aged in American oak barrels from Missouri. Eucalyptus and sweet spice aromas dominate the nose, followed by nice blackberry and currant fruit in the mouth.

Raul A. Randon | 2005 | SERRA GAÚCHA, BRAZIL

★ ★ $ $ Legendary wine consultant Michel Rolland had a hand in this 60/40 Cabernet-Merlot blend. Made with grapes grown at 3,000 feet above sea level, the licorice- and eucalyptus-scented red has tight tannins, loads of blackberry fruit and a touch of fennel.

Stratus Red | 2005 | NIAGARA PENINSULA, CANADA

★ ★ ★ $ $ $ Considered one of the Niagara region's best crafters of Bordeaux-style blends, French winemaker J.-L. Groux assembled this massive, wonderfully complex amalgam of mostly Bordeaux grapes. It shows cigar box, eucalyptus, black fruit and sweet spice, followed by pepper, black fruit and an earthy richness in the mouth.

Viñedo de los Vientos Tannat | 2006 | ATLÁNTIDA, URUGUAY

★ $ This Uruguayan Tannat exhibits the spiciness and rusticity of those traditionally made in France's Madiran region. Licorice and caramel share the stage with blackberry fruit from start to finish, accented nicely by sweet spice nuances.

champagne & other sparkling wines

There's no need to save Champagne and the world's countless other sparkling wines just for big occasions. Crafted in many styles and available across the price spectrum, these versatile, food-friendly wines are perfect for everyday sipping as well as celebratory toasting.

Sparkling Wine: An Overview

Though there are several ways to make sparkling wine, by far the finest—as well as the most time-consuming and expensive—is the traditional method (*méthode tradition-nelle*), in which vintners create and trap carbon dioxide bubbles in a still wine by activating a second fermentation in sealed bottles. Other less costly techniques include inducing a second fermentation in large tanks, or, the crud-est method, simply forcing carbon dioxide into still wines. Sparkling wines of all quality levels vary greatly in style: Some are dry, others sweet, and while some bubble aggres-sively in the mouth, others have a subtle effervescence. Nearly every major wine region produces sparkling wines, although the highest-quality examples come from cool regions with mineral-rich soils, which allow the grapes to develop a wide range of flavors while retaining their essential high levels of acidity. The pinnacle of sparkling wine regions is Champagne in northern France. Exceptional sparklers are also made in France's Loire Valley, northern Italy and Spain, California's Anderson Valley and Carneros regions, as well as the Australian island of Tasmania.

champagne

Champagne is undeniably the world's greatest sparkling wine. Only wines made in northern France's Champagne region are entitled to be called "Champagne," yet the word is often wrongly used to refer to any wine with bubbles, and those that falsely bear the name are invariably of inferior quality. The Champagne region possesses all the hallmark qualities for superior sparkling wine production: The cool climate slows the ripening of the grapes and maintains acid levels, while the chalk-rich soil gives these wines their distinctive mineral flavors.

Champagne Grapes & Styles

Grape-growing is a precarious business in the cool climate of Champagne, and grapes often struggle to achieve ripeness. For this reason, vintners traditionally blend grapes from various vintages and villages, though the only permitted grapes are Chardonnay, Pinot Noir and Pinot Meunier. *Blanc de Blancs* are made from 100 percent Chardonnay, whereas *Blanc de Noirs* are produced with red grapes Pinot Noir and/or Pinot Meunier. Rosé wines are created by either blending red wine into the white sparkling wine or by soaking pigment-rich red grape skins in pressed juice to "bleed" in some color. The most popular Champagnes are dry ("Brut"), although several sweeter styles are also made (see Champagne Labels, on the next page).

Champagne Labels

Look for the word "Champagne" on the label to make sure it's the real thing. Most Champagnes are "NV," or non-vintage, meaning they are blends of wines from different years, a practice that allows each Champagne house to create a distinctive and consistent taste from year to year. Vintage Champagnes are made only in exceptional years. Top Champagnes are labeled with unofficial terms such as "Tête de Cuvée" and are often given proprietary names such as Moët's Dom Pérignon. Sweetness levels are categorized as follows, from driest to sweetest: *Brut Nature* (also known as *Brut Zéro, Pas Dosé* or *Sans-Dosage*), *Extra Brut, Brut, Extra Dry* (or *Extra Sec*), *Sec* (or *Dry*), *Demi-Sec* and *Doux*. "Brut" is the most common style on the market.

star producers
champagne

Alfred Gratien

One of Champagne's lesser-known gems, Gratien crafts vintage cuvées that remain fresh for decades, and non-vintage wines that age well, too.

Dom Pérignon

Dom Pérignon was a monk who is credited with perfecting Champagne production in the 1600s. The legendary sparklers that bear his name are long-lived and complex.

Gosset

The consistently great Gosset is especially lauded for its Brut Excellence as well as its prestige cuvée Célébris and its vintage cuvée Grand Millésime.

Goutorbe

While Goutorbe is one of the larger growers in Champagne, it produces a relatively modest 10,000 cases a year; its cuvées are rich and well structured.

Henriot

Established in the early 1800s, Henriot carries on the tradition of Champagne production today with wines famous for their complexity and creamy, often biscuity characteristics.

Krug

One of the finest and most expensive Champagnes, Krug is dedicated to quality, and its wines inspire an elite and devoted following.

champagne recommendations

WHITES

Alfred Gratien Cuvée Paradis Brut | NV |

★★★ $ $ $ $ By aging still wines in barrels before the second fermentation, Gratien makes Champagnes that stand out for their richness and restraint. Cuvée Paradis, their flagship wine, is regal, playing plush, yeasty baked apple flavors off powerful acidity.

De Meric Grande Réserve Sous Bois Premier Cru Brut | NV |

★★★ $ $ $ For those who can't afford Bollinger, De Meric is a great alternative at a friendly price. This is 80 percent Pinot Noir and wonderfully rich: Wood and baking spice notes infuse apple pie flavors.

Dom Pérignon | 1999 |

★★★★ $ $ $ $ Dom Pérignon was the world's first "prestige" cuvée—a vintage 1921 released about a dozen years after it was bottled—and it's still the most famous. In this example, warm, sunny weather in 1999 made for a plush, powerful wine, gamey and sultry with expansive flavors of Bartlett pears, roses, smoke and spice.

Gosset Excellence Brut | NV |

★★★ $ $ $ Gosset, said to be the oldest Champagne house, makes rich wines with an opulent, old-fashioned elegance. Their "Excellence" is savory and broad, full of dark berry, wood and spice flavors.

Goutorbe Cuvée Prestige | NV |

★★★★ $ $ $ From a family-owned estate in the Grand Cru of Aÿ (and just recently introduced to the U.S.), this is ripe, generous Champagne. The predominance of Pinot Noir in the blend gives it heft and spiced red fruit flavors; lemon and hazelnut notes lend it grace.

Henriot Blanc Souverain Pur Chardonnay | NV |

★★★★ $ $ $ Henriot, which celebrated its 200th anniversary in 2008, focuses on Chardonnay in all its wines. This bottling shows the grape in all its splendor, with chalky minerality and tight acidity holding down the lemon and cream flavors.

Jacques Lassaigne Les Vignes de Montgueux Blanc de Blancs Brut | NV |

★★★ $ $ $ In the Côte des Bar region, the Montgueux area stands out for its chalky soils, and unlike most of the Côte des Bar (which is planted with Pinot Noir), Chardonnay thrives here. This is a blend of grapes from several parcels of vines, and it's downright hedonistic, combining cream, hazelnut and brioche notes with fine bubbles.

Krug Grande Cuvée | NV |

★★★★ $ $ $ $ Krug's extensive stock of older vintages allows the house to compose a consistently complex cuvée with intense flavors. Deep notes of wood spice, nuts and smoke underline brighter citrus and apple tones, the whole melded by a creamy texture. Delicious.

Moët & Chandon Nectar Impérial | NV |

★★★ $ $ $ This venerable Champagne house produces an extremely sophisticated demi-sec. With notes of pineapple, pear and mango, it's sweet enough to pour for dessert, but it also has the spice and acidity to match foie gras or cheese.

Nicolas Feuillatte Blue Label Brut | NV |

★★ $ $ $ This is one of the best deals in Champagne. Crisp with fine bubbles and gentle pear and red apple flavors, it's a bargain, usually selling for around $30 to $40.

ROSÉS

Veuve Clicquot Rosé | NV |

★★★ $ $ $ $ Veuve Clicquot was the first house to produce a rosé Champagne, and theirs remains one of the best. Pink and red berry aromas plus whiffs of acacia and honeysuckle rise from the glass; biscuity cherry flavors lead into a dry, pleasantly chalky finish.

other sparkling wines

Champagne will always be the benchmark by which other sparkling wines are measured. Still, regions all over the world produce a wide range of quality sparklers, many of them selling at a fraction of Champagne's cost.

france

Beyond Champagne, France abounds with sparkling wines, most notably from the Loire Valley, Alsace and Languedoc's Limoux subregion. Most are made with grapes typical to each region and are labeled *méthode traditionnelle*, *méthode classique* or "Crémant" if made the same way as Champagne. Others are labeled "Brut" or "Mousseux."

other french sparkling wine recommendations

Jaillance Cuvée Impériale | NV | CLAIRETTE DE DIE

★★ $ $ Made from Muscat with a dash of Clairette, this Rhône Valley sparkler is aromatic and pretty, with soft bubbles and a slightly sweet peach flavor. It would make an excellent brunch pour or an easy refresher on a hot day.

Langlois-Château Brut | NV | CRÉMANT DE LOIRE

★★★ $ $ Langlois-Château has been synonymous with sparkling wines almost since its inception in 1885. This basic Brut demonstrates why: It's crisp and clean with fine bubbles, as well as powerful acidity that drives the dry fruit flavor through a long, invigorating finish.

Lucien Albrecht Blanc de Blancs Brut | NV |
CRÉMANT D'ALSACE

★★★ $ $ From one of the oldest estates in Alsace, this is an elegant sparkler, fragrant with apple blossom tones. The tiny bubbles create a creamy fizz that holds aloft soft, dry apple flavors—excellent for stoking the appetite before dinner.

Maison Parigot et Richard Blanc de Blancs | NV |
CRÉMANT DE BOURGOGNE

★★★★ $ $ Made in the Champagne method from Chardonnay and Aligoté grapes grown in Savigny-lès-Beaune in Burgundy, this is a shoe-in for true Champagne, with rich, creamy, baked apple flavors and a gentle, tiny-bubbled texture—and it's only about $23.

italy

Italian *spumante* (sparkling) wines are crafted primarily in the country's northern regions. One of Italy's finest sparkling wines comes from Lombardy's Franciacorta zone, with its mineral-rich soil and variable climate of warm days and cool nights. Made by the *méthode traditionnelle* (or *metodo classico*, as it is known locally), Franciacorta sparklers often taste similar to Champagne. The Piedmont region's flowery and fresh Moscato d'Asti and the light red, berry-scented Brachetto d'Acqui are also worth noting. An increasingly popular sparkler from Veneto, Prosecco provides an affordable and tasty alternative to many pricier sparkling wines made elsewhere.

italian sparkling wine recommendations

Ca' del Bosco Cuvée Prestige Brut | NV | **FRANCIACORTA**
★★ $ $ $ From one of Lombardy's finest sparkling wine producers comes this crisp wine with bright apple flavors and rich brioche notes.

Collalbrigo Brut | NV | **PROSECCO**
★★★ $ $ Collalbrigo makes serious Prosecco just outside Valdobbiadene. Their very dry Brut shows lean yet fragrant peach flavors powered by citric acidity. With its fine fizz, it's an elegant Prosecco.

Col Vetoraz | NV | **PROSECCO DI VALDOBBIADENE**
★★★★ $ $ Located in the heart of Valdobbiadene, Col Vetoraz makes some of the most stunning Proseccos on the market. The high altitude of the vineyards makes for a particularly fresh wine, with crisp peach flavors carried on satin-textured fizz.

Le Bellerive | NV | **PROSECCO**
★★ $ $ This small-production bottling from a family-run winery offers a rare combination of power and grace: Crisp lemon flavors take on an extra dimension with an underlying chalky richness.

Medici Ermete Malvasia Frizzante Secco Daphne | 2007 | **EMILIA-ROMAGNA**
★★★ $ $ Not your typical sparkling wine, this is as spiced as a *digestivi*, with a heady mix of floral notes and ripe yellow apple flavors. As honeyed as the flavors taste, the wine finishes clean and dry.

Michele Chiarlo Nivole | 2007 | **MOSCATO D'ASTI**
★★ $ Piedmont's white wines often get overlooked in favor of the region's reds, but this is a lovely bottle to have around for impromptu desserts; light and peachy, it boasts a gentle, creamy mousse.

spain

Spanish Cavas, by law made entirely from local grapes using the traditional method, have historically been marketed as less-expensive fill-ins for Champagne. The vast majority come from the Catalonia region near Barcelona and are made mostly from Macabeo, northern Spain's most planted white grape. In general, the best Cavas come from larger firms that control their own vinification, though some small vintners are producing high-quality examples.

spanish sparkling wine recommendations

WHITES

Avinyó Brut Reserva | NV | CAVA

★★★★ $ $ Avinyó started out as little more than a hobby for Joan Esteve Nadal, who established the winery in Penedès about 50 years ago. Today, the estate's old vines play into the complexity of this Cava, as elegant as it is lively, with spicy scents, delicate bubbles and fruit as crisp as a fresh green apple.

Freixenet Brut Nature | 2000 | CAVA

★★★ $ Freixenet, the largest Cava house in Spain, makes a Brut Nature only in exceptional years. The 2000—a bargain at $12—is built like a racehorse, slender yet powerful. It's bone-dry, with spicy, salty mineral flavors that beg for oysters or anything else from the sea.

Paul Cheneau Blanc de Blancs Brut | NV | CAVA

★ $ $ It's nice to still be able to purchase a decent sparkling wine for less than $16. This value pour is a simple yet pleasing bubbly with yeasty, ripe apple flavors, a touch of sweetness and another of earth.

Segura Viudas Reserva Heredad | NV | CAVA

★★★ $ $ Heredad began as a bottling for family and friends. Now it's Segura Viudas's flagship wine. Made from estate-grown fruit and aged in bottle for five years, it blends fresh, delicious pear flavors with deeper notes of toasted brioche, luxurious yet restrained.

ROSÉS

Segura Viudas Aria Sparkling Pinot Noir | NV | CAVA

★★ $ An untraditional *rosado* made from Pinot Noir, this Cava has a deep pink color that leads into sweet strawberry and cherry flavors. The vibrant acidity keeps it fresh and lively, finishing dry.

united states

The quality of American sparkling wine has been rising in recent years. Northern California is still the best source, especially the cooler-climate appellations such as Carneros and the Anderson and Green Valleys. Other states, though, including Washington, Oregon, New York and New Mexico, are making a growing number of flavorful, complex and vibrant sparkling wines.

u.s. sparkling wine recommendations

WHITES

Argyle Brut | 2003 | **WILLAMETTE VALLEY, OREGON**
★★★★ $ $ $ Argyle has become synonymous with sparkling wine in the Pacific Northwest due to wines like this one. Made in the *méthode traditionelle,* this predominantly Pinot Noir blend is rich in red berry flavor, with a hedonistically full, broad texture.

Chandon Reserve Pinot Noir Brut | NV |
NAPA COUNTY/SONOMA COUNTY, CALIFORNIA
★★ $ $ Moët & Chandon was the first French company to establish a sparkling wine house in California back in 1973. This bottling, made mostly from Pinot Noir, is its most lavish cuvée, with deeply smoky, savory cherry flavors and a hint of brown sugar.

Christian Wölffer Cuvée Sparkling Wine Brut Méthode Champenoise | 2004 | **THE HAMPTONS, NEW YORK**
★★★ $ $ $ Wölffer winemaker Roman Roth consistently crafts elegant sparkling wines. His 2004, a blend of Chardonnay and 41 percent Pinot Noir, is light and crisp, with subtle notes of toast and nuts under its fresh apple flavor.

Iron Horse Classic Vintage Brut | 2003 |
GREEN VALLEY, CALIFORNIA
★★★★ $ $ $ All of the wines from the family-run Iron Horse estate are top-quality; if you must choose just one, try the Classic Vintage. Shimmering acidity reins in this bottle's plump, creamy flavors, striking a fine balance between richness and restraint.

Mumm Napa DVX | 2000 | **NAPA VALLEY, CALIFORNIA**
★★★ $ $ $ The top-of-the-line cuvée from the California arm of the Mumm Champagne company, DVX is named for Guy Devaux, who founded the respected Napa estate in 1983. The wine is remarkably reserved, with cool, delicate apple fruit flavors and vibrant acidity that lingers long on the palate.

ROSÉS

Gloria Ferrer Brut Rosé | 2004 | **CARNEROS, CALIFORNIA**
★★★ $ $ $ José Ferrer (owner of Catalonia Cava house Freixenet) was the first to produce sparkling wine in Carneros, setting up shop in the early 1980s. Today, the Carneros-based winery makes a range of great sparklers; the rosé stands out for its Pinot Noir flavor—all cherry and raspberry, dry and spicy, with mouthwatering acidity.

other countries

Vintners in many other corners of the world craft sparkling wines, ranging from countless average examples to a few great ones. German and Austrian winemakers use Riesling and Pinot Blanc to make some fine (and a lot of mediocre) sparkling wine, called "Sekt." Portugal and Greece offer middling sparklers at fair prices, as do Georgia, Armenia and Moldova. South Africa, Argentina, Australia and New Zealand produce sparkling wines modeled after Champagne, some of them excellent. Australia's offerings include lovely examples from the island of Tasmania as well as dark red and tannic sparkling Shirazes.

other countries sparkling wine recommendations

WHITES

No. 1 Family Estate Cuvée No. 1 Blanc de Blancs | NV |
MARLBOROUGH, NEW ZEALAND
★★ $ $ Originally from Epernay in Champagne, the Le Brun family established the No. 1 winery in 1996. This 100 percent Chardonnay cuvée was their first wine; it's lively and fresh, with bright apple fruit.

Szigeti Brut Grüner Veltliner | NV | **BURGENLAND, AUSTRIA**
★★ $ $ This unusual sparkler comes from the sunniest spot in Austria: Burgenland, just east of the Neusiedlersee. Made from Grüner Veltliner, the wine is exotic and wild, with notes of cumin and smoke blending with blackberry and pear flavors, and tiny bubbles.

Tselepos Amalia Brut | NV | **GREECE**
★★★ $ $ Yiannis Tselepos is the master of Moschofilero in Greece. From his high-altitude vineyards in Mantinia, he crafts this fragrant sparkler, with orange blossom and white pepper scents decorating ripe pear and peach flavors.

ROSÉS

Altenburger Brut Rosé Sekt | NV | **BURGENLAND, AUSTRIA**
★★★ $ $ As elegant as its spare and modern label, this blend of Zweigelt (25 percent) and Blaufränkisch has savory, deep cherry flavors kept buoyant by a fine, lively fizz. It has the heft to pour with dinner, or very hearty hors d'oeuvres.

fortified & dessert wines

Fortified and sweet wines typically serve as the bookends of a meal, enjoyed as aperitifs or as a delectable finale. Despite the immense versatility of these wines, with styles ranging from dry, palate-stimulating Sherries to intensely sweet red and white dessert wines, they remain unknown to many wine lovers. Luckily, this makes it possible to find true bargains on high-quality examples from countries around the world.

fortified wines

The practice of fortifying wines—by adding a neutral spirit, such as clear grape brandy, before bottling—began as a way to ensure the wines' stability over long ocean voyages. Traditional fortified wines include Sherry, Port, Madeira and Marsala, although variations abound. The alcohol content of these wines is higher than that of most unfortified wines, usually between 16 and 20 percent. A fortified wine's style depends largely on when the spirit is added during its production. Adding it during fermentation, as in most Port and Madeira, halts the process, and the resulting wines retain a good deal of natural grape sugar. When brandy is added after fermentation to fully fermented dry wine, the result is much drier, a good example being Fino Sherry.

sherry

Sherry (a.k.a. Jerez or Xérès) has the unfortunate reputation in America of being a "little old lady" drink. In truth, this distinctive wine has a noble heritage. Made in southern Spain's Jerez region, Sherry gains its complex flavors from the area's chalky soils and a peculiar indigenous yeast that appears on the wine's surface after fermentation. Sherry's many styles range from utterly dry to incredibly sweet.

Sherry Grapes & Styles

Most Sherries are blends of wines from different years. The dominant grape is Palomino, though sweeter styles often contain Pedro Ximénez or Moscatel. Vintners employ a fractional blending system called "solera," which combines barrel-aged liquids from different vintages in such a way that all Sherries bottled contain a portion of the oldest wine in that specific solera. Sherry comes in two basic varieties, Fino and Oloroso, both of which have subcategories.

• **FINO SHERRY** gets its unusual flavors from a yeast called *flor,* which grows on the surface of the wine as it matures in wooden casks and protects it from oxygen. Two basic types of Fino are **Manzanilla Sherry** and the typically dry **Amontillado.** The first displays notes of chamomile (*manzanilla* in Spanish) and a fresh, salty tang. Amontillado, on the other hand, shows nutty qualities and profound mineral flavors. **Pale Cream Sherry** is a Fino sweetened by the addition of Pedro Ximénez wine or grape juice concentrate.

• **OLOROSO SHERRY** does not develop flor, so the presence of oxygen during aging creates a nutty, smoky, earthy flavor and a darker hue. Most Olorosos are sweet, though some are sweetened further by adding Pedro Ximénez, creating **Cream Sherry. Palo Cortado** is a chestnut-colored Sherry that begins to develop flor but then backtracks, ending up somewhere between Oloroso and Amontillado in style.

• **PEDRO XIMÉNEZ** (or PX for short) is produced in many Sherry houses even though it is not technically considered a Sherry. Crafted from grapes of the same name grown primarily in the Montilla-Moriles region just outside of Jerez, PX tends to be rich, thick and sweet, exhibiting intense, dried fruit flavors.

sherry recommendations

Bodegas Hidalgo La Gitana Pastrana Single Vineyard Manzanilla Pasada

★ ★ ★ ★ **$ $** La Gitana is the definitive Manzanilla; this aged, single-vineyard version, conceived in conjunction with Port vintner Cristiano van Zeller, builds on the salty freshness of the regular bottling, adding delicate, stony minerality and an intriguing caramel-soy note.

Bodegas Toro Albalá Don PX Pedro Ximénez | 2005 |

★ ★ ★ ★ **$ $ $** Exceptional Pedro Ximénez, this is intensely sweet yet not cloying at all. The flavors are like a cascade of warm, buttery caramel wrapped around golden raisins, figs and almonds; and while the acidity is imperceptible, the wine finishes totally clean.

Bodegas Tradición Palo Cortado Muy Viejo 30 Years

★ ★ ★ ★ **$ $ $ $** Established in 1998, Bodegas Tradición specializes in blending old wines, some dating to the 18th century, which owner Joaquín Rivero has purchased from different houses. His Palo Cortado is complex, with notes of nuts, mushrooms, earth and caramel; strong acidity keeps it dry and long.

El Maestro Sierra Amontillado 1830 Viños Viejos

★ ★ ★ **$ $ $ $** (375 ml) The family-owned Maestro Sierra house, founded in the 1800s, only recently began selling Sherries abroad, so they have deep stocks of old wines. This one spent at least 50 years in the solera; it's as intense as a buttery caramel, and just as smooth.

Gutiérrez Colosía Moscatel Soleado Dulce

★ ★ ★ ★ **$ $** (375 ml) Not officially a Sherry but made by a venerable producer in the area, this is made from sun-dried Muscat grapes. It's concentrated and sweet yet delicate, with flavors that range from golden raisins to tangelos, licorice, cedar and orange blossoms.

Osborne Pale Dry Fino

★ ★ **$** Today, Osborne makes Port, brandy, Rioja (Montecillo) and even food, but its origins are in Jerez. Its Fino is a good introduction to the category: crisp, light and just salty enough to be palate-whetting.

port

Portugal's second-largest city, Oporto, gave its name to the country's emblematic wine. Made in the Douro Valley and fortified with brandy to arrest fermentation, Port is a dark, sweet wine with a high alcohol content.

Port Grapes & Styles

The grapes most often used in Port production are Touriga Nacional, Touriga Franca and Tinta Roriz (Tempranillo). Categorized by style, Port comes in three basic types: White, Ruby and Tawny (the last two have subcategories).

• **WHITE PORT** exhibits the slightly sweet, citrusy flavors of the white grapes from which it is produced. Some houses make oak-aged, subtly oxidized, orange-hued versions.

• **RUBY PORT** is the most common style of Port. Inexpensive and straightforward, Rubies are blended from a variety of young wines. **Ruby Reserve Ports** (formerly known as Vintage Character Ports) are more complex blends, often carrying proprietary names like Graham's Six Grapes. **Late Bottled Vintage (LBV)** Ports are single-vintage Rubies that have been aged four to six years in barrel and are drinkable upon release, unlike most Vintage Ports. Made from the best grapes in the finest years and aged in oak for several years, **Vintage Port** requires decades of bottle aging to reach its maximum potential. **Single Quinta Vintage Ports** are produced with grapes from a single vineyard.

• **TAWNY PORTS** are, in theory, wines that have been aged in wood longer than a Ruby and thus take on a tawny hue. In reality, many of today's Tawny Ports are the same age as most Rubies; they're just made with lighter wines. Aged Tawny Port is authentic, however, made from blends of the highest-quality Ports that might otherwise have been bottled as Vintage Port. Tawny Port labels include an indication of the blend's age (10, 20 or 30 years old, for example). Tawnies are ready to drink upon release and generally exhibit delicate nutty aromas and dried-fruit flavors.

port recommendations

Churchill's White
★ ★ ★ $ $ Aged ten years in wood barrels, this golden wine has more character than most white Ports. Its sweet caramel notes merge into spice and hazelnut tones, finishing dry. As such, serve it chilled, without the typical soda and twist.

Croft Quinta da Roeda Vintage | 2005 |
★ ★ ★ $ $ $ The Quinta da Roeda vineyard has been called the diamond of the Douro. This 2005 is a dark, smooth Port brimming with chocolate and figs; subtle herbal and nutty nuances add complexity.

Fonseca Unfiltered Late Bottled Vintage | 2001 |
★ ★ ★ $ $ Fonseca is known for its voluptuous Ports; this LBV is no exception. It's warm, soft, and sweet as a triple chocolate cake, with drier herbal and earth tones in the background keeping it in balance.

star producers
port

Croft
Founded more than 300 years ago and boasting one of the best vineyards in the Douro, Croft remains one of the world's finest Port producers.

Quinta de Ventozelo
For years, Quinta de Ventozelo made wine in bulk for large shippers. A decade ago, the estate began producing under its own label and has earned an impressive reputation for it.

Ramos Pinto
Noted for its research into native grapes and vineyard management, Ramos Pinto has been instrumental in the Douro's recent quality strides.

Sandeman
The first Port company to brand its wines (beginning in 1880), Sandeman has a long history of smart marketing; its wines are impressive, too.

Warre's
Arriving in Portugal in 1670, the Warre's company began trading English goods in return for wine; the company's Port empire remains one of the most respected today.

W.&J. Graham's
The Scottish Graham brothers established one of the first vineyards on the Upper Douro, launching high-quality Port production in the region.

Quinta de Ventozelo 10 Year Tawny

★ ★ ★ **$ $ $** Although Ventozelo dates back to the early 1800s, the quinta only began bottling wine under its name in 1999. It has quickly established itself as a major player with wines like this Tawny, an elegant Port with light caramel, fig and herbal flavors.

Ramos Pinto Vintage | 2003 |

★ ★ ★ ★ **$ $ $ $** This stellar Port, from a house started by Adriano Ramos Pinto in 1880, has outstanding chocolate and blackberry flavor kept on the restrained side by fierce tannins and smoky herbal notes. It could easily age for 20 years.

Sandeman Limited Edition 40 Year Tawny

★ ★ ★ ★ **$ $ $ $** The most coveted of Sandeman's "Century of Ports"—a collection of Tawnies aged 10, 20, 30 and 40 years—this 40-year-old is wildy flavorful and fragrant, with hazelnut and praline notes underscored by spiced golden raisin and caramelized orange.

Warre's Warrior Special Reserve

★ ★ ★ **$** Founded in 1670, Warre's claims to be the oldest British Port house. Their Warrior is a good introduction to Port: It's as smooth as satin, with spiced fig and bright cassis flavors ending relatively dry.

W.&J. Graham's 20 Year Tawny

★ ★ ★ ★ **$ $ $** The Symingtons, who also own Dow's, Quinta do Vesuvio, Smith Woodhouse and Warre's, have run W.&J. Graham's since 1970. The house's 20 Year Tawny is smooth and mellow, with walnut, orange and cherry flavors wrapped in dark caramel.

FORTIFIED WINES

madeira

Like other fortified wines, Madeira has fallen out of fashion despite having been an iconic American drink in the 19th century. Named for the Portuguese island off the coast of Morocco where it's produced, Madeira comes in a variety of styles, suitable for drinking before, during and after meals.

Madeira Grapes & Styles

Most Madeiras are a blend of grapes, but the best carry the name of one of four: Sercial, Verdelho, Bual or Malmsey (Malvasia). Sercial Madeira is the driest, while Verdelho, Bual and Malmsey are progressively sweeter. Most age designations indicate the youngest wine in the blend.

madeira recommendations

Blandy's 5 Year Rich Alvada

★★★ $ $ (500 ml) The fuchsia label is the first hint that this isn't traditional Madeira. With Alvada, Blandy's bucks the single-varietal tradition to blend Bual and Malvasia grapes; the result is a rich, hedonistic wine with lots of soft spice and toffee tones.

Cossart Gordon Medium Rich Bual Colheita | 1995 |

★★ $ $ $ (500 ml) Colheita Madeiras are vintage wines that have been aged in wine lodges for years before bottling; this one was bottled in 2005. As thick as maple syrup, it's as golden in flavor as it is in color, with lots of dried fruit and nut flavors.

D'Oliveira Harvest Malvasia | 1987 |

★★★★ $ $ $ $ D'Oliveira is famous for the old stocks of wines it has—some from 1850 are still being sold. This one is a comparative infant, vibrant with notes of peaches, oranges, cashews and spice, and an acidity that keeps the flavors weightless and long.

The Rare Wine Co. Historic Series Charleston Sercial

★★★★ $ $ $ Made in the style that Charlestonians of the 18th century preferred, this is a dry, elegant Madeira. It combines a salted cashew richness with earthy, delicate flavors like fresh chanterelles and chicken broth; it would be delicious as an aperitif or with cheese.

The Rare Wine Co. Historic Series New York Malmsey

★★★★ $ $ $ The Rare Wine Co. works with the Madeira-based Vinhos Barbeito to craft wines that drink like vintage Madeiras but cost a fraction of the price. The New York Malmsey is incredibly rich, with dark fruitcake flavors and dry spice that balances its sweetness.

dessert wines

As their name implies, dessert wines are typically enjoyed with or in place of dessert. Sauternes from France's Bordeaux region has long held court as perhaps the most prestigious of all sweet wines and continues to command high prices. But wine drinkers today can experiment with many other reasonably priced and high-quality sweet wines, as interesting examples are being produced in Australia and Canada, brimming with sweet fruit, zippy acidity and even the addictive, honeyed aroma of botrytis (see below).

white dessert wines

The finest white dessert wines are intense nectars bursting with powerful flavors of flowers, spice, honey and smoke. All well-made examples possess high levels of acidity, which keeps them refreshing in spite of a high sugar content.

White Dessert Wines Grapes & Styles

• **LATE-HARVEST** wines are made from grapes left on the vine late into the season, allowing them to develop especially high sugar levels; any grape can be used to make them. The most famous examples come from Germany (marked *Spätlese,* which means "late," or *Auslese,* which is even sweeter) and Alsace (where they're called *Vendanges Tardives*). California, Australia, South Africa, Chile and the Greek isle of Samos also make good versions.

• **PASSITO** wines are an Italian specialty made from grapes that have been dried before pressing. Tuscan vintners use Trebbiano to make the local version, *Vin Santo,* while Sicilian vintners use the Zibibbo grape for their passito wines.

• **BOTRYTIS** wines obtain their unique and highly praised flavors from *Botrytis cinerea,* a mold referred to as "noble rot," which concentrates the wine's fruit flavors while adding hints of smoke and truffle. Some of the best are made in the Sauternes region of Bordeaux, where Sémillon, Sauvignon Blanc and Muscadelle are blended to craft wines of exceptional flavor and longevity. Bordeaux's Barsac subregion makes outstanding examples, while neighboring Loupiac and Cadillac yield similar, though less expensive, versions. The Loire subregions of Quarts de Chaume, Vouvray, Coteaux du Layon, Montlouis and Bonnezeaux use Chenin Blanc to produce their generally outstanding sweet wines. Alsace vintners utilize the region's finest grapes for their *Sélection de Grains Nobles* wines, and German and Austrian vintners produce sublime botrytized wines from Riesling and other grapes, which they designate *Beerenauslese* (BA) or *Trockenbeerenauslese* (TBA) according to sugar levels (see p. 132). California, Australia and South Africa also make wines from botrytis-affected grapes.

• **ICE WINE/EISWEIN** is made from grapes that have been left on the vine until after the first freeze. The grapes are pressed while frozen, which yields small amounts of sweet, concentrated juice. The finest ice wines are crafted in Germany and Austria with Riesling, though almost any grape can be used. Some beautifully made versions come from Canada, New York and Washington State. In warmer regions some vintners simply put extra-ripe grapes in a freezer and then press them for the same effect.

• **VINS DOUX NATURELS** are fortified with brandy during fermentation, which preserves the grape's sugars. They are made mainly in southern France, with the two most noteworthy examples being Muscat de Beaumes-de-Venise from the Rhône Valley and Muscat de Rivesaltes from Roussillon.

• **TOKAJI** is a unique wine infused with a mash of botrytis-affected grapes (*aszù*). Produced mainly in Hungary, Tokaji is graded by the amount of crushed grapes added to the base, on a scale measured by *puttonyos;* the more puttonyos, the more intense the wine. All tend to exhibit delicious apricot, orange and almond flavors and high acidity.

white dessert wine recommendations

Beringer Nightingale | 2005 | **NAPA VALLEY, CALIFORNIA**
★★ $ $ $ (375 ml) First created by Beringer winemaker Myron Nightingale in 1971, this wine is like a New World Sauternes, fuller-bodied and riper than the French original. With apricot, peach and nectarine, along with hints of caramel, it's a fine imitation.

Carabella Late Harvest Pinot Gris | 2006 |
CHEHALEM MOUNTAINS, OREGON
★ $ $ (375 ml) From a vineyard planted with Oregon stalwarts comes this late-harvest Pinot Gris. It's redolent of melon, red apple and honeyed fruit, and nice acidity balances the sweetness.

Carl Ehrhard Rüdesheimer Riesling Auslese | 2004 |
RHEINGAU, GERMANY
★★ $ $ $ (375 ml) This sweet German wine from a 150-year-old estate shows good Riesling character: red apple, ripe apricot and some minerality and white pepper on the palate. Impeccably balanced, it has a generous body and bright acidity.

Castello Banfi Florus | 2005 |
MOSCODELLO DI MONTALCINO, ITALY

★★ **$ $** (500 ml) Rich, yet well balanced, this late-harvest wine has a grapey quality, coupled with layers of honey, caramel, dried apricot and almonds. It also offers intoxicating floral and citrus aromas.

Château de Jau | 2002 | **GRAND ROUSSILLON, FRANCE**

★★ **$ $** (500 ml) This amber wine is defined by flavors of sweet orange marmalade and apricot preserves, with honey flavors pleasingly balanced against the crisp acidity. Made from 100 percent Grenache Blanc, it's fortified and aged in new Bordeaux barrels for three years.

Château Haut-Bergeron | 2004 | **SAUTERNES, FRANCE**

★★★ **$ $** (375 ml) With vineyards that neighbor Château Climens as well as the famous Château d'Yquem, this Sauternes, though not inexpensive, represents a great value. It's full-bodied and displays complex honey, apricot, candied citrus and stewed fruit flavors with subtle hints of tangerine.

Château Puy-Servain Terrement | 2004 |
HAUT-MONTRAVEL, FRANCE

★★ **$ $ $** (500 ml) Haut-Montravel is a designation for sweet whites in the Bergerac region, just west of Bordeaux. This wine offers white flower aromas and fleshy peach flavors, touched with grapefruit and zesty orange peel, and a waxy texture.

C.H. Berres Ürziger Würzgarten Goldkapsel Riesling Auslese | 2006 | **MOSEL-SAAR-RUWER, GERMANY**

★★★ **$ $ $** (375 ml) The 2006 vintage marks the third with Markus Berres at the helm, making him the 21st generation to uphold his family's legendary reputation in the Mosel. Their Riesling Auslese is perfumed with peach and apple aromas, plus a hint of acacia flower, leading to honeyed citrus flavors that last long into the finish.

Clos des Camuzeilles | 2005 | **MUSCAT DE RIVESALTES, FRANCE**

★★ **$ $** (500 ml) Made from organically farmed grapes in France's southern region of Languedoc-Roussillon, this wine has nice apple and pear fruit along with a fresh and beguiling seawater quality. There are also delicate flavors of peach and orange blossom.

d'Arenberg The Noble Chardonnay/Semillon | 2006 |
ADELAIDE, AUSTRALIA

★★ **$ $** (375 ml) d'Arenberg's The Noble shows honey aromas and some of the distinct flavors of botrytis (a.k.a. "noble rot"), making it a perfect introduction to the style. Intense and unctuous on the palate, the wine has delicious peach and candied orange flavors.

Dr. Loosen Riesling Beerenauslese | 2006 | MOSEL, GERMANY

★ ★ ★ $ $ (187 ml) This late-harvest German gem offers ripe apple flavors laced with peach and nutmeg. Refreshing acidity and mineral notes provide nice balance, accented by star anise on the finish.

Gunderloch Nackenheim Rothenberg Riesling Auslese | 2006 | RHEINHESSEN, GERMANY

★ ★ ★ $ $ (375 ml) This superripe German Riesling has nicely concentrated aromas of apple and peach with some rigid minerality and spice peering through. Full-bodied and long on the palate, the finish is dry and beautifully balanced following the initial sweet fruit.

Klein Constantia Vin de Constance | 2002 | CONSTANTIA, SOUTH AFRICA

★ ★ $ $ $ (500 ml) South African icon Klein Constantia's Vin de Constance deserves its reputation as a rival of Yquem and Tokaji. Its intense aroma of grapey Muscat, marzipan and orange peel is followed by dried fruit, with plenty of structure and a long finish.

star producers
white dessert wines

Château Haut-Bergeron

The Lamothe family has made stellar Sauternes at this château since the end of the 18th century; winemaker Hervé Lamothe is in charge today.

C.H. Berres

Slate-rich soils and a family with centuries of winemaking experience make up the winning recipe for this German vintner's fine sweet Rieslings.

Clos des Camuzeilles

In addition to its superb sweet Muscat de Rivesaltes, this Languedoc producer makes delicious dry wines from old Carignane and Grenache vines.

Dr. Loosen

Dr. Loosen's ungrafted Riesling vines average 60 years in age and are located on some of the best sites in Germany's Mosel region. The result? Luscious, complex, terroir-driven wines.

Gunderloch

Germany's Hasselbach family crafts superb dessert Rieslings from their estate's top site, the Nackenheim Rothenberg.

Kracher

Considered one of the world's best dessert winemakers, this Austrian producer makes wines from a surprising array of grape varieties.

Kracher Trockenbeerenauslese | NV | BURGENLAND, AUSTRIA

★ ★ ★ ★ $ $ (187 ml) This amazingly rich, perfumed apricot nectar of a wine was crafted by the legendary Alois Kracher, who died in 2007 and was considered by many to be one of Austria's finest winemakers. Hazelnut, baking spice and quince aromas continue to emerge from the glass with time, followed by dense honey and apricot flavors and a full-bodied, creamy mouthfeel.

Les Petits Grains | NV | MUSCAT DE SAINT JEAN DE MINERVOIS, FRANCE

★ ★ $ (375 ml) Intense aromas of orange peel and grape juice and flavors of apricot and honey mark this gently fortified wine. It has a tactile, seductive texture and plenty of acidity to keep it fresh.

Nittnaus Premium Eiswein | 2004 | BURGENLAND, AUSTRIA

★ ★ $ $ $ (375 ml) Made from Grüner Veltliner grapes, this Austrian ice wine enchants with its white-peach-meets-white-pepper notes and intense flavors of tropical and red apple fruit. The creamy texture leads to a mouth-coating, fruit-filled finish.

Paradise Ranch Late Harvest Pinot Blanc | 2006 | OKANAGAN VALLEY, CANADA

★ $ $ (375 ml) This Canadian late-harvest wine contains less sugar and acidity than the more famous ice wines, but still offers plenty of excitement with its tart green apple, zesty grapefruit and lively lemon flavors. The finish has citrus and clean mineral notes.

Peter Lehmann Botrytis Semillon | 2006 | BAROSSA VALLEY, AUSTRALIA

★ $ $ (375 ml) The 2006 vintage in Australia offered excellent botrytis development, giving this "sticky" a vaguely Sauternes-like nose. The flower and tropical fruit aromas are met by fresh green apple and honeyed fruit, all balanced with generous acidity.

Quinta do Alqueve Colheita Tardia | 2005 | RIBATEJO, PORTUGAL

★ $ $ (500 ml) Like liquid peach cobbler, this wine from Portugal's central province of Ribatejo has a nectarlike intensity and nice aromas of ripe peaches with hints of cinnamon and cloves.

RoxyAnn Winery Late Harvest Viognier | 2006 | ROGUE VALLEY, OREGON

★ ★ $ $ (375 ml) This wine shows classic Viognier aromas of stone fruit—nectarines and white peaches—along with orange blossom and hints of jasmine. The honeyed fruit is supple and silky on the palate with a touch of restrained sweetness and perfect balance.

Ruffino Serelle | 2003 | **VIN SANTO DEL CHIANTI, ITALY**
★★ $ $ (375 ml) There's more to Chianti than red wine, as this sweet white shows. Deftly balancing dried apricot flavors with notes of caramel and candied almond, it finishes with sweet spice.

Santa Julia Tardío | 2007 | **MENDOZA, ARGENTINA**
★★ $ (500 ml) Santa Julia features the aromatic Torrontés grape in this sweet wine of moderate alcohol and light body. It's effusive in its floral and citrus notes, turning to pineapple and peach on the palate.

Sigalas Vin Santo | 2003 | **SANTORINI, GREECE**
★★ $ $ $ (500 ml) Massive and viscous, with apricot preserve and orange marmalade flavors that'll make you want to spread it on breakfast toast, this Greek Vin Santo is as dense as motor oil. The long finish and jammy consistency make it a dessert in itself.

Styring Vineyards White Riesling | 2003 |
WILLAMETTE VALLEY, OREGON
★ $ $ (375 ml) This wine is classic Riesling, exhibiting red candy apple and slight petrol aromas. The alcohol and sugar are both nicely restrained, making for a dessert wine of good balance and precision.

Wenzel Riesling Beerenauslese | 2006 |
BURGENLAND, AUSTRIA
★★ $ $ $ (375 ml) From an Austrian winery founded in 1647, this is less intensely fruit-filled than most Beerenauslese. Flinty minerals balance lean apple and lemon flavors with subtle notes of pineapple.

red dessert wines

The renown of Port and Madeira should not overshadow the red dessert wine contributions of Italy, France, California and Australia, all of which produce intriguing versions ranging in style from light and bubbly to dark and rich.

Red Dessert Wines Grapes & Styles

Red dessert wines vary greatly from region to region. From northern Italy comes Recioto della Valpolicella, the sweet sibling of bittersweet Amarone (see p. 89), as well as pink Muscat (Moscato Rosa) and the lightly sparkling Brachetto. France's Roussillon region offers the fortified wines of Banyuls and Maury, both made with Grenache. California and Australia produce sweet late-harvest and Port-style wines from many different grape varieties.

red dessert wine recommendations

Chateau Reynella Old Cave Fine Old Tawny Port |
MCLAREN VALE, AUSTRALIA
★ ★ ★ ★ $ $ (500 ml) Some recalcitrant Aussies insist on using the term "Port" (traditionally reserved for the famed fortified wines of Portugal), but this comes very close to the real thing, and is, in fact, better than most true Ports. This Tawny, aged for 12 years in oak casks, is nutty and honeyed, with baked fruit evolving on the long finish.

Dashe Late Harvest Zinfandel | 2006 |
DRY CREEK VALLEY, CALIFORNIA
★ $ $ (375 ml) This dessert wine never fails to serve up enough acidity to balance the intense fruit sweetness of a late-harvest Zin. Flavors of raisins, blueberry and chocolate meet soft tannins on the palate.

Domaine de Nidolères Grenat Vin Doux Naturel | 2004 |
RIVESALTES, FRANCE
★ ★ $ $ (500 ml) This Grenache-based wine nicely disguises its 15.5 percent alcohol content with ample fruit and balanced sweetness. The dried fruit flavors of raisin, fig and plum evolve into black cherry and dark chocolate in a richly layered wine.

Feiler-Artinger Zweigelt Beerenauslese | 2005 |
BURGENLAND, AUSTRIA
★ ★ $ $ $ (375 ml) While the nose is earthy and herbal, the palate of this 100 percent Zweigelt red is like watermelon Jolly Rancher candy (in a good way), with abundant fruit and a lovely sweet-tart balance.

M. Chapoutier Vin Doux Naturel | 2006 | BANYULS, FRANCE
★ ★ $ $ (500 ml) This traditional fortified wine of southern France serves up loads of dark cherry and raspberry fruit along with chocolate and spice. Medium-bodied, it's an approachable crowd-pleaser.

Peller Estates Cabernet Franc Icewine | 2006 |
NIAGARA PENINSULA, CANADA
★ ★ ★ $ $ $ $ (375 ml) A true ice wine, this Canadian gem offers typical Cabernet Franc aromas: berries, tea and rhubarb, along with dried apricot. Its sweet maple syrup flavors never become cloying.

Troon Vineyard Insomnia Reserve "Port" | 2005 |
APPLEGATE VALLEY, OREGON
★ ★ ★ $ $ (375 ml) Made from Tempranillo and Dolcetto, this delicious fortified wine from a small Oregon operation is full of dried red fruit, plum and cherry. On the smooth, lush palate, dark chocolate and sweet spices join the chewy fruit, leading to a date-filled finish.

how to pair wine & food

The old adage "White wine with fish and red with meat" has been replaced with "Drink whatever you like with whatever you want." Both approaches have advantages, but you're bound to encounter pitfalls by adhering too closely to either. The trick is to pair food and wine so that neither distorts or overwhelms the other. Ideally, you want to bring together dishes and wines that highlight each other's best qualities. In the next three sections, you'll find general matching rules, a host of ideas for pairing by grape variety and a pairing "cheat sheet."

general rules for matching

be body-conscious Delicately flavored food goes best with a light and delicate wine; heavy, full-flavored dishes call for heftier wines. The subtle flavors of sole meunière are going to get lost if paired with a big, oaky Chardonnay, and a light Beaujolais will seem like water if served with braised short ribs.

balance extremes If a dish is rich and creamy, you need a tart, high-acid wine to cut through the fat and to cleanse your palate. A bit of sweetness in wine balances salty or spicy foods. If you can't wait to drink those young and astringent Bordeaux, Barolos or California Cabernet Sauvignons, the protein and fat of a rich cut of meat will help moderate their tannins.

pair likes Peppery meat dishes work well with spicy red wines like those from the Rhône Valley. Play fruit sauces off rich and fruity wines. Grassy, herbal whites tend to go beautifully with green vegetables.

look to the locals Wines from a particular region often match well with foods from the same place.

mix & match The "red with meat, white with fish" rule is a good fallback when you're unsure what to pair with a dish, but it's a rule made to be broken. Try a light, acidic red such as a Burgundy with a rich fish like salmon; or pair a rich Chardonnay with grilled chicken.

bridge the gap If your table has ordered steak, salmon and sea scallops and you have to pick the wine, choose one that offers a bit of something for each dish. Full-bodied rosés such as those from Bandol or Tavel or lighter-bodied reds like non-Riserva Chianti Classico or a light-style Oregon Pinot Noir have the subtlety not to overwhelm delicate dishes and the substance to stand up to a hearty steak.

pairing by grape

Of the thousands of different grape varieties in the world, only about 20 are regularly represented on American wine shelves. Each variety has its own particular characteristics that yield different styles of wine and result in a greater affinity with certain foods than others. Here is a guide to the most common varieties, with suggestions for dishes that pair especially well with each and a selection of wines that express each grape's typical qualities.

cabernet franc

Cabernet Franc adds spicy pepper and bright red cherry flavors to Bordeaux red wines, but it stars in France's Loire Valley, where it makes light, spicy reds. California and Long Island also make some good examples.

BEST PAIRINGS Cabernet Franc tends to be a bit lighter and more herbal than Cabernet Sauvignon, so pair it with dishes like herb-rubbed roast chicken (or any light meat involving a lot of herbs), roast pork loin or veal chops. Earthier, more structured Old World bottlings—for instance, those from the Chinon region of the Loire Valley—are ideal with roast duck or other game birds.

Catherine & Pierre Breton Clos Sénéchal | 2005 | ★★★ $ $ | P. 56

Domaine Bernard Baudry Clos Guillot | 2006 | ★★★★ $ $ $ | P. 56

Langlois-Château Les Montifault | 2006 | ★★ $ $ | P. 57

Macari | 2004 | ★★★ $ $ | P. 213

Peju Province | 2005 | ★★★ $ $ $ | P. 193

cabernet sauvignon

Cabernet Sauvignon is revered for its cedary black currant and blackberry flavors bolstered by tannin. The best expressions come from Bordeaux, California's Napa Valley and Chile's Alta Maipo region, although stellar examples are made worldwide.

BEST PAIRINGS Cabernets from California, Australia and South America, with their rich fruit and substantial tannins, pair best with meat—well-marbled steaks, braised short ribs, hearty roasts. European Cabernets and Bordeaux blends tend to have higher acidity and less overtly ripe flavors; lamb is a great match for them, or game of any kind.

Château Brane-Cantenac Grand Cru | 2005 | ★★★★ $ $ $ | P. 32

Cuvaison | 2005 | ★★★ $ $ $ | P. 172

Elyse Morisoli Vineyard | 2004 | ★★★ $ $ $ $ | P. 173

Hundred Acre Kayli Morgan Vineyard | 2005 | ★★★★ $ $ $ $ | P. 174

Peju H.B. Vineyard | 2004 | ★★★ $ $ $ | P. 174

chardonnay

Chardonnay grows almost everywhere. It reaches its apex in France's Burgundy, where it produces elegant, mineral-laden whites. Elsewhere it is responsible for full-bodied, fruit-driven wines, toasty Champagnes and dessert wines.

BEST PAIRINGS Lighter, unoaked Chardonnay and Chablis pair well with fish, shellfish and salads. Oakier versions (most California Chardonnays, for instance) are better with more substantial dishes like roast chicken, pork tenderloin or richer fish or shellfish such as salmon or lobster.

Albert Bichot Domaine du Pavillon | 2005 | ★★★ $ $ $ | P. 40

Geyser Peak Winery | 2006 | ★★ $ | P. 162

Gilbert Picq & ses Fils | 2006 | ★★ $ $ | P. 39

Jean-Marc Boillot St. Jacques | 2005 | ★★★ $ $ | P. 46

PlumpJack Reserve | 2006 | ★★★★ $ $ $ | P. 164

chenin blanc

Full of fruit and high acidity, Chenin Blanc produces some of France's best wines, like the Loire Valley's full-bodied, long-aging dry whites, dessert elixirs and sparklers. South Africa and California also produce enjoyable examples.

BEST PAIRINGS Dry Chenin Blanc is a good partner for white-fleshed fish, chicken or even lighter veal or pork dishes. Off-dry (lightly sweet) versions pair better with spicy foods such as Indian or other Asian dishes.

Domaine des Aubuisières Cuvée Silex | 2006 |
★★★★ $ $ | P. 52

Domaine Laffourcade Clos la Royauté | 2006 |
★★ $ $ | P. 52

Marc Brédif | 2006 | ★★★ $ $ | P. 53

Nicolas Joly Clos de la Coulée de Serrant | 2005 |
★★★ $ $ $ $ | P. 53

Simonsig | 2007 | ★★ $ | P. 247

gewürztraminer

Pink-skinned Gewürztraminer offers flamboyant flavors ranging from honeysuckle to lychee, apricot, mineral and spice. It's especially important in the white wines of Alsace and Germany. New York and California are also home to some excellent versions.

BEST PAIRINGS Gewürztraminer almost always pairs well with Asian and Indian food—for spicy dishes, choose an off-dry (lightly sweet) bottling; for less spicy dishes, dry Gewürztraminer is better. It is also good with strong cheeses like Epoisses or Münster.

Domaine Weinbach Cuvée Théo | 2006 | ★★★ $ $ $ | P. 26

Hugel & Fils Hugel | 2006 | ★★ $ $ | P. 27

Léon Beyer | 2005 | ★★ $ $ | P. 27

P.J. Valckenberg Estate | 2006 | ★★ $ | P. 139

Weingut Herbert Messmer Burrweiler Altenforst Spätlese
| 2007 | ★★ $ $ $ | P. 139

grenache/garnacha

The fresh, spicy cherry flavors of Grenache are essential to many southern French red wines, such as Châteauneuf-du-Pape and Côtes-du-Rhône. Spanish winemakers rely heavily on Grenache (Garnacha in Spanish), particularly in Priorat. It is also important in Sardinia (where it's called Cannonau) and shows up in California and Australia.

BEST PAIRINGS Grenache, with its warm, quintessentially Mediterranean flavors, pairs well with hearty dishes like grilled sausages, lamb chops and rustic stews.

Argiolas Costera | 2006 | ★ ★ $ $ | P. 109
Chateau Reynella Basket Pressed | 2004 | ★ ★ ★ $ $ | P. 225
Costers de Mas Igneus | 2001 | ★ ★ ★ $ $ $ $ | P. 119
J. Vidal-Fleury | 2004 | ★ ★ $ $ $ | P. 68
La Font du Vent Confidentia | 2005 | ★ ★ $ $ | P. 68

malbec

Malbec is the signature red wine grape of Argentina, where it yields wines that are bursting with lush, dark berry fruits and rich chocolate flavors. It is no longer important in Bordeaux, its place of origin, but dominates red wine production in the French region of Cahors, where it goes by the name Auxerrois, and shows up in the Loire Valley, California, Australia and Chile.

BEST PAIRINGS Malbec's full-bodied dark fruit flavors and light peppery spiciness make it a natural partner for beef, lamb, venison or other substantial meats.

Château Lagrézette Cru d'Exception | 2003 |
★ ★ $ $ $ | P. 77
Inacayal Select | 2005 | ★ ★ ★ $ $ | P. 238
Kaiken Ultra | 2006 | ★ ★ ★ $ $ | P. 238
Kokomo Windsor Oaks Vineyards | 2006 |
★ ★ $ $ $ | P. 193
Susana Balbo Signature | 2006 | ★ ★ ★ $ $ | P. 239

marsanne

Most at home in France's Rhône Valley, the white wine grape Marsanne is prized for its succulent honey flavors and full body. Good versions are found throughout California and Australia. It often appears as part of a blend, usually with the Roussanne grape, but also with Viognier and other grapes.

BEST PAIRINGS Marsanne's gentle stone fruit and melon flavors and moderate acidity make it a good all-around white wine for pairing with chicken, white-fleshed fish and main-course salads.

d'Arenberg The Hermit Crab | 2006 | ★ ★ ★ **$ $** | P. 218
M. Chapoutier Les Meysonniers | 2006 | ★ ★ ★ **$ $** | P. 61
Perrin Réserve | 2006 | ★ ★ **$** | P. 64
Treana Mer Soleil Vineyard | 2006 | ★ **$ $** | P. 169

merlot

With its plum and chocolate flavors, Merlot is one of the most popular grapes in the world and is responsible for some of the greatest red wines, such as those from Bordeaux's Pomerol and Washington State. Terrific examples are also produced in California and northeastern Italy.

BEST PAIRINGS Merlot's plummy, spicy notes and full-bodied texture make it a good match for everything from pork chops or roasts to pasta in meat sauces or sausages off the grill.

Château de Bel-Air | 2005 | ★ ★ **$ $** | P. 32
Duckhorn Vineyards Estate Grown | 2005 |
★ ★ ★ **$ $ $ $** | P. 179
Dunham Cellars Lewis Vineyard | 2005 |
★ ★ ★ **$ $ $ $** | P. 204
Novelty Hill | 2005 | ★ ★ **$ $** | P. 206
Shinn Estate Vineyards Nine Barrels Reserve | 2005 |
★ ★ ★ **$ $ $** | P. 213

muscat

All Muscat, both red and white, bursts with fragrant flavors such as honeysuckle, orange blossom and musk. It's grown throughout the world, most famously in Italy as Moscato and in Spain as Moscatel, as well as in Alsace, southern France, Greece, California and Australia.

BEST PAIRINGS Most Muscat bottlings are lightly sweet; that, together with the grape's tangerine-scented fruitiness, makes it a natural partner for fresh fruit desserts.

Clos des Camuzeilles | 2005 | ★ ★ **$ $** | P. 273
Gutiérrez Colosía Moscatel Soleado Dulce |
★ ★ ★ ★ **$ $** | P. 266
Les Petits Grains | NV | ★ ★ **$** | P. 275
Michele Chiarlo Nivole | 2007 | ★ ★ **$** | P. 260

nebbiolo

Nebbiolo achieves its greatest glory in Italy's Piedmont region, where its cherry, tar and tobacco flavors define the elegant, long-lived reds of Barolo and Barbaresco. A small number of vintners outside of Italy work with Nebbiolo, too, particularly in California and Australia, though away from home, the grape tends to express different characteristics.

BEST PAIRINGS This structured, aromatic red grape pairs particularly well with any dish involving mushrooms, but it is also good with lamb, venison and beef (beef braised in Barolo is a classic Piedmontese dish). Older vintages go perfectly with truffles.

Ceretto Bricco Rocche Brunate | 2004 | ★ ★ ★ $ $ $ $ | P. 82
Damilano Lecinquevigne | 2003 | ★ ★ $ $ $ | P. 82
Gaja | 2004 | ★ ★ ★ ★ $ $ $ $ | P. 83
Giuseppe e Figlio Mascarello Monprivato | 2003 |
★ ★ ★ ★ $ $ $ $ | P. 83
Massolino | 2004 | ★ ★ ★ $ $ $ $ | P. 83
Pio Cesare Il Bricco | 2003 | ★ ★ ★ $ $ $ $ | P. 83

petite sirah

Petite Sirah (not to be confused with Syrah) yields wines that are lusty and dark with chewy tannin. Originally from France's Rhône Valley, the grape is believed to be a cross between the Peloursin variety and Syrah, and grows well in California, Mexico, South America, Australia and parts of the Middle East.

BEST PAIRINGS Almost invariably full-bodied and bursting with blackberry and spice flavors, Petite Sirah is ideal with saucy barbecued meats or rich braised short ribs prepared with an array of sweet or savory spices.

Concannon Limited Release | 2005 | ★ $ | P. 192
Earthquake | 2005 | ★ ★ $ $ | P. 192
Epiphany Rodney's Vineyard | 2005 | ★ ★ $ $ $ | P. 192
Lolonis Orpheus Heritage Vineyards | 2005 |
★ ★ $ $ $ | P. 193
Stags' Leap Winery | 2005 | ★ ★ ★ $ $ $ | P. 193

pinot blanc

Winemakers in Alsace, California and Italy craft wines from Pinot Blanc (also called Pinot Bianco) that tend to be medium-bodied and mildly fruity. In Austria, where the grape goes by the name Weissburgunder, it expresses richer, more concentrated flavors and greater overall character than in typical Pinot Blanc styles found elsewhere.

BEST PAIRINGS Pair Pinot Blanc with delicate freshwater fish like trout or perch, or light meat dishes involving chicken breasts or veal scallops. Italian Pinot Biancos tend to be leaner and are best with raw shellfish or fresh green salads lightly dressed.

Domaine Mittnacht Frères Terre d'Etoiles | 2006 | ★★ $ $ | P. 24

Josmeyer Mise du Printemps | 2005 | ★★ $ $ | P. 24

Lieb Reserve | 2006 | ★★ $ $ | P. 210

Lucien Albrecht Cuvée Balthazar | 2006 | ★★ $ $ | P. 24

Trinitas | 2006 | ★ $ $ | P. 169

pinot gris/pinot grigio

In Alsace and Oregon, Pinot Gris produces full-bodied, nutty white wines. In Italy, where it is called Pinot Grigio, the grape makes light, brisk whites. It also has success in California's cooler regions.

BEST PAIRINGS Light and simple Pinot Grigios make a good match for equally light fish dishes and green salads. Alsace-style Pinot Gris tends to be richer and goes better with flavorful pasta dishes or chicken in cream-based sauces; it also pairs well with modestly spiced Asian and Indian dishes.

Domaine Marcel Deiss | 2004 | ★★★ $ $ $ | P. 25

Domaines Schlumberger Grand Cru Spiegel | 2005 | ★★★ $ $ | P. 25

Heidi Schröck Grauburgunder | 2006 | ★★★ $ $ | P. 144

King Estate Signature Collection | 2007 | ★★ $ $ | P. 197

Lucien Albrecht Grand Cru Pfingstberg | 2003 | ★★ $ $ $ | P. 25

pinot noir

Called the heartbreak grape, Pinot Noir is difficult to grow and make. At its best, Pinot Noir is incredibly seductive, with aromas of roses, smoke, red fruits and earth. The red wines of Burgundy are regarded as its ultimate expression, but excellent Pinot Noir also comes from Australia, California, the Loire Valley, New York, New Zealand and Oregon.

BEST PAIRINGS Old World Pinot Noir (Burgundy, for instance) goes best with flavorful, simple dishes like steaks, lamb chops or wild game birds. Fruitier, more straightforward New World bottlings are good with duck, dishes involving mushrooms and richer fish, particularly salmon.

Craggy Range Te Muna Road Vineyard | 2006 | ★★★ $ $ $ | P. 232

Domaine Jessiaume Les Combottes | 2006 | ★★ $ $ | P. 44

Jean-Marc Boillot Jarollières | 2005 | ★★★ $ $ $ $ | P. 45

Joseph Drouhin | 2005 | ★★★ $ $ $ | P. 45

Retour | 2006 | ★★★★ $ $ $ $ | P. 200

riesling

Riesling can make white wines of incredible complexity with high acidity and lots of mineral flavors, in styles that range from bone-dry to sumptuously sweet. Riesling is made all around the world, but the best are from Alsace, Germany, Austria, Australia and New York. Many can age for decades.

BEST PAIRINGS Off-dry (lightly sweet) Rieslings pair very well with Asian cuisines, especially Thai and Vietnamese. Dry Riesling is a good accompaniment to freshwater fish such as trout, as well as dishes with citrus flavors.

Domaine Weinbach Cuvée Ste-Catherine | 2006 | ★★★ $ $ $ | P. 26

Dönnhoff Schlossböckelheimer Felsenberg Spätlese | 2006 | ★★★ $ $ $ | P. 134

Hunt Country Vineyards Dry | 2006 | ★★ $ | P. 210

Joh. Jos. Prüm Wehlener Sonnenuhr Auslese | 2006 | ★★★★ $ $ $ | P. 134

Trimbach | 2005 | ★★ $ $ | P. 26

roussanne

White wine grape Roussanne is at home in France's northern Rhône Valley, where it yields wines with nutty, unctuous flavors. It is often blended with Marsanne for the esteemed white wines of Crozes-Hermitage, Hermitage and St-Joseph, and appears as well with Viognier and other grapes. California also grows Roussanne, with some good results.

BEST PAIRINGS With its mineral notes and hints of melon and herbs, Roussanne makes an ideal partner for herb-based sauces on lighter meats and more substantial fish. It's also good with simple roast chicken and with vegetables like parsnips, fennel and celery root.

Andrew Rich Vintner | 2006 | ★ ★ ★ $ $ | P. 202
E. Guigal | 2006 | ★ ★ ★ $ | P. 63
Jean-Luc Colombo La Redonne Blanc | 2006 | ★ ★ $ $ | P. 60
La Vieille Ferme | 2006 | ★ ★ ★ $ | P. 63
Perrin Réserve | 2006 | ★ ★ $ | P. 64

sangiovese

Sangiovese is an important grape in Italy, where it is prized for its red cherry and leather flavors and high acidity. It is most common in Tuscany, where it makes most of the red wines of Chianti and many of the exalted Super-Tuscans. The grape is also grown in California.

BEST PAIRINGS Sangiovese's bright cherry-berry flavors, firm acidity and moderate tannins are all characteristics that make it ideal for pastas with tomato-based sauces as well as pizza. Rich, starchy dishes such as risotto or full-flavored salami Toscana and other dry-cured sausages are some other good partners.

Antinori Marchese Antinori Riserva | 2003 | ★ ★ ★ $ $ $ | P. 94
Castello di Ama | 2005 | ★ ★ ★ ★ $ $ $ $ | P. 94
Col d'Orcia | 2003 | ★ ★ ★ $ $ $ | P. 97
Fuligni | 2003 | ★ ★ ★ $ $ $ $ | P. 97
Kuleto Estate | 2005 | ★ ★ $ $ $ | P. 193

sauvignon blanc

Sauvignon Blanc's finest expressions are the lemony, herbaceous white wines of the Sancerre and Pouilly-Fumé regions of France's Loire Valley, but many New Zealand examples, with flavors of zingy grapefruit and fresh-cut grass, are also outstanding. Winemakers in parts of California, Austria and South Africa produce excellent Sauvignon Blancs as well.

BEST PAIRINGS With its bright acidity, mixed citrus (most commonly grapefruit) fruit flavors and herbal notes, Sauvignon Blanc makes an ideal partner for raw shellfish, light fish dishes, salads and fresh vegetable dishes; it's also a classic partner for anything involving goat cheese.

Château de Sancerre | 2006 | ★★ $ $ | P. 55
de Ladoucette | 2005 | ★★★ $ $ $ | P. 55
Kim Crawford | 2007 | ★★ $ $ | P. 231
Pascal Jolivet Sauvage | 2007 | ★★★ $ $ $ $ | P. 55
Robert Mondavi Winery To Kalon Vineyard Reserve Fumé Blanc | 2005 | ★★★ $ $ $ | P. 167

semillon

The second of Bordeaux's great white grapes after Sauvignon Blanc, Semillon is the primary component of the region's luxurious, sweet Sauternes wines. It also appears on its own or blended with Sauvignon Blanc to make some delicious, full-bodied dry wines in Bordeaux and Australia.

BEST PAIRINGS Semillon's notes of lemon and honey are an ideal complement to light fish in butter-based sauces, as well as simple baked or roast fish; it's also good with light chicken dishes.

Château Carbonnieux Grand Cru | 2005 | ★★★★ $ $ $ | P. 30
Château Olivier Grand Cru | 2005 | ★★★ $ $ $ | P. 30
Domaines Barons de Rothschild Lafite Réserve Spéciale | 2006 | ★ $ $ | P. 31
St Hallett Poacher's Blend | 2007 | ★ $ | P. 219
Vieux Château Gaubert | 2006 | ★★ $ $ | P. 31

syrah/shiraz

Typically full-bodied and tannic, with berry, pepper and smoky flavors, Syrah is capable of wines that show both power and finesse. Its most renowned domain is the Rhône Valley of France, but California's Central Coast, Washington State and Australia, where it's called Shiraz, also make impressive versions.

BEST PAIRINGS Pair spicy, structured Old World Syrahs with big steaks, or game such as venison and lamb. Fruitier New World bottlings, like most examples from Australia, also work well with lamb and can go with rich, cheesy dishes like eggplant Parmesan or hamburgers topped with blue cheese.

Beckmen Vineyards Purisima Mountain Vineyard | 2006 | ★★★ $ $ $ | P. 185

Delas Frères Seigneur de Maugiron | 2004 | ★★★ $ $ $ $ | P. 61

Domaine Alain Voge Vieilles Vignes | 2005 | ★★★ $ $ $ $ | P. 61

Peter Lehmann Stonewell | 2002 | ★★★ $ $ $ $ | P. 224

Two Hands Bella's Garden | 2006 | ★★★★ $ $ $ | P. 224

tempranillo

Grown throughout Spain, Tempranillo is best known as the grape responsible for Rioja's reds. Tempranillo tends to give spicy aromas, red fruit flavors and medium body.

BEST PAIRINGS Lamb in almost any form is a classic pairing for Tempranillo. Tempranillo-based wines are also good partners for hard sheep cheeses like Manchego and lighter roast meats like pork or veal; its typically cherrylike fruit also makes it nice with duck.

Allende | 2004 | ★★★★ $ $ $ | P. 115

Faustino I Gran Reserva | 1996 | ★★★ $ $ $ | P. 115

R. López de Heredia Viña Bosconia Reserva | 2000 | ★★★★ $ $ $ | P. 115

Sierra Cantabria Crianza | 2004 | ★★★ $ $ | P. 116

Viña Real Reserva | 2001 | ★★★★ $ $ $ | P. 116

viognier

The basis of many of the famed white wines of France's northern Rhône Valley, Viognier has become a favorite in California for its lush peach, citrus and floral flavors.

BEST PAIRINGS Pair low-acid, lush Viognier with fruits such as apples, pears and peaches; richer shellfish such as scallops or lobster; and white-fleshed fish with butter or cream sauces. French versions, which tend to be leaner and spicier, are also good partners for guinea hen, quail, rabbit or sweetbreads.

Chateau Lorane | 2006 | ★★ $ $ | P. 197

Fess Parker | 2006 | ★★★ $ $ | P. 168

François Villard Les Contours de DePoncins | 2006 | ★★★ $ $ $ | P. 60

Maison Alain Paret Lys de Volan | 2006 | ★★★ $ $ $ | P. 61

Routas Coquelicot | 2006 | ★★ $ $ | P. 74

zinfandel

California's own red grape (by way of Croatia), Zinfandel assumes many forms, from off-dry pale rosés and simple reds to full-bodied, tannic wines with blackberry and spice flavors. Zinfandel also makes thick Port-style dessert wines.

BEST PAIRINGS Zinfandel's robust, dark berry flavors, spice notes and moderate tannins make it an ideal partner for simple, hearty meat dishes like hamburgers, sausages or lamb chops. It's also a great match for barbecue, where the wine's sweet-spicy flavors complement the sweet, spicy sauce, and for Mexican food.

Alexander Valley Vineyards Alexander School Top of the Crop Old Vine | 2005 | ★★ $ $ $ | P. 188

Clos du Bois Sonoma Reserve | 2005 | ★★ $ $ | P. 188

Dashe | 2006 | ★★★ $ $ | P. 188

Francis Ford Coppola Director's Cut | 2005 | ★★★ $ $ | P. 189

Lolonis | 2005 | ★★ $ $ | P. 190

wine & food pairing cheat sheet

CLASSIC DISHES	THE WINES
RAW OYSTERS	Muscadet
TUNA STEAK	Rosé
GRILLED SALMON	Pinot Gris
CRAB CAKES	Sauvignon Blanc
LOBSTER	Chardonnay
SALAD WITH VINAIGRETTE	Pinot Grigio
ROAST CHICKEN	Pinot Noir
PORK TENDERLOIN	Merlot
HAMBURGERS/SAUSAGES	Zinfandel
SPAGHETTI WITH RED SAUCE	Sangiovese
STEAK	Cabernet Sauvignon
PIZZA	Barbera
INDIAN CURRIES	Gewürztraminer
SPICY ASIAN FOOD	Off-dry Riesling

WHY THE MATCH WORKS	BOTTLE TO TRY
This white has an almost briny note that's great with raw shellfish.	Sauvion Château du Cléray Réserve Muscadet sur Lie | 2007 | ★★★ $ | P. 54
Rosés have the fruit to stand up to meaty fish, but lack tannins that can make fish taste metallic.	Bieler Père et Fils Sabine Rosé | 2007 | ★★★ $ | P. 74
Salmon and other rich fish can pair with either full-bodied whites or lighter reds.	Domaines Schlumberger Grand Cru Spiegel | 2005 | ★★★ $ $ | P. 25
Tangy, high-acid whites cut through the fat of pan-fried or deep-fried seafood.	Brancott B | 2007 | ★★★ $ $ | P. 230
Lobster's luscious sweet flavor calls for a substantial white.	Patz & Hall Zio Tony Ranch | 2006 | ★★★ $ $ $ | P. 164
A salad with a tangy dressing will overwhelm low-acid whites but not tart whites.	Schiopetto | 2006 | ★★★ $ $ $ | P. 89
Pinot Noir is light enough for white meat, yet flavorful enough for dark.	Miner Garys' Vineyard | 2006 | ★★★ $ $ $ | P. 184
Medium-bodied Merlot is a good red wine for lighter meats like pork or veal.	Duckhorn Vineyards Estate Grown | 2005 | ★★★ $ $ $ $ | P. 179
Big, juicy reds have the substance to match robust meats.	Dashe | 2006 | ★★★ $ $ | P. 188
Red wines with bright acidity complement tomato-based pasta sauces.	Antinori Marchese Antinori Riserva | 2003 | ★★★ $ $ $ | P. 94
The tannins in Cabernets balance the richness of well-marbled beef.	Artesa Reserve | 2005 | ★★ $ $ $ | P. 171
This Italian red has enough acidity to cut through cheesy pizza slices.	Vietti Tre Vigne | 2005 | ★★★ $ $ | P. 84
Gewürztraminer's exotic aromas complement Indian spices like cumin and coriander.	Hugel & Fils Hugel | 2006 | ★★ $ $ | P. 27
Light sweetness can help cool the heat of spicy foods.	Dönnhoff Schlossböckelheimer Felsenberg Spätlese | 2006 | ★★★ $ $ $ | P. 134

bargain wine finder

Great wine does not have to be expensive. Good value for money was an important consideration in the process of selecting the wines recommended in this guide. Following is an index of many different wines whose quality (★) to price ($) ratio makes them exceptional values and well worth stocking up on.

Whites

★★★★ $ $

Domaine des Aubuisières Cuvée Silex, Vouvray, France, p. 52

Elena Walch Kastelaz Gewürztraminer, Alto Adige, Italy, p. 88

Gérard Boulay Chavignol, Sancerre, France, p. 55

Montenidoli Fiore, Vernaccia di San Gimignano, Italy, p. 93

Nikolaihof Grüner Veltliner Hefeabzug, Wachau, Austria, p. 143

R. López de Heredia Viña Gravonia, Rioja, Spain, p. 114

Spy Valley Sauvignon Blanc, Marlborough, New Zealand, p. 231

Vare Bianco, Napa Valley, California, p. 169

★★★★ $

Monarchia Cellars Olivier, Buda-Etyek, Hungary, p. 154

★★★ $

Cave Spring Estate Bottled Riesling, Beamsville Bench, Canada, p. 251

Clos du Bois Pinot Grigio, California, p. 168

De Martino Sauvignon Blanc, Maipo Valley, Chile, p. 241

Domaine de la Louvetrie Hermine d'Or Muscadet sur Lie, Sèvre-et-Maine, France, p. 54

Domaine de la Pépière Muscadet sur Lie, Sèvre-et-Maine, France, p. 54

Drylands Sauvignon Blanc, Marlborough, New Zealand, p. 230

E. Guigal, Côtes-du-Rhône, France, p. 63

Horton Vineyards Rkatsiteli, Orange County, Virginia, p. 210

Inacayal Vineyards Pinot Grigio, Mendoza, Argentina, p. 236

La Vieille Ferme, Côtes du Luberon, France, p. 63

Loimer Lois Grüner Veltliner, Kamptal, Austria, p. 143

Naia, Rueda, Spain, p. 121

Prà, Soave Classico, Italy, p. 88

Pullus Sivi Pinot, Maribor, Slovenia, p. 154

Sauvion Château du Cléray Réserve Muscadet sur Lie, Sèvre-et-Maine, France, p. 54

Tenuta di Salviano, Orvieto Classico, Italy, p. 104

Willamette Valley Vineyards Riesling, Willamette Valley, Oregon, p. 197

Rosés

★ ★ ★ ★ $

Muga Rosado, Rioja, Spain, p. 115

★ ★ ★ $

Artazu Artazuri Rosé, Navarra, Spain, p. 122

Bieler Père et Fils Sabine Rosé, Coteaux d'Aix-en-Provence, France, p. 74

Le Printemps Rosé, Mendocino, California, p. 170

Reds

★ ★ ★ ★ $ $

Antucura Calvulcura, Uco Valley, Argentina, p. 237

Argiano Non Confunditur, Tuscany, Italy, p. 100

Bodega Norton Privada, Luján de Cuyo, Argentina, p. 237

Charles Cimicky The Autograph Shiraz, Barossa Valley, Australia, p. 222

Domaine Skouras Grand Cuvée, Nemea, Greece, p. 151

Il Poggione, Rosso di Montalcino, Italy, p. 97

Intriga Cabernet Sauvignon, Maipo Valley, Chile, p. 242

Isole e Olena, Chianti Classico, Italy, p. 95

Layer Cake Shiraz, Barossa Valley, Australia, p. 223

★ ★ ★ $

Capezzana, Barco Reale di Carmignano, Italy, p. 99

Chalone Vineyard Pinot Noir, Monterey County, California, p. 182

Château Tellagh, Medea, Algeria, p. 157

Clos Siguier, Cahors, France, p. 77

El Burro Kickass Garnacha, Cariñena, Spain, p. 122

Furque 3 Cepas, Mendoza, Argentina, p. 238

Kanonkop Kadette, Stellenbosch, South Africa, p. 249

Maison Champy Signature, Bourgogne, France, p. 45

Marqués de Cáceres Crianza, Rioja, Spain, p. 115

Stormhoek Pinotage, Western Cape, South Africa, p. 249

Tres Barcos, Toro, Spain, p. 123

Sparkling & Sweet

★ ★ ★ ★ $ $

Avinyó Brut Reserva, Cava, Spain, p. 261

Bodegas Hidalgo La Gitana Pastrana Single Vineyard Manzanilla Pasada Sherry, Spain, p. 266

Chateau Reynella Old Cave Fine Old Tawny Port, McLaren Vale, Australia, p. 277

Col Vetoraz, Prosecco di Valdobbiadene, Italy, p. 260

Gutiérrez Colosía Moscatel Soleado Dulce, Spain, p. 266

Kracher Trockenbeerenauslese, Burgenland, Austria, p. 275

Maison Parigot et Richard Blanc de Blancs, Crémant de Bourgogne, France, p. 259

★ ★ ★ $

Freixenet Brut Nature, Cava, Spain, p. 261

Warre's Warrior Special Reserve Port, Portugal, p. 269

top wine websites

The ever-increasing number of wine websites and blogs is making it easier to learn about wine and find great bottles. Here are a dozen of the most informative sites both for beginner oenophiles and connoisseurs.

allaboutwine.com

A large catalogue of wine websites covering a wide range of topics and interests.

allamericanwineries.com

A comprehensive winery and vineyard guide for locating producers in every U.S. state.

burgundy-report.com & burghound.com

Two fonts of wisdom and opinion for Burgundy lovers.

cellartracker.com

An interactive site for sharing tasting notes and a virtual wine cellar for tracking purchases and consumption.

erobertparker.com

A website and chat forum devoted to in-depth discussion of wine and events in the wine world.

foodandwine.com

Expert advice on bottles to buy and perfect food pairings from America's premier culinary magazine, FOOD & WINE, plus deputy wine editor Ray Isle's lively Tasting Room blog.

jancisrobinson.com

One of the world's most admired wine critics offers her insights as well as the complete text of her invaluable *Oxford Companion to Wine.*

localwineevents.com & wineevents-calendar.com

Find a local wine tasting or plan a wine-oriented vacation.

wine-searcher.com & winezap.com

Find obscure bottles and compare prices worldwide.

reliable importers

Not sure which bottle to choose? Look for the importer's name on the label. These importers, grouped by specialty, offer excellent wines that are among the best of their type.

Australia The Australian Premium Wine Collection, Epicurean Wines, Epic Wines, The Grateful Palate, Old Bridge Cellars, Pasternak Wine Imports

Austria Domaine Select Wine Estates, Terry Theise Estate Selections, Vin Divino, Winemonger

France European Cellars, Jenny & François Selections, Kermit Lynch Wine Merchant, Kysela Père et Fils, Louis/Dressner Selections, North Berkeley Imports, Pasternak Wine Imports, Robert Chadderdon, Robert Kacher Selections, Rosenthal Wine Merchant, Terlato Wines International, VOS Selections, Wilson Daniels

Germany Classical Wines, Rudi Wiest Selections, Terry Theise Estate Selections, Valckenberg

Greece Athena Importing, Athenee Importers

Italy Dalla Terra, Domaine Select Wine Estates, Empson USA, John Given Wines, Kobrand, Marc de Grazia Selections, Montecastelli Selections, Panebianco, Summa Vitis, Terlato Wines International, Vias Imports, Vin Divino, Vinifera, Winebow

Portugal Aidil Wines & Liquors, Broadbent Selections, Signature Imports, Tri-Vin Imports

South Africa Broadbent Selections, Cape Classics, Vineyard Brands

South America Billington Wines (Argentina & Chile), Brazilian Wine Connection, Vine Connections (Argentina)

Spain Classical Wines, De Maison Selections, European Cellars, Europvin, Jorge Ordoñez

index

b

l

m